CAN ACADEMICS CHANGE THE WORLD?

EASA Series

Published in Association with the European Association of Social Anthropologists (EASA)
Series Editor: Aleksandar Bošković, University of Belgrade

Social anthropology in Europe is growing, and the variety of work being done is expanding. This series is intended to present the best of the work produced by members of the EASA, both in monographs and in edited collections. The studies in this series describe societies, processes, and institutions around the world and are intended for both scholarly and student readership.

Recent volumes:

39. CAN ACADEMICS CHANGE THE WORLD?
An Israeli Anthropologist's Testimony on the Rise and Fall of a Protest Movement on Campus
Moshe Shokeid

38. INSTITUTIONALISED DREAMS
The Art of Managing Foreign Aid
Elżbieta Drążkiewicz

37. NON-HUMANS IN AMERINDIAN SOUTH AMERICA
Ethnographies of Indigenous Cosmologies, Rituals and Songs
Edited by Juan Javier Rivera Andía

36. ECONOMY, CRIME AND WRONG IN A NEOLIBERAL ERA
Edited by James G. Carrier

35. BEING-HERE
Placemaking in a World of Movement
Annika Lems

34. EXPERIMENTAL COLLABORATIONS
Ethnography through Fieldwork Devices
Edited by Adolfo Estalella and Tomás Sánchez Criado

33. BACK TO THE POSTINDUSTRIAL FUTURE
An Ethnography of Germany's Fastest-Shrinking City
Felix Ringel

32. MESSY EUROPE
Crisis, Race, and Nation-State in a Postcolonial World
Edited by Kristín Loftsdóttir, Andrea L. Smith, and Brigitte Hipfl

31. MANAGING AMBIGUITY
How Clientelism, Citizenship, and Power Shape Personhood in Bosnia and Herzegovina
Čarna Brković

For a full volume listing, please see the series page on our website:
https://www.berghahnbooks.com/series/easa

CAN ACADEMICS CHANGE THE WORLD?

An Israeli Anthropologist's
Testimony on the Rise and Fall
of a Protest Movement on Campus

Moshe Shokeid

berghahn
NEW YORK • OXFORD
www.berghahnbooks.com

First published in 2020 by
Berghahn Books
www.berghahnbooks.com

© 2020, 2025 Moshe Shokeid
First paperback edition published in 2025

All rights reserved. Except for the quotation of short passages for the purposes of criticism and review, no part of this book may be reproduced in any form or by any means, electronic or mechanical, including photocopying, recording, or any information storage and retrieval system now known or to be invented, without written permission of the publisher.

Library of Congress Cataloging-in-Publication Data
Names: Shokeid, Moshe, author.
Title: Can Academics Change the World? An Israeli Anthropologist's Testimony on the Rise and Fall of a Protest Movement on Campus / Moshe Shokeid.
Other titles: EASA series; v. 39.
Description: First edition. | New York: Berghahn Books, 2020. | Series: EASA series; vol. 39 | Includes bibliographical references and index.
Identifiers: LCCN 2020006103 (print) | LCCN 2020006104 (ebook) | ISBN 9781789206982 (hardback) | ISBN 9781789206999 (ebook)
Subjects: LCSH: Shokeid, Moshe. | Ad Kan (Organization) | Universitat Tel-Aviv. | College teachers—Political activity—Israel—Tel Aviv. | Protest movements—Israel—Tel Aviv. | Anthropologists—Israel—Biography. | College teachers—Israel—Biography. | Palestinian Arabs—Politics and government. | Arab-Israeli conflict.
Classification: LCC LG341.T47 S5 2020 (print) | LCC LG341.T47 (ebook) | DDC 378.1/981095694—dc23
LC record available at https://lccn.loc.gov/2020006103
LC ebook record available at https://lccn.loc.gov/2020006104

British Library Cataloguing in Publication Data
A catalogue record for this book is available from the British Library

ISBN 978-1-78920-698-2 hardback
ISBN 978-1-80539-721-2 paperback
ISBN 978-1-80539-909-4 epub
ISBN 978-1-78920-699-9 web pdf

https://doi.org/10.3167/9781789206982

To:

AD KAN activists,

colleagues and comrades in protest

Contents

List of Illustrations viii
Preface ix
Acknowledgments xiii

Introduction.	On Memory	1
Chapter 1.	A Personal Note	7
Chapter 2.	The First Palestinian Intifada	16
Chapter 3.	Intellectuals'/Academics' Engagement in the Public Forum	33
Chapter 4.	Israeli Academics' Political Involvement Prior to the First Intifada	53
Chapter 5.	The Founding of AD KAN	56
Chapter 6.	Opening the Sealed Box of AD KAN	64
Chapter 7.	The Operation of a Protest Organization	68
Chapter 8.	The Media Coverage	79
Chapter 9.	The Moving Scene Observed from Afar and Near	85
Chapter 10.	The Senate Debacle	93
Chapter 11.	Raising the PLO Presence on Campus	98
Chapter 12.	Toward the Last Stage	104
Chapter 13.	The Aftermath: "When Prophecy Fails"	107
Chapter 14.	Listening to AD KAN Veterans	126
Chapter 15.	Past and Present Israeli Protestors Reconsidered	142
Chapter 16.	Israeli and Other Critics' Commentary on the Continuing Occupation	155
Chapter 17.	Israeli Society Revisited: An Anthropological Perspective	167

Epilogue 182
References 187
Index 195

Illustrations

7.1. AD KAN members protesting the continuing occupation and the construction of Jewish settlements beyond the Green Line (*from left:* Avishai Ehrlich, Moshe Shokeid, Ariella Friedman, Ruth Berman, Israel Gershoni), ca. 1989 — 77
7.2. Button with logo, "AD KAN! Speak to the PLO" — 78
7.3. "AD KAN, the University's Peace Movement Calling [PM] Rabin! Instead of More Knives Cut off Now: Two States," a poster inviting faculty and students to attend a demonstration on campus, March 1993 — 78

Preface

The following chapters, relaying the evolution of a protest movement, represent a somewhat unusual document in the record of my ethnographic research engagements. It is also equally uncommon in the tradition of anthropological reports. I graduated from the Manchester School of Anthropology during the late 1960s, where my instructor, Max Gluckman, used to tell his students before departure to the field, "Have your data right." True, these were the days before the era of "reflexivity" and "critical" analysis that have transformed the style of ethnographic writings, challenging the authority of subjectivity and the endurance of the ethnographer's "facts." Thus, there was ample space for the practitioners' revelations about their own personal experiences and feelings in the field, from Turnbull's *The Mountain People* (1972) and Rabinow's *Reflections on Fieldwork in Morocco* (1977) to Geertz's *After the Fact* (1995).

Contrary to the norms of my old school, the present ethnographic material is significantly based on my participation as chief "informant" in the ethnographic scene under investigation. Consequently, the ethnographer combines the dual identity of researcher and subject. It calls to mind the moving testimony *I Will Bear Witness* (1998) by Klemperer, the German linguist whose diaries produced a monumental ethnography about Jewish life under the Nazi regime. Though this book is no comparison with Klemperer's horrific experiences and agonizing narrative, I take the liberty of employing the anthropologist's toolkit and private persona to testify about my own society, stepping out of the normative, mainstream professional task to bear witness to other societies. Incidentally, this research procedure connects with a recent discourse about the parallel worlds of ethnography and biography.[1] However, my testimony integrates the reports and discourses exposed by other Israeli researchers and critics representing various vocational perspectives.

It took me a long time to take on the role that seems to extol the anthropologist as major protagonist. No doubt, the founding of the state of Israel presents a unique story in world history, a consequential outcome of the major events that reconstructed global politics, society, and culture during the twentieth century. Israeli scholars, anthropologists included, have been raised under the national banner and vision, but they are simultaneously expected to prove that they are accomplished citizens of the Western Euro-American scientific world. Indeed, to this day, publications in Hebrew weigh less in considerations of academic appointments and promotions.

Israeli anthropologists who were first recruited and promoted by a research project under the leadership of Gluckman (see Shokeid 2004), but who also came from other schools, have mostly investigated Israeli communal-ethnic-cultural issues. They thus deviated from their Euro-American colleagues' dominating field-sites and anthropological concerns, typically engaged in "other," third-world societies. In any case, my subject today, though signifying the tradition of research "at home," deviates again both in method and ethnographic mission. The initial field-site, a protest group at Tel Aviv University campus, but also its wider ethnographic objective makes inquiries into Israeli academics' terms of engagement and disengagement in view of acute national sociopolitical issues: in particular, the continuing tragic conflict with the Palestinians.

As related in later chapters, Euro-American academics of all disciplines have rarely engaged in joint action during critical national conflict situations at home. Anthropologists, almost as a rule, avoided expressing their moral judgment about the routine behavior, culture, and politics they observed in the societies they studied. They have usually developed an attitude of commitment and gratitude toward the people who allowed them to penetrate their lives and cultures. They made their careers on "the shoulders" of the "natives" in the various close or remote field-sites. Naturally, they refrained from risking positive relationships with their subjects.[2]

However, a few among the founding generation, Franz Boas and Margaret Mead in particular, were not hesitant to express their viewpoints and advice on various critical issues in the surrounding "real world." In later generations, other individuals voiced their value judgment on controversial social problems observed in the field or at home: notably, Laura Nader and Nancy Scheper-Hughes. Though less publicly visible, anthropologists have sometimes expressed their views on current issues in newspapers' op-eds and other venues.

In recent years, however, a new trend that has expanded the borders and mission of the anthropological project has been initiated under the banner of "public anthropology" or "public ethnography." Its appropriation involves "liberating" ethnographic observations and interpretation from their seclusion among the limited audience of close professional colleagues and journal reviewers. It entails transforming that knowledge into practical orientations addressing a wider world of readers, including the studied people and more diverse professional and civil audiences. Among the promoters of public anthropology, it deserves mentioning Albert Borofsky's exceptional contribution to that field (see Vine 2011, Borofsky 2019). However, as suggested by Fassin (2018: 7–8), public ethnography produces unique effects compared with other modes of apprehending social worlds; the presence of the ethnographer in the field attests to the veracity of his/her account of facts and events; the researcher and author's personal involvement with the work and the people who inhabit it calls for a critical take on the deceptive transparency of what is related and offers an effect of realism—a description and narration that generate more concrete and lively knowledge than other rhetorical forms do. In conclusion, Fassin claims, "What is at stake in the project of public ethnography is the sort of truth that is produced, established, and, in the end, told" (p. 8). The present exposition might suit the textual construction and the advocated agenda of public anthropology.

And last, the reality presented in this text is not bounded by the time span of the major events that triggered its recording. It includes short and long experiences and observations I engaged in during my later years as a citizen and commentator. That mode of presentation reflects the terms of the "ethnographic present" (Sanjek 2013), expanding the provisions of the "normative" fieldwork endeavor. However, never before have I been engaged in a field-site that attracted a comparable number of researchers and commentators who produced a wealth of reports representing various disciplines, methods, political-ideological perspectives, and narration genres. Inevitably, I introduce a limited selection of relevant sources that might disappoint some critical readers.

How should one categorize my work: as auto-ethnography, anthropological autobiography, memoir (e.g., Okely and Callaway 1992, Reed-Danahay 1997)? Reed-Danahay has applied auto-ethnography to a category of counternarratives, politicized texts that resist ethnographic presentation by outsiders (1997: 139). It seems my writing is a mix of all these textual categories in the list.

I hope the reader would tolerate my *hutzpah* in holding on to the role of key witness—"informant" in the anthropological convention—expressing his personal prospect on the scene investigated, hopefully absolved under the prerogative of a "native anthropologist."

Notes

1. *Social Anthropology* 26(1), February 2018.
2. Among the exceptional cases of antagonistic relationships, see Scheper-Hughes 2000.

Acknowledgments

I am deeply grateful to my colleagues and friends, dedicated members of AD KAN, those introduced in the text and many others, who shared with me their frustrations and hopes for changing Israeli realities. For a while they helped transform an institution representing an arena of individuals' lone achievements and competition into a space of comradery and teamwork. I regret I could not introduce many among them in more detail.

I thank Professor Aleksander Boskovic, EASA series editor, and the reviewers who commented on the text. I am grateful to Tom Bonnington, Ryan Masteller, and Elizabeth Martinez, Berghahn Books' editorial team, for their impressive care of the book production.

Introduction
On Memory

> *I have never attached so much importance to my own person that I would have been tempted to tell others the story of my life. Much had to occur, infinitely more events, catastrophes, and trials than are usually allotted to a single generation had to come to pass, before I found the courage to begin a book in which I was the principle person or, better still the pivotal point. Actually, it is not so much the course of my own destiny that I relate, but that of an entire generation.*
> —Stefan Zweig, *The World of Yesterday*

The following narrative intends to present a past social reality engaging the personal experiences of the author as member of AD KAN (NO MORE), a group of Israeli academics at Tel Aviv University (TAU) representing various disciplines, who came together to protest against their government's uncompromising positions in a long-standing binational conflict. It is part of the story of the first (1987) Palestinian intifada (uprising), the emergence of the Palestinians' effective public response after twenty years of subjugation to Israeli control of the West Bank and Gaza, since the aftermath of the 1967 war. And last, it is an account inquiring into the role and consequences of academics, or in broader terms "intellectuals," their active engagement in issues affecting the common good of their respective society. That discourse will naturally connect our case with past and present representations of academics' involvement with social-political conflict situations in Israel and other countries.

However, the return story of my engagement with the intifada, twenty-five years after I was first caught in its rolling events, cannot be compared with my other ethnographic accounts. It was not a planned professional fieldwork assignment that occupied me for many years of investigation and writing, a method one can identify in the long-term studies among the first generations of anthropologists. As later indicated, I rely on many documents at my disposal comparable with the ethnographer's "fieldnotes" as well as on present-day interviews with past participants. Nevertheless, the impact of memories on all involved, the author included, must be reckoned with more than ever before as an active element in the following exposition.

The spectrum of the studies inquiring the origin, contents, meaning, presentations, and consequences of memory in human life is wide and complex, including the biological, psychological, sociological, and other research dimensions (e.g., Mendels 2007). The founders of the modern ethnographic tradition claimed to offer descriptions of human behavior based on direct observations. They made great efforts to separate their personal narratives and their interpretations from the scientific domain of their colleagues the psychologists. Citing a known witness's account, "Received anthropological wisdom warns against using statements that people make about their past lives in constructing their histories" (Rosaldo 1980: 31). The long absence of "memory" from the anthropological dictionary is clearly visible in the *Anthropology of Experience* (Turner and Bruner 1986), a collection of essays that included a list of vanguard anthropologists who contributed to new genres, concepts, and metaphors in ethnographic writing. Mainstream anthropologists were also no less careful to restrain a hidden temptation for a literary career reflecting on their memories from the field, even though they all had the stuff for many exciting novels.

I experienced that "taboo" early in my career, as a student returning from the field participating at the Manchester staff seminars and in later writings; I felt inhibited, compelled to report directly on the continuing references of my subjects—immigrants from the Atlas Mountains in an Israeli village—to the stratification ladder that had existed in their past community in Morocco and that seemed to influence their present-day relationships. Instead, I referred to these "memories" as a myth of some sort (Shokeid 2007a). The method of life history, a literary model and style presenting the ethnographer's chosen subject's life, partly based on memories, also remained suspect. It was employed by a few "deviants," such as Lewis's *La Vida* (1967) describing the life of a Puerto Rican prostitute. However, from the late 1970s, anthropologists started publishing ethnographies based on memories and making no effort to disguise the use of the term. Myerhoff's acclaimed *Number Our Days* (1978), about a group of aging Jews who made their home in Los Angeles after retirement, concentrated on the memories that took them back to their earlier days of work, and also prior to their immigration to America.

It seems that memory's recognition as a promising vehicle for ethnographic work was encouraged by the growing impact of reflexivity in anthropology. The genre demanded the researcher's increased presence in the ethnographic text to allow for better information about his/her relationships with the people studied, as well as about his/her feelings and role in the field. In that new construction and style of ethnographic text, the authors transformed the memories that nourished their personal stories assembled in their fieldnotes into a coherent document that produced a collective memory representing the ethos of a particular group. This method had actually borrowed a sociological strategy when the writers chose the framework for a paradigmatic narrative that suited their leading thesis.

The sociological approach, geared mostly to the conception of collective memory, considered the past a social construction that shapes the various views of the past as they are manifested respectively in every historical epoch, though it treated the significance of autobiographical memory with suspicion. Halbwachs (1992), the first sociologist who stressed that our conceptions of the past are affected by the mental images we employ to solve present problems, argued that collective memory is essentially a reconstruction of the past in the light of the present. But anthropologists, whose research deeply engaged the company of the studied society, had inevitably relied and constructed autobiographical reports on past experiences—though sensitive to the observed participants' acceptance or refutation of their fellow community members' records.

Committed to a rigorous tradition of fieldwork, I have tried to maintain the role of a neutral and uninvolved observer, the recorder of memories, throughout my engagements. Naturally, I was unaware I might have harbored some social or ideological biases. In the ethnographic projects of later years, I limited the impact of informants' references to personal memories and maintained a low profile in the observed scene. However, more recently, I could not hide a feeling of nostalgia for a lost world shared with my veteran informants at the gay synagogue (CBST) in New York. On return to the "field" ten years later, I discovered the dramatic changes that took place with the transformation of a lay-led synagogue into an organization run by salaried professionals (Shokeid 2007b). I missed an important cohort among my friends who had died of AIDS or left for other places in the United States. Not a few reduced their participation in the congregation's affairs because they could not adapt to the changing social atmosphere and religious style. I could not help comparing and judging the present social ambience with my memories of life at CBST a decade earlier, in the late 1980s and early 1990s. I "went native" to an extent, sharing memories with veteran congregants and envisaging the present congregational reality, screened through the same mental apparatus as my subjects.

No doubt, under the growing impact of reflexivity in recent decades, ethnographic writing has withdrawn the old taboos regarding the role of memories and of the ethnographer. The genre demanded the researcher's increased presence in the text to allow for better information about his/her relationships with the studied people, as well as about the reporter's own mindset and performance in the field (e.g., Rabinow 1977, Behar 2003). I experienced that notion of emotional engagement and professional responsibility of informing on the ethnographer's "true" feelings during fieldwork already in the stage of the first ethnographic account, though published in an article not included in the PhD dissertation: "Fieldwork as Predicament rather than Spectacle" (1971).

However, the most "notorious" deviation from the old tradition of excluding the researcher's presence from the ethnographic text was exposed in an impromptu piece of writing: "Exceptional Experiences in Everyday Life" (1992). Not only was the material for that article based entirely on memories, it was also based upon my own self, recording personal uncanny events from young age to later years conceived as sort of an invisible rite of passage. Again, a Hebrew book, *An Israeli's Voyage: Tel Aviv, New York and Between* (2002), portrayed the social ambience of the Tel Aviv downtown neighborhood I was raised in during the 1940s/1950s. However, I never considered my writings as representing a literary narrative compared with Stefan Zweig's celebrated memoir and other known "pure" novelists and biographers. It was always the anthropologist's perspective, the tools and terms of reference when recording the present-day or past life experiences of the author and the "others" in his research.

As later clarified, the following record of the protest activities on TAU campus during the first intifada is mostly based on a large pile of documents that amount to ethnographic "fieldnotes," as well as on recent interviews with other participants. Nevertheless, one cannot erase the notion of personal memories affecting the perceptions of all involved, inevitably influenced by present-day experiences. Here we turn to Aristotle's distinction between memory and recollection, as introduced by Bloch (2007: 72): "Unlike the passive state of memory, recollection is a kind of active search, or, even more revealing, a kind of deduction."

The following text offers a tapestry composed of threads of "facts" of the day (based on documents related to AD KAN's activities as well as on reports by other observers in "real time"), memories of the narrator and a few close colleagues, as well as the views of other unrelated commentators. Moreover, I use that opportunity as vehicle to express a veteran observer's perspective and feelings about current developments in Israeli society. Thus, contrary to an earlier claim, I apparently concur with certified literary biographers, but in the role, or the pretension, of a "professional observer." Although the reporter's lifetime experiences are far remote from the dramatic and tragic transformations narrated by Zweig and others (e.g., Haffner's *Geschichte Eines Deutschen*, 2000), the story of the founding of the state of Israel in 1948 and the later transformations of its social, territorial, and political construction, all within a short epoch, seems deserving of Zweig's epitaph at our opening page: I bear witness to that extraordinary national saga unique in world history.

Finally, one cannot escape narrating the personal circumstances that have preceded and might have been instrumental in the development of an anthropologist as "activist." I hope the following presentation does not appear intended to glorify the narrator's persona.

1
A Personal Note

I was born in Tel Aviv a few years before the 1948 founding of the state of Israel. My father arrived in Palestine in 1924 from Lithuania, a young Zionist pioneer trained as a carpenter to help build the new Jewish sanctuary. My mother came about the same time with her family, who left their town in Poland in fear of a forthcoming pogrom. I was raised as one of the promising children of the Sabra generation,[1] the first harvest of Israeli native offspring free from the history of Jewish oppression and limited opportunities, brought up as Hebrew speakers avoiding the Diaspora languages of our parents. I served for two years in the Israeli army with the antiaircraft regiment and enrolled as a student at the Hebrew University in Jerusalem, the leading academic institution at the time except for the Technion, the engineering school in Haifa.

Expecting a career in the diplomatic service, I joined two BA major programs: Middle East history and sociology (though I had only a vague idea about the second subject). However, I was soon disappointed with the Middle East studies taught mostly by the esteemed representatives of an old-style Germanic encyclopedic tradition. But I enjoyed the sociology courses taught by younger Anglo-American-trained scholars headed by Professor S. N. Eisenstadt, who took over Martin Buber's chairmanship. We were introduced to Talcott Parsons's functionalist theories that dominated American sociology at that time.

It was during the MA studies that I was recruited to assist a research project on the second generation in the new cooperative farming villages. These villages were founded in the periphery of the post-1948 map of Jewish settlements to absorb the immigrants coming mostly from Muslim countries. That task led me to the position of rural sociologist of the semiarid Negev region with the administration of the Jewish Agency Land Settlement Department, consulting on the complex problems of transforming craftsmen and peddlers—Jewish immigrants mostly from Middle Eastern countries (Morocco, Tunisia, Yemen, Kurdistan, Cochin, etc.)—into farmers, members of the newly established cooperative communities (2015b).

Having conducted research in the field of immigration, and after enduring a fascinating experience of consulting with TAHAL (the Israel water planning company) on a development project in Iran (following the 1962 earthquake in the Qazvin region), I was left with the impression that one can indeed influence the lives of people entangled in the intricacies of bureaucratic constraints (Shokeid 1963). But applying the Jerusalem sociological toolkit of modernization theories made me aware of the limits of mainstream sociological research. I looked for another, more satisfying way of research, studying the human condition "in vivo": the reality beyond the campus offices, libraries, statistical data, scheduled interviews, experts' seminars, etc. Thus, I began my "discovery" of anthropology and ensuing journey to Manchester. From here started a life-long career as an anthropologist conducting ethnographic studies in Israel and later in the United States.

However, my "formal" anthropological assignment started with a fieldwork project among immigrants from the Atlas Mountains in a farming cooperative Negev village. The research recorded their memories of life in Morocco (where they served their Berber neighbors as traders and craftsmen—carpenters, shoemakers, blacksmiths, etc.), their adaptation to modern farming and cooperative organization, their family life and traditions, their religious comportment and leadership, and the emergence of a new communal order under the impact of the social-economic and political circumstances in a Jewish nation-state. The ethnography presented a successful case of social and economic transformation of the newcomers who became prosperous farmers engaged in a vast network of family relations settled elsewhere in Israel and preserving much of their cultural heritage (Shokeid 1985 [1971]).

No doubt, that success story was not the fortune of all other new arrivals in the 1950/60s—particularly those who settled in the new "development towns" in the Israeli periphery with few economic assets and poor employment opportunities. However, that research experience made a profound impact on my own life. Feelings of wonder and admiration at that tremendous social drama, and gratitude for the warm hospitality extended to me during my eighteen months of fieldwork, made me adopt the name of that village, Shokeid, instead of my Eastern European surname.[2] True, I am sometimes embarrassed by that exposure of personal identification with a remote corner of Israeli geography, but I do not regret that act of personal engagement and gratitude to the people who enabled the start of a gratifying professional vocation.

I returned to Israel in 1968 on the completion of my doctoral dissertation. This coincided with the aftermath of Israel's stunning 1967 victory following the preceding scary weeks when the existence of Israel seemed in peril. It seemed inevitable a peaceful solution would soon be reached with the establishment of a Palestinian state alongside Israel in the West Bank and Gaza. Before departure, I was deeply impressed watching the optimistic future illustrated by Abba Eban, the Israeli foreign minister at that time, who interviewed in London, reiterated Churchill's avowal: "We shall be magnanimous in victory."

My return to Israel, as appointed lecturer at the newly instituted Tel Aviv University, also coincided with the founding of anthropological studies as an autonomous subject integrated into Israeli academia in the joint departments of sociology and anthropology. The 1970s and 1980s were productive years of professional accomplishments. Anthropology made its modest impact at all Israeli faculties of social sciences. I served twice as chair of the joint department at Tel Aviv and as chair of the Israel Anthropological Association.

I spent a short spell writing letters to the Israeli popular newspaper *Yediot* during my five-month conscription to the army reserves in the 1973 war (on combat duty in the Sinai and the Golan Heights). These letters expressed my rage against Golda Meir's government. Obsessed with the glory of the 1967 war, the PM and her partners failed to initiate peace negotiations with the neighboring Arab states.

This was a hectic moment in Israeli history following the debacle of the Yom Kippur War (1973), for the first time shaking my viewpoint on academics' retreat from the public arena. I was personally engaged, as were many other civilians called to serve in the war and its aftermath. Cut off from civilian-academic work for nearly five months, I found refuge in expressing frustration and anger, sending handwritten short letters to my girlfriend (later my spouse) who typed them and forwarded them to the editor.

One of these last communications shortly after returning to civilian life was titled "The Scientists and Public Engagement" (*Ha'aretz*,

6 May 1974). At that era of demonstrations against the government of Golda Meir and Moshe Dayan (the defense minister blamed for the military mishap), an impressive list of Tel Aviv academics publicly supported political action and the founding of a new, more radical party (SHINUI-change). My short article was meant to congratulate their coming out of the academic closet, their departure from the traditional position of neutral observers—reporting but not judging the natives' comportment. That position of academic "purity," I argued, has been responsible for the minimal impact of Israeli social scientists on the life of their society. The piece ended indicating that this "innocence" raises some association with historical events in other societies where intellectuals kept aloof from responsibility as tragedy developed around them, assuming they did not take part in these happenings (one had to be careful not associating by name the German example—a continuing taboo in Israeli public culture). Disappointedly, that episode of Israeli academics' involvement ended on a humiliating note when PM Menachem Begin coopted the crew of intellectuals headed by Professor Yigael Yadin (a distinguished Jerusalem university archeologist), and the party soon disintegrated. I regretted that I did not have the stamina to visit Professor Yadin and express my revulsion at his submissive comportment under PM Begin's cunning manipulation.

Since then, I retreated from the public forum and came to consider the positive quality of the "ivory tower," the exclusive commitment to one's professional occupation. Disillusioned, I nourished a somewhat romantic perception of the university role in society as recorded since the dark days of the Middle Ages, the citadel preserving "culture" from the teeth of politicians, greedy tycoons, and the uninformed masses.

But other than these letters during the 1973 war, I was never active in the public forum, neither registering as a party member nor participating in a nonpartisan voluntary association, and was reluctant to participate as an expert in political-intellectual discussions or popular talk shows on television. On return to civilian life, I declined an invitation from the editor of *Yediot* (Mr. Dov Yudkovsky) to contribute some of my social-cultural observations more regularly. A "100 percent" academic, fully engaged in teaching and ethnographic research, I believed that academics should spend their time and energies mostly in the service of their professional vocation and resented "professors" who seemed to display a need for public attention in the media or who engaged in the political arena. Why assume that academics are better informed or endowed with superior judgement when dealing with public issues?

It is not an easy task to try and comprehend the vast literature dealing with the terms and scope of personal identities, an issue that has engaged an army of psychologists, sociologists, anthropologists, novelists, and other practitioners for over a hundred years. How many identities does an ordinary academic possess, considering his/her family, gender, nationality, religious, civil, professional, and other roles? Am I satisfied with those ascribed to me? Thus, for example, when asked abroad "Where do you come from?" I usually respond "Tel Aviv," confusing sometimes an innocent investigator unfamiliar with that spot on the world globe. Am I disguising my "official" Israeli-Jewish identity, naturally assumed by ordinary bystanders? True, I pretend to separate myself from Israeli politics and from certain sociocultural segments in Jewish-Israeli society.

However, excluding the official, biological, and other intrinsic life signifiers, what are those dimensions in one's persona he/she might prefer and emphasize as chief element of their self-presentation, embodying a major existential lifetime fulfilment? No doubt, as is probably true for many others, my professional occupation and the credentials of a social/cultural anthropologist represent a major element in my core identity: "I am an anthropologist!" is not simply a professional designation of an employment record for the last few decades. That personal presentation has become a key guide navigating my stance in daily life and reflecting a wide spectrum of experiences and social/cultural perspectives. It seems, however, that element in my self-perception locates me as member in the tribe of "intellectuals."

Basic education in British anthropology of the late 1960s seemed to situate the practitioner in a neutral professional position aimed to examine the "natives," the society observed on another continent removed from the ethnographer's present life situation. Most anthropologists had no intention of influencing their subjects in the field or the audience at home, or any desire to change their perspective about their personal or public lives. True, in the United States, Margaret Mead got the mythical reputation of effecting norms of parental authority and sexual conduct among the younger American generation as consequence of her studies in Samoa. But at the same time, most American anthropologists made it their mission to present and interpret other cultures, thus informing but not transforming their home society.

No doubt, my position was somewhat "problematic," scheduled to conduct my PhD research in Israel—my home, though I was trained in the company of teachers and students whose major ethnographic fieldwork destination was among rural and urban African communities far remote from their home societies. Actually, my first anthropological article, "Fieldwork as Predicament rather than Spectacle" (1971), presented the exceptional research situation among immigrants from the Atlas Mountains (Morocco), sharing with them as I did the status of citizenship and cultural roots (as Jews and Israelis though from a different socio-economic-cultural background). That early encounter with the emerging genre of reflexivity in anthropology was concerned with the relationship between the ethnographer and his subjects during the stage of fieldwork, and later was presented in the published ethnography.

However, though different in training and practice, the anthropologists shared with their Israeli sociologist colleagues the ethos of studying Israeli society, immigrant absorption in particular. Yet, teachers and students were mostly disinterested in national politics. There was no expectation to engage in civil activities beyond the ordinary obligations of Israeli citizens, such as military service. Except for a few short-lived interventions in the public arena described earlier, the sociopolitical ambience of university life was overwhelmingly consensual for many years. These were the days immediately after the establishment of the state of Israel; the arrival of many thousands of Jewish immigrants from Europe (Holocaust survivors) and from the Middle East; the expansion of the economy, the social services, and other public agencies; and the continuing security tensions around the borders with the neighboring Arab states.

A general atmosphere of optimism seemed to engulf the founding of the new nation, based on the biblical myth remodeled by the Zionist movement's ideology and invigorated by horror and international guilt following the Holocaust. The new democracy surrounded by belligerent and feudal regimes seemed to enjoy the sympathy and support of the free progressive world. The astonishing victory of the 1967 war seemed to testify to that immense national achievement. Israeli intellectuals, including the leading authors, sociologists, anthropologists, and other academics, seemed to support the project of a new democratic society absorbing of massive immigration that doubled the country's population within ten years.

My next ethnographic project took place in Jaffa, the pre-1948 Arab major city in Palestine, now part of Tel Aviv's municipality—a field-site close to home, representing a wider context of major sociopolitical issues. The previous project among Moroccan immigrants was part of a research scheme initiated by Manchester University, but the study among the Muslims and Christians in Jaffa was an impromptu personal decision (Shokeid and Deshen 1982). It was the consequence of a meeting with an Arab student who attended the introductory anthropology course at Tel Aviv University and invited me to attend Christmas mass at his Catholic church.

No doubt, my immediate engagement with that fieldwork site was a response to a sort of guilt about ignorance if not detachment from the most acute social-political-moral issue affecting Israeli life. "Israeli Arabs," a major social-cultural ethnic constituency among my compatriots, officially equal citizens, though they are profoundly alien in Jewish public perception and everyday experiences. Moroccan Jewish immigrants were expected to quickly integrate into mainstream Israeli society and culture, but the Arabs left in Israel after the 1948 war of independence (the Nakba in the Palestinian narration) were not supposed to change their communal organization, culture, and lifestyle. The Druze, however, began to more closely participate in Israeli life, as their young men are conscripted into the regular army (at age eighteen) and many stay on as career military personnel. The Arabs in Jaffa in the late 1970s composed a small minority of about ten thousand left of its former population of about one hundred thousand Muslims and Christians of various denominations.

The sudden awareness of an Arab community in close proximity to my Tel Aviv neighborhood seemed an invitation for research I could not let go. The following observations revealed a major difference in family and communal life separating the Christians from the Muslim residents of Jaffa. The Christians seemed better organized. Their religious leadership—clergy recruited mostly from abroad—supported extensive communal services centered on churches of various denominations. By contrast, a major theme that seemed to represent family and political comportment among the Muslims was their cultural allegiance to the "code of honor." I interpreted that commitment as a mode of behavior supporting their sense of a distinct national-cultural identity surrounded by Jewish neighbors and under Israeli rule, which pervaded most aspects of their daily lives. It was no less a symbolic claim for their continuing association with the Arab world surrounding Israel and, in particular, their relatives and co-religionists in the West Bank and Gaza.

The next ethnographic project took me to New York. Nevertheless, it was an Israeli issue that raised much concern in the public media: a growing awareness of the phenomenon of the derogatively nicknamed Yordim ("those who go down"), Israeli-born citizens who migrated to other countries, the United States in particular. It was sort of a "return trip" research mission, from the early observations of Moroccan Jews considered Olim ("going up") arriving in "the promised land" to the subjects of the researcher's own generational cohort of native Israelis abandoning their shared homeland for another "land of promise." For two years, 1982–84, I stayed with my family in a Queens neighborhood attracting many Israelis, socializing mostly in their company. Observations at that time revealed that they departed from Israel mostly due to impromptu circumstances, such as professional training, work contracts, post–army service tourist trips, family ties, etc., that were extended beyond the original plan of the scheduled stay. That reality gained the ethnography's title "Children of Circumstances: Israeli Emigrants in New York" (1988). Incidentally, the book came out during the hectic first year of AD KAN's emergence, and despite my original intention to produce a Hebrew version, I was too busy and possibly lost the motivation to invest time in what seemed a far less urgent issue in Israeli life.

The three ethnographic projects preceding the explosion of the intifada were all related to what might be considered major social issues in Israeli contemporary life. That choice of research engagement became typical to many Israeli anthropologists, partly because of the lack of funding for ethnographic work outside the country, but more due to the tradition that began with the first cohort of anthropologists who were recruited to study the establishment and transformations of the new Jewish/Israeli society. However, my ensuing projects were not only separate from Israeli topics, they were also far remote from traditional mainstream anthropological fieldwork sites and subjects of interest: observing gay organizations in New York (Shokeid 2003b [1995], 2015a). One might guess that transformation of sites and research issues was not unrelated to a state of mind and emotions impacting the personal national commitments of an Israeli academic.

But regardless of that later detour of research sites, I have remained an "Israeli anthropologist" in terms of my continuing close association and inescapable engagement with Israeli socio-cultural-political issues and divisions. That position seems to differentiate anthropologists who have studied "at home" from their colleagues mostly engaged in the study of "other" societies.

Promoted to full professor, I joined the laudable society of the university senate. Familiar with that leading institution years earlier as an elected representative of the lower ranks, I was never comfortable at the senate meetings. Only rarely did its monthly meeting's agenda seem of particular interest. Meetings were mostly occupied with technical matters such as confirming new teaching programs, institutes, honorary chair incumbents, etc. The senate was seldom the site for lively discussions on subjects that reflected, at least in my view, some relevance to the advancement of science, culture, society, and politics. Was I a naïve newcomer to the "hall of mirrors"? Those who had the stamina to attend more regularly preserved the ethos of a self-governing academic institution. True, some among them have been rewarded for their loyalty and taken on leading positions and honors in the campus organization. Actually, I attended the senate meetings regularly to represent the lower ranks, but I lost motivation to continue when granted full membership and upon discovering as, later narrated, how ineffective one could be in aiming to promote an issue of moral-national-academic importance.

Anyhow, considering this record of field-site research and teaching experience since returning from Manchester, I had no complaints about life and work, which seemed quite satisfactory.

Notes

1. The "Sabra generation" refers to the first Israeli-born youth. A symbolic, affectionate projection of the "free"-born children, away from their parents' Diaspora environment, resembling the cactus fruit: prickly outside but sweet inside.
2. Revealed in "What Is There to a Name? The Ethnographer and His Moroccan Subjects in Shokeida" (Shokeid 2009).

2

The First Palestinian Intifada

The first intifada (Palestinian uprising against the Israeli occupation) that started on 9 December 1987 drew back the curtain on the extraordinary drama begun in June 1967, when the Israeli army astounded the world with its quick victory (the Six-Day War) over the massive Arab armies that intended to overturn the humiliating failure of 1948 and regain Palestine. Consequently, the state of Israel gained control of the West Bank (until then under the rule of the King of Jordan), the Sinai Peninsula and the Gaza Strip (by then under the rule of Egypt), and the Golan Heights (a Syrian territory overlooking the Sea of Galilee). Although the Sinai Peninsula was returned to Egypt with the Begin-Sadat peace accord in 1979, the Gaza Strip remained under Israeli control.

It is difficult to compare the impact of two historical moments that both happened in the span of twenty years: the founding of the State of Israel in 1948 and the 1967 war against the Arab armies. The 1967 epic victory seemed to embody a "rebirth" of a nation, taking on a completely new form and destination. It seemed a far more miraculous happening compared with the UN recognition of a Jewish state and the outcome of the war of independence. Caught in the euphoric atmosphere of that eventuality, it seemed almost a sign of divine intervention. For many Israelis, it promised a final reconciliation with the Arab states (the Palestinian refugees included), but for many others it was the fulfilment of messianic hopes: a return of the Jewish nation to the promised land undivided by the pre-1967 borders (the Green Line) that kept apart East Jerusalem and other sacred historical sites, especially Hebron (site of the Cave of the Patriarchs).

It is beyond the terms of this presentation to expand on the complex failed attempts to construct a new political order in Palestine. That perplexing process engaged the Israelis' political-ideological and security considerations, the Arab states' positions, as well as the international powers and intermediaries who tried to intervene and terminate the continuing conflict. The Israelis were mostly unwavering about the annexation of East Jerusalem, but they were divided on whether to hold on to other parts of the occupied territories. The Arab partners could not accommodate any serious change to the pre-1967 borders. The Palestinians at that early phase were considered citizens of Jordan and Egypt, internally divided by family and regional loyalties. However, with the withdrawal of King Hussein from his legal claims to the West Bank, the 1967 war turned into the "hour of the Palestinian people." The Arab League recognition in 1974 of the Palestine Liberation Organization (PLO) as the sole legitimate representative of the Palestinian people initiated the Palestinian identity as a separate national entity (e.g., Gelber 2018).

However, with the failure of all proposals for a final solution, it seemed for a while that the "temporary" Israeli occupation had benefitted the Palestinian residents. Their standard of living improved considerably with the opening of the Israeli labor and commercial markets, a level of affluence far more favorable than the economic conditions during the Jordanian and Egyptian regime era. The apparently peaceful acceptance of the Israeli rule seemed to indicate, at least among the Israeli leaders and citizenship, the successful ad hoc implementation of an "enlightened occupation" (*kibush naor*) unprecedented in other conflict situations. That does not, of course, consider the strict control of Palestinians' political activities, but again, this control did not seem dramatically conspicuous compared with the limits on free politics under the Arab states' former rule. That early stage of the apparently consensual period of a peaceful routine in the occupied territories was thoroughly described by General Shlomo Gazit (1999; 2016) who served for seven years as first coordinator of the government's defense and civil operations in the territories beyond the Green Line (the 1948 universally recognized postwar border between Israel and its Arab neighbors).

Assuming the occupation regime would not last for long, Moshe Dayan, the defense minister at that time, and his deputy general Gazit, implemented a civil-political strategy intended to avoid drastic changes in the lives of the Palestinians in the territories as much as possible. Moreover, they enabled a free movement of Israelis and Palestinians crossing through the Green Line, offering a "normal" exchange of visitors, labor, and commerce. However, many years later, Gazit sadly concluded: "Twenty years of success and peace [1967–87] caused Israel a colossal disaster. We deluded ourselves it could last forever" (2016: 385).

I have no intention to expand on the history of the Zionist movement and the stages that have led to the settlement of Jews in Palestine: the 1917 Balfour declaration, a public statement issued by the British government announcing support for the establishment of a Jewish homeland in Palestine; the United Nation partition plan for a Jewish and an Arab state in Palestine; the following war and the founding of the State of Israel in 1948; the aftermath of the 1967 Six-Day War—the Israeli occupation of the West Bank, Gaza, and Golan Heights; and the missed efforts of reconciliation between the two national movements. However, I mention in this context *The Question of Palestine* (1980) by Edward Said, the most eloquent public intellectual of Palestinian descent. His detailed narrative presenting the Palestinian cause, written about ten years after the start of the 1967 occupation of the Palestinian territories, predicted the eruption of the first intifada, expressed in the last sentences of his chronicle: "We must look forward realistically to much turbulence, much ugly human waste in the short term" (p. 238).

Edward Said, the celebrated author of *Orientalism* (1978), a critique of the cultural representations underpinning "Orientalism" (how the Western world perceives the Orient), analyzed the Palestinians' destiny as part of that legacy: "By the middle of the twentieth century there was a willing identification between Western liberal discourse and Zionism. In Zionism, the liberal West saw the triumph of reason and idealism. … The Zionist had become the *only* person in Palestine as because the Arab's negative personality; oriental, decadent, inferior" (p. 37–38). Considering Zionism as basically a product of European colonialism, Said introduced the counter-response movement of the dispossessed Palestinian natives (himself a member of the Palestinian National Council). They seemed to him ready to accommodate the Israelis who occupied much of their homeland and drove them out as stateless refugees. Edward Said passed away in 2003 during the outbreak of the second round of violence (the second intifada), which confirmed his prediction of a volatile future in contested Palestine.

A road traffic collision that killed four laborers from the Gaza Strip on their way home after a day of work in Israel triggered the first intifada eruption. Apparently, though the accident was unintentional (a frequent occurrence on Israeli roads), a rumor nonetheless spread among the Palestinians that the deaths were in retaliation for the murder of an Israeli in the center of Gaza City the preceding day. In the next few weeks, seemingly unorganized protests by Palestinians took place across the occupied territories, blocking roads and impeding Israeli army movements. Despite the tear gas and rubber-coated bullets used against them, demonstrators remained in the line of fire, throwing stones and heading unarmed toward the soldiers. Shopkeepers played an important role in maintaining the daily and general strikes. On 9 March 1988 the labor boycotts started, and no workers from Gaza went to their jobs in Israel. The intifada gradually grew more organized. It ended five years later with the signing of the first Oslo Accords in 1993 (e.g., Lockman and Beinin 1990; Nassar and Heacock 1990; Schiff and Ya'ari 1990; Freedman 1991; Lustick 1993; King 2007).

Leaflets served as informal leadership at the start of the uprising, coordinating the daily events of protest. In *Speaking Stones: The Words Behind the Palestinian Intifada*, Mishal and Aharoni (1989) recorded nearly eighty flyers advertised around the territories during 1988 by the various major secular and religious organizations that took the lead; these impacted the lives of Palestinians—in Gaza and the West Bank—in key spheres of life: strikes at work, transport and education, closure of shops, calling on local employees to resign from their posts at the Israeli civil administration (the police in particular), boycotting Israeli products, appealing for mutual help and contributions, etc. Most residents considered these fliers executive commands.

Among the early reporters, Lockman and Beinin (1990) introduced a wide spectrum of observers and commentators, outsiders and insiders, Palestinians, Israelis, and international reviewers who followed the start and escalation of the intifada. Edward Said, who signed his chapter in that volume in January 1989, watched his predictions coming true: "the intifada accomplished a number of unprecedented things ... Palestine and Israel will never be the same again ... collaborators with the occupation were encircled and gradually rendered ineffective ... the old social organizations that depended on notables, on family, on traditional hierarchy—all these were largely marginalized. A new set of institutions emerged ..." (p. 20). Another contributor, Salim Tamari, a leading Palestinian sociologist at Birzeit University in the West Bank, highlighted the demographic pattern of the intifada participants: roughly 60 percent of the people of the West Bank and Gaza were under seventeen years of age. "These are the core of the people you watch every day confronting Israeli soldiers ... it suggests the context in which young people lose fear in facing death or mutilation of their bodies" (p. 127). But, most important, the insurrection unified all Palestinian political factions that were previously divided.

Naturally, the list of texts reporting on the intifada have often presented similar observations and conclusions, though, expressing personal viewpoints, expectations, and sentiments. Among the outside observers is Ian Lustick, an expert on the Israel-Palestine conflict, whose *Unsettled States, Disputed Lands* (1993) was authored during the first intifada and compared the Israel-Palestine conflict with "similar" struggles: Britain-Ireland, France-Algeria. Demonstrating a deep knowledge about Israeli inside politics, Lustick offered sharp insights on the transformations Israeli society has experienced since 1967. In particular, he emphasized the change of the "hegemonic conception" concerning the borders of the state: the hectic political-ideological debates since 1967 about the fate of the Green Line and the growing political power of Jewish settlers in the occupied territories. However, like most other early and later commentators, he highlighted how the shocking eruption of the intifada erased the comfortable public notion of a "benign occupation" and the standard accusation of the PLO (Palestine Liberation Organization) as instigators of disturbances.

No doubt, the flare-up of the intifada had deep causes: economic, social, and political deprivation culminating in Gaza. Gaza was one of the most populous sites on the planet with 1.391 people per kilometer at the time, a high birthrate, and more than 50 percent of its workforce employed in low-income occupations in Israel with little options for the better educated. These grave demographic and economic circumstances added to other developments in Gaza and the West Bank, such as, the emergence of a young generation born under Israeli rule, who took on a growing part in the conflict that was led hitherto mostly by outside Arab players. A classified survey conducted in 1985 for the Israeli PM office described the Gaza Strip as an economic and demographic time bomb presenting a severe political and security threat (Gazit 1999). However, that serious alert left no impact on its recipients in Israeli governmental agencies.

As mentioned briefly above, outside scholars and professional observers reported extensively on the intifada outburst. However, I intend to expand on that story based on the observations of Israeli reporters close to the scene, prominent media commentators, and those in leading administrative positions. Ze'ev Schiff and

Ehud Ya'ari, preeminent TV and newspaper military and national defense journalists, published among the earliest exposures of the sociopolitical context, the developing events on the ground, and an analytical perspective on the potential consequences of the revolt (*Intifada: The Palestinian Uprising—Israel's Third Front*, 1990). Meron Benvenisti served as vice mayor of Jerusalem during the 1970s and was responsible for municipal affairs of the annexed Arab East Jerusalem. His *Fatal Embrace* (1992) was also published during the events of the intifada. David Hacham was a high-ranking Israeli officer who served for eight years (before and up to the end of the uprising) as head of the Arab affairs department in the Israeli civil administration apparatus, responsible for the Gaza Strip. Hacham's later report, subtitled *The Inside Story of the Intifada* (2016), offers a comprehensive record displaying the role of a "participant observer" in the real sense of the term.

Schiff and Ya'ari have portrayed the two sides of a blind mirror confronting the upcoming revolt, across the apparently unmarked Green Line border separating two national destinies. With the intifada still in progress, they presented an extensive description of the history, politics, and ongoing events at both sides of the conflict. In a cynical tone, the authors claimed that the Israelis discovered the occupied territories twice: at the end of the Six-Day War and again twenty years later, in December 1987. In the meantime, they related to the Palestinian issue, the territories, and Palestine's inhabitants as though a reality was taking place in a distant land. As from the Palestinian side, Schiff and Ya'ari argued, the intifada began not as a national uprising but as a rebellion of the poor. It was the despair of a generation of Palestinian youth who felt bereft of a promising future and thousands of laborers who made their living in Israel but were expected to remain invisible. Even Yasser Arafat (leader of the PLO staying in Tunisia at the time) failed to see anything out of the ordinary in early reports about the eruption of riots in the territories. However, Israelis of all political convictions have now come to feel that their country has been living a lie. They have been deceived believing that the status quo of occupation could be maintained indefinitely.

No surprise, the political, intelligence, and military apparatus were totally unprepared for the upsurge of mass demonstrations and other manifestations of civil disobedience. That late realization, together with rage at the Palestinians for breaking the delusion of consensual occupation, led to a wave of extremism in Israel. The ensuing sharp turn toward the right-wing aspirations and the spread of fanatic behavior were at times reminiscent of the Palestinians' frenzied expressions during the uprising. Nevertheless, Schiff and Ya'ari considered the option of a peaceful arrangement based on political compromise. At that time, they noticed that the demographic map of the occupied territories, including Jewish settlers, had not changed much. They concluded that Israel must insist on the solution to the conflict be a confederative arrangement that will include Israel, Jordan, and the Palestinian entity constituted in the West Bank and Gaza. In retrospect, the intifada acted as an earthquake, raising far-reaching expectations and visions on both the left and right of the Israeli ideological-political national spectrum and widening its divisions.

Benvenisti, who developed an academic career since his days in Jerusalem's municipal organization, engaged his commentary within a broad social-historical perspective. He aimed to explain the underlying motives and the combative strategies employed by both sides of the conflict. The spontaneity of the uprising seemed "irrational" considering the heavy price the Palestinians paid in material and other existential terms, although their social-economic circumstances improved compared with the pre-occupation Jordanian and Egyptian regimes' living conditions. He offered a sociological perspective: the Palestinians' notion of "relative deprivation," comparing their present-day socio-economic-political position with the Jewish community of occupiers and settlers representing a classical colonialist situation (reminiscent of Ireland, Algeria, and South Africa). On the Israeli side, however, he called on the founding myth of a persecuted ethnic minority returning to an ancient deserted homeland—thereby liberating its dispersed tribes around the globe—and surrounded by powerful enemies scheming its brutal destruction. He also pinpointed the changing composition of Israeli social structure, the ideological transformations strengthening right-wing constituencies, and religious trends supporting the continuing occupation and land annexation. Benvenisti's 1992 account and his instructive warnings authored during the hectic days of the intifada were critical of the changing social-political texture of Israeli society (reminiscent of Lustick's observations reported above), and his analysis of the intracommunal Jewish-Palestinian conflict has not lost its relevance for present-day readers.

As for Hacham, he was in close day-to-day contact with representatives of both protagonists during the developing intifada conflict: the Israeli military and civil agencies on the one hand, and the Palestinians employed in local public municipal services on the other. An Israeli agent, he nevertheless cultivated intimate relationships with many locals (the traditional leadership in particular) and revealed a deep understanding of local cultural traditions— becoming an anthropologist in disguise. No doubt, his stance and obligations were fully subjected to the interests of the Israeli regime. Nevertheless, he developed a keen perspective and empathy toward the changing public mood in Gaza City and its surrounding villages. I feel a sort of kinship with Hacham, who, like myself, drew on memories and records from the intifada to return to that period many years later, describing it as "an experience of once in a lifetime" (2016: 369).

He confesses: "The intifada got us in complete surprise, totally spontaneous with no prior planning and with no Palestinian organization initiating its sudden emergence" (p. 17). Like all other observers, he reports that the trigger was the road accident at the entry gate to Gaza that killed a few returning laborers. But obviously, he concluded, that accident must have just released the cork off the top of the simmering mount of resentment ready to erupt. Protest against the Israeli regime mostly consisted of market strikes and the closure of shops announced by daily leaflets, as the impromptu uprising was gradually institutionalized. As also recorded by Nassar and Heacock (1990), there were hundreds of monthly strikes and parades of angry protestors barricading main roads during the first two years of the intifada.

However, Hacham admits, "we [military and civil administration] were completely ignorant of the depth of the social-political-religious transformations Palestinian society has went through" (p. 17). As suggested by other observers, the sudden spontaneous uprising surprised the Palestinian elites no less than anyone else (Freedman 1991: 15). Hacham's observations emphasize the changes of leadership: the decline of the authority of traditional kin group elders and communal venerated headmen who were collaborating with the regime of occupation and enjoying its rewards, and the emergence of a new militant generation born into the reality of occupation free of old alliances and traditional obligations. Moreover, he was aware of the growing prominence and influence of religious leaders and their constituencies (tolerated at an earlier stage by the Israelis) competing with the PLO's popular position in the territories. The mosques have changed their function from sites of prayer and ritual, instead becoming centers of uprising that enjoy the safety of sacred places. This was the road by which Hamas soon became a major player in the radicalization of the intifada, adding a powerful Islamic element to the ideology of Palestinian nation-building and rejecting compromise with the Israelis. The universities in Gaza and the West

Bank have also developed into a public forum for political expression, enlisting hundreds of college students and high-school youth.

However, the Israeli civil and military leadership were slow to realize the seriousness of the eruption of protest, assuming it was a short-lived flare-up of violence to be easily contained. Thus, for example, the defense minister at that time (Yitzhak Rabin) left for a two-week trip to the United States, leaving behind a rude suggestion "to break hands and legs" as an efficient method to calm down the protest. Delegations of Knesset members who visited local dignitaries returned convinced that the majority of Palestinians preferred a return to normal life along the model of peace and order provided by the Israelis. However, local residents employed in the civil administration apparatus, hitherto seemingly content and cooperative, suddenly expressed resentment against the Israeli regime. They were thought unusual and punished, losing their jobs. No doubt, for many years it was assumed that Gaza Strip residents' dependency on shared interests with the Israeli economy as its major source of work (in industry, construction, services, and agriculture) and on the bounding effect of the exchange of commerce would prevent political revolt.

It seems it took some time also for Hacham to comprehend the magnitude of antagonism and the determination of the protesters. The protesters were ready to pay heavy economic penalties that would impact wide sectors of the Palestinian population (a communal combative notion Benvenisti comprehended much earlier). Contrary to the assumptions considering their "reasonable" economic interests, many Palestinian employees in the Israeli-led municipal and governmental administration agencies resigned voluntarily, and thousands of workers gave up daily employment in Israel.

The intifada's impact was also cast on the social structure of Palestinian society: political organization affiliation replaced family loyalties, and families known for close ties with the Israelis lost respect or were under pressure to dissociate themselves from hitherto-esteemed relatives now stigmatized for collaborating with the enemy. In fact, during the early stage of the intifada (January 1988), Hanna Siniora, the editor of *Al-Fajar*—the daily Palestinian newspaper published in East Jerusalem—had already advocated for civil disobedience, a form of nonviolent resistance: stop working in Israel, stop paying taxes, and avoid buying Israeli products.

The harsh reprisals assumed to calm down the revolt were of little effect and actually achieved the opposite result. Hacham explains, for example, the failed idea of a psychological contra campaign, such as the promotion of fake fliers to confuse the authentic intifada messages. In particular, following the escalation of violence—the killing of an Israeli policeman and three soldiers—415 militant participants from Gaza and the West Bank, many from Hamas and other religious organizations, were deported to Lebanon. However, their camp in southern Lebanon became a center for pilgrimage, inviting the international media and promoting the personal reputation of its inmates. Israel was finally compelled to let them return, thus elevating their reputation and influence among the younger generation in the territories. Moreover, it boosted the growth of Hamas, the later most ardent enemy of Israel. In retrospect, Hacham admits this was a grave mistake, although at the time he thought it was a legitimate response to the brutal killing of the Israeli personnel.

My appreciation of the report and empathy with an agent representing the regime of occupation relates also to his account about a few Palestinians I came to know during the activities of AD KAN, the peace/protest organization on campus. As later described, leading professionals, from Gaza in particular, were invited to take part in AD KAN's public events to report on local conditions and suggest their viewpoint on the politics of the day and future options. A few members of the organization went to visit them in Gaza. However, the report by an Israeli insider revealed some sensitive information unknown to us at the time, such as his own people's brutal attack on a Gaza lawyer who played an important role in the history of AD KAN. He must have irritated members of a radical Palestinian group by advocating for compromise, contrary to the growing preference for non-negotiation with the Israelis during the heyday of the intifada. Media reporters were probably uninformed about the inner conflicts and competitions inflicting the ongoing turmoil among the intifada's active participants.

Before the eruption of the intifada, the Palestinians were permitted to travel and visit all sites in Israel, and there was no system to monitor who came in and out of Gaza and other occupied territories. I remember visiting the Gaza main food market with friends in the Negev village where I studied for my PhD dissertation, and a few years later visiting residents and restaurants in the West Bank in the company of my Jaffa research Arab companions. The Israeli defense methods introduced during the intifada included a security system of personal magnetic IDs enabling identification of suspect individuals when going through the main checkpoints at the Gaza gate and other major entry points. Thus, in response to the intifada disturbances, the separation between the Israeli and the Palestinian geographical and residential entities grew a visible dimension, alerting sensitive observers to the potential development of an apartheid regime. Not surprising, the public mood in Israel during the first year of the intifada seemed to reflect a stronger opposition to negotiations with the PLO and a preference for tougher military measures against the intifada uprising (Arian and Ventura 1989).

However, the academic report closest in time to the eruption of the intifada has been revealed in a small collection of contributions by leading Israeli social scientists based on a conference conducted during the early years of the intifada (*The Seventh War: The Effects of the Intifada on the Israeli Society*, Gal 1990). The veteran sociologist Moshe Lissak pinpointed the positive impact of the uprising on Palestinian society as a moment of nation-building. In contrast, he showcased its negative effects on Israeli society, such as the growing political divisions over the future of the state's borders, the potential conflicts between the civil and army leadership, the potential impact of Palestinian nationalism among Israeli Arabs, the degradation of the rule of law and the rising of Jewish ethnocentrism, the growing public opinion of apathy toward the mounting of brutal treatment of Palestinian civilians caught in the dynamics of communal uprising. No doubt, Lissak's guesses soon materialized.

Communication experts (Elihu Katz and Hanna Levinson) surveyed Israelis' public opinion during the intifada's first two years. Their findings revealed public insecurity but little change in the majority opposition (70 percent) to negotiate with the PLO on peace arrangements, and also that nearly 50 percent refused to give up occupied territories—although a growing constituency seemed to believe a Palestinian state might finally be founded alongside Israel. The authors of that survey closed their report with two major questions: would there be a change in public opinion around the possible recognition of the PLO as legitimate partners for peace negotiations, and would a growing constituency reconcile with withdrawal from the occupied territories?

The psychologists in that early intifada report considered various facets of individuals' and groups' responses to the situation of growing insecurity, emotional stresses among young and older army recruits, as well as moral dilemmas affecting ordinary citizens (leftists in particular) over the military and civil agencies' treatment of the Palestinians. Of particular relevance to our present agenda was a report by Eyal Ben-Ari, the anthropologist on that team who reported on his one-month experience in 1988 as an IDF reserve officer with his unit, who for the first time were conducting their military duty in the occupied territories. It was a major change for a combat unit to act as a police force implementing security measures among Palestinian civilians in villages and towns in the West Bank. Naturally, Ben-Ari, who conducted long-term fieldwork in Japan, had no prior intention of conducting fieldwork during his military service. I thus share with him the characterization of "accidental ethnographer," reporting on the activities we performed, voluntarily or involuntarily drawn into the events of the first intifada.

Ben-Ari was aware of the limited scope of his exploration based on his personal experience, a few interviews he conducted with his fellow servicemen, and newspaper reports from the time. However, in examining his own and his colleagues' comportment during their stint of duty, which often included intimidating local Palestinians in search of hidden ammunition or looking for persons implicated in radical activities, Ben-Ari revealed a "masking" strategy that helped individuals to separate between true identity from their role performance under the shield of their masks. Acting under the protection of that mask, individuals felt free to express hostility with no fear of punishment because it was not their real persona: "During the limited period of their army reservist role, these military men stop being 'regular' people" (p. 111). Thus, the author concluded, we can better understand the dynamics of military service during the intifada by realizing these men are not themselves: they are people acting under special circumstances that permit unusual behavior. The unit went through a process of "naturalization," adjusting to the intifada's unique terms of social, moral, and technological existence.

Ben-Ari's short span of unplanned and undocumented fieldwork experience revealed a wider phenomenon of "masking" that seemed to engulf a majority of Israeli citizens during the start of the first intifada.[1] In retrospect, the later-described AD KAN participants, together with other protest movements, tried to tear off that masking strategy and "open the eyes" of a wider public to the reality of continuing occupation and its effects on Israeli society.

However, a few years of resistance and suffering on both sides ultimately reached a point of no return. Rabin, then in the role of PM, realized the futility of responding to the uprising through force alone and finally entered into negotiations with the PLO leadership. That process eventually led to the Oslo Accords, which culminated in the historical signing on 13 September 1993 of the peace agreement between the government of Israel and the Palestinian Liberation Organization (PLO) on the White House lawn: the mutual recognition of both nations' right to self-government as separate political entities. It is beyond the framework of this book to examine the details of that first experiment's tragic failure (and last attempt, to this day) at instigating a peace process, starting with the assassination of PM Rabin (4 November 1995), PLO chairman Arafat's fall from grace, the Israelis' withdrawal from the Gaza Strip in 2005 (led by PM Sharon) and its takeover by Hamas, as well as the continuing expansion of Jewish settlements in the West Bank. Twenty-five years later, one can see no peaceful solution on the horizon to end the lingering, bleeding conflict.

Above was presented the story of the first intifada as recorded by Hacham, an Israeli close witness and active participant in the Israeli apparatus of occupation, situated in Gaza. However, I conclude the story of the first intifada and its observers with two reflections from exceptionally knowledgeable Israeli analysts (each of whom wears both the hat of a security expert and an academic), one written before the eruption of the first intifada and one twenty years later. And finally, I present an overview of the intifada saga and its interpreters as proposed by an Israeli social scientist who framed the intifada events in more conclusive sociological terms of "collective action."

I start with Yeoshafat Harkabi (professor of international relations at Hebrew University, retired army intelligence general), whose scholarly yet evocative *Fateful Decisions* (1986) appeared shortly before the intifada. Long before the Palestinians' uprising, Harkabi was convinced that Israeli leaders must recognize the PLO activists as representatives of the Palestinians' national leadership. He insisted that any attempt at political negotiation with the Palestinians without involving the PLO has no credibility and proves the lack of a serious wish to reach a peaceful settlement between the protagonists. He passionately argued that a peace agreement constitutes a major Israeli interest, given the Arabs' greater ability to endure the human and material toll of long-term warfare, comparing the Palestinians' struggle with the Vietnam War. Moreover, he claimed, one can identify among leading PLO members new voices expressing more "rational" and "realistic" opinions supporting accommodation with the Israeli government.

Harkabi considered the West Bank Jewish settlements a major obstacle for peace; although they represent a successful project in the physical domain of constructing buildings, roads, and the "amount of concrete" produced in its expansion, they constitute a colossal failure in the human domain (p. 63). An annexation of West Bank territories might offer more comfortable security borders, but "would there remain a country worth protection" (p. 68)? The French moved a million settlers out of Algeria after 130 years of colonization, so the removal of thirty thousand West Bank settlers cannot be considered an impossible undertaking (compared with about four hundred thousand at present time—thirty years later).

Harkabi warned his readers of the consequences of continuing occupation, predicting the escalation of conflict, the increase of terror activities, the intensification of suppression on both sides of the Green Line, the growth of Jewish religious extremism, and the loathing of foreigners. And last, he cautioned that the spread of international criticism of Israeli colonialism might also affect world Jewry. He confessed that he wrote his assessment and verdict about the continuing Israeli occupation of the West Bank in the midst of emotional turmoil, indeterminateness, and acute pain: "I recognize the democratic right of the Jews in Israel to commit a national suicide, but I try, as much as I can, to warn them. I am aware of the little influence I command, but writing is the only means at my disposal" (pp. 7–9). Later in his book he made an allusion to the destruction of Jerusalem and the dispersal of the Jews as consequence of the futile uprising against the Roman Empire, which was instigated by a radical minority that imposed its extremist agenda on a dissented society. That moment in Jewish history became a major myth in Israeli youth education as an example of courage and national dedication. Harkabi compared this myth with the Likud Party and its right-wing allies, the West Bank settlers in particular, who imposed a disastrous future on the state of Israel. In reading that evocative testimony, I was reminded of the biblical prophets who tried to speak "truth" to stubborn rulers absorbed in their grandiose dreams and personal interests.

I turn now to Matti Steinberg, faculty member at the Israel Democracy Institute and former advisor to the Israel Security Agency. Harkabi's student, Steinberg became a leading expert on the Palestinian national movement, the development of its central institutions, the conflicting factions inside the organization, and their disparate methods for achieving the liberation of Palestine. His *Facing the Fate: Palestinian National Consciousness 1967–2007* (2008), published long after the collapse of the Oslo Accords, offers a wide perspective, revealing a composed analysis of historical records and the incisive knowledge of an intelligence officer. Steinberg followed the changes in ideology and practice that initiated a shift of orientation among Chairman Arafat and his close colleagues from a position of total refusal to consider any loss of territory of historical Palestine, and a dedication to an armed conflict (expressed in the 1968 PLO proclamation). Instead, he concluded, they have begrudgingly adopted a more accommodating "realistic" stance—accepting the idea of two national entities on the same territory (displayed in the 1988 PLO proclamation).

Steinberg closely followed the process leading to the Oslo Accords and the aftermath of its collapse, offering a "clinical" history and a prognosis for the future awaiting both national patients. However, Steinberg played an important role as professional informant during the later-described meetings of AD KAN core membership, supporting the movement's push to recognize the PLO leadership as the legitimate Palestinian partner for peace negotiations. I will not repeat the details of the breakdown of the Oslo Accords presented by Steinberg and others, but I will illustrate in a later chapter the reasons for the continuing tragic failure to secure a peaceful binational pact as suggested by AD KAN veteran members whom I interviewed in 2016–17, as well as other commentators' accounts.

In conclusion, Israeli and other reporters emphasized the sudden eruption of the first intifada that seemed to take everyone by surprise. The Palestinians' spontaneous, apparently irrational resistance in Gaza and the West Bank violently crushed the status quo of a "benign occupation" that seemed acceptable on both sides. It turned into a political, military, economic, and emotional earthquake, revealing the unfinished consequences of the 1967 war.

However, the prevalent perception of the sudden, unexpected eruption of the intifada was challenged by Eitan Alimi (2007), a sociologist at Hebrew University, who conceptualized the various facets of the conflict situation that culminated in December 1987 as "an exceptional manifestation of collective action: a voluminous episode of contentious politics for shaking off the Israeli military occupation of the West Bank and Gaza" (p. 6). His analysis of collective action is rooted in the writings of Marx, Simmel, Durkheim, and Weber. He went on to document the structural and cultural dynamics that operated in both sides of the conflict (some mentioned by earlier observers). Twenty years of occupation impacted both sides: the Palestinians, now closely familiar with Israeli society, were highly aware of the disintegration of Israeli unity, mindful of how domestic divisions over the continuing occupation impacted the presentation of "Israeliness."

Moreover, the many thousands of Palestinians who served time in Israeli jails had learned a great deal about Israeli society and participated in political group discussions. They emerged highly motivated to fight the occupation and played a major role in the intifada. The expansion of Israeli settlements in the occupied territories with better living conditions intensified the level of frustration and deprivation, adding to the objective and subjective inequalities within Palestinian society: in particular, between the 1948 war refugees' and the veteran Gaza and West Bank inhabitants' residential conditions, income, education, and other public services. The radicalization process inside the arena of contention leading toward a collective action included other elements, some of which I mentioned above, such as the rise of a younger generation, the rise of Hamas, and disappointment with the Arab states' treatment of the Palestinian question both regionally and internationally. No less, the unprecedented proximity between Palestinians and Israelis brought about a sharp contrast between the two societies, raising a shared awareness among the Palestinians of their situation and national sentiments.

But, the radicalization process inside the arena of contention is not entirely confined to the Palestinian side; it is interactive, affecting both protagonists, systematically fed by the extremists on both sides. Twenty years of occupation have left an immense impact on Israeli society, widening the gaps between its social, political, and ideological divisions: specifically, the conflicting views about the future of the occupied territories and the expectations of a political accord with a Palestinian neighboring state. In the meantime, the continuing expansion of Jewish settlements in the West Bank has changed the landscape of Israeli visions and options as a major visible factor in the interactive process of the contentious politics, interlocking the protagonists preparing for the eruption of an open conflict.

Observing the failure of the Oslo Accords that was finally chronicled with the 2000 outbreak of the second intifada, which the Palestinians named the "Al-Aqsa Intifada" (the intifada of the Al-Aqsa Mosque), Alimi considered it another cycle of contention, although more violent in nature, rather than speaking about a "new" or "second" intifada (p. 176). In conclusion, Alimi reminds us of Harkabi's final words of faith: "For Israel, the resolution of conflict is not a matter of choice, it is a necessity. It is imperative for Israel policy makers, regardless of ideological orientation, to grasp to the full the devastating damage the occupation has inflicted on Israeli society" (p. 170).

Above, I presented a vast panorama of Israeli and other commentators who described and analyzed the first intifada from both sides of the conflict. Its achievement culminated with the signing of the Oslo Accords, and its abysmal failure started soon with PM Rabin's assassination. No doubt, that intifada saga remains a most traumatic experience for Israelis and Palestinians, becoming a major turn in the one-hundred-year history of the binational conflict. The majority of

AD KAN membership attended the demonstration of many thousands of enthusiastic Israelis celebrating the Oslo Accords. Gathering on the evening of 4 November 1995 at Tel Aviv main square (later renamed Rabin Square), they sang songs of peace and listened to PM Rabin the night he was fatally shot on his way out by a young Jewish right-wing zealot. In retrospect, they observed that night the demise of a dream they had nourished since the start of the intifada.

Ironically, the dramatic events leading to the Oslo Accords came back to me recently during a short visit to New York in spring 2017. Planning to attend a Wednesday matinee play, I selected a last-minute recommendation of a not-yet-reviewed production under the title *Oslo* (by J. T. Rogers). I believe I was among a few in the audience who were not enthusiastic and joyfully entertained, observing the "happy end" of a drama reconstructing the process initiated by two resourceful Norwegian diplomats: a charismatic couple, who orchestrated the negotiations between the Israeli and Palestinian delegates leading to the 1993 Oslo Accords. That piece of history, dramatized and improvised with some amusing scenes to entice Lincoln Center theatergoers, was not the anticipated prescription to elevate the spirits of an Israeli visitor familiar with the sad end of the Oslo Accords.

Note

1. See Ben-Ari's (1989) separate publication.

3

Intellectuals'/Academics' Engagement in the Public Forum

As mentioned in earlier chapters, the ethnographic field-site and analytical trigger for the following discourse is the case of a group of academics at TAU who founded a protest movement against the continuing Israeli rule of the Palestinians in the West Bank and Gaza. However, before narrating the story of their initiative and its consequences, I intend to explore the history and the role of academics in modern societies as perceived by a wide spectrum of commentators.

Examining the sociological, historical, and philosophical literature dealing with the society of academics often considered "intellectuals," one reveals a complex picture. The list of writers, past and present, is overwhelming, demanding a separate volume. One could start with early commentators such as Julien Banda, the French author of *The Betrayal of the Intellectuals*, (1955 [1928]). He blamed nineteenth- and twentieth-century European intellectuals who turned passionate about political and military matters, becoming apologists for crass nationalism instead of adopting the dispassionate outlook of classical civilization. However, I introduce a limited, more recent sample of that wide repertoire representing some general relevant assessments about the roles, types, and personal characteristics of potential participants, as well as a few major historical records portraying the engagement of intellectuals/academics in acute national social-political conflicts.

Like other observers, D. L. Schalk (1991), a leading historian on the intellectuals' engagement in politics in France and the United States, commented that a social and cultural category of the "intellectual" was born in Paris at the moment of the Dreyfus affair. Thus, echoing Banda's view, intellectuals are defined by their more "distantiated" social role, which sharply contrasts with all others in a modern society, often applying ideas in an ethical way that may question the underlying values of society and the legitimacy of the established authorities (p. 39). However, as pinpointed by Richard Bellamy (1997), when intellectuals attempt to position themselves as social critics, they are often caught in a difficult dilemma: if they remain outside politics, they are charged with aloofness and a selective blindness to injustice, but if they enter the political arena, they appear condemned either to prostrate themselves before the powerful or to illegitimately impose their ideas on others (reminiscent of Max Weber's "value neutral" postulate, advising the academic or scholar to be aware of their own moral judgments and values). Bellamy provoked a profound question: is there an acceptable form of intellectual engagement with politics? "Can intellectuals play a distinctive political role without either trimming their ideas in despicable ways, or indulging in the sorts of reprehensible behavior associated with various kinds of elitism?" (p. 25).

Gramsci (1971 [1929–35]) defined various types of representatives in that category and their different effects in society. They do not represent a "class" in Mannheim's perspective because they are too differentiated (1968 [1952]:186–87). The humanities and social sciences produce more radicals compared with the natural-scientific fields or the professions (Brym 1980: 14). That observation was made by other leading social analysts. Thus, Merton (1957: 211) made a similar differentiation:

> The intellectual dealing with human conduct and culture is concerned with alternatives which have immediate and obvious value implications. He is peculiarly subject to attack by those whose interests and sentiments are violated by his findings. For those reasons, and doubtless others, intellectuals concerned with human affairs in general find themselves in a less secure status than the physical and biological scientists who affect public policy.

That viewpoint is shared by Rieff (1969), who differentiated between the less progressive applied professions and other intellectuals who express a right to be heard and to exert influence. Coser (1965: viii–x) described the intellectuals as descendants of the biblical prophets who castigate the men of power for the wickedness of their ways, who never seem satisfied with things as they are, and who are upsetting to the routine of ordinary citizens. However, he claimed, not all scientists equally share that concern with public issues and social responsibility. Shils (1969) equally emphasized the intellectuals' resentment of religious and secular authority, while Dahrendorf (1969) compared the intellectual with the royal clowns, the "fool," who had the freedom to express their critical opinions about the social order and to ask questions that no one else dared to ask. That representation of the intellectual is recapped in Said's (1996) description of the exiled, marginal man, who tries to speak truth to power. He has to choose to support the weak over the powerful, and he is always challenged by the problem of primordial loyalties to the protestor's own community, nationality, religion, etc. Nisbet, however, claimed that campus settings are not hotbeds for political or social radicals. These institutions remain a setting for the scientific imagination (1997).

Conversely, a more militant position was voiced by Kaufman (*The Radical Liberal,* 1968), who attacked the university guise of political neutrality: "Universities should instead encourage skepticism of official action, promote social criticism and dissent, do whatever is consistent with the university's basic functions to reinforce committed, thoughtful, political action" (p. 128). He went on to emphasize the special role of teachers in the processes that build political commitments. They have a heavy obligation to display in their own behavior the ways in which intelligence and dedication can be welded and translated into political activity.

However, the most striking model of an academic's engagement seems to be E. P. Thompson, the Warwick University leading social historian. He withdrew from campus life, dedicating himself to the promotion of various social-political issues of the day, such as an international peace movement, demonstrating against the race to nuclear armament, the sins of colonialism, the Korean War, etc. He resented and satirized the *Academicus superciliosus*, consumed by the enormous pomp and self-important propriety and succinctly portrayed in *Warwick University Ltd* (1970). As bluntly stated in describing the Warwick students' revolt: "A university is not born when the Privy Council grant it a charter; it is born when its members come to realize that they have common interests and a common identity" (p. 53). He supported the students' fight against the administration exposing the close power relations that connected capitalism and higher education. The university-ensconced academics, Thompson complained, however liberal and humane, were "alienated from the people as a mass ... deeply skeptical about working class movements ... impotent in social or political terms." On leaving his academic post, he spoke at hundreds of meetings, rallies, and tours; "he spoke to the world" (B. D. Palmer 1994: 99, 126).

But, a more accommodating critical approach was suggested by Jenni (2001), who presented two contradicting positions. On one side of the issue, there are those who claim that academics ought to avoid direct public service, both because they are ill-suited to that task and because it undermines professional integrity. To exemplify that viewpoint, Jenni introduced Gracia (1999), who considers philosophers unsuited to a role in public life because they are skeptical about the possibility of finding the truth: "They are contentious, ideological, callous, arrogant, and lack experience addressing social problems." Similar observations, no doubt, could be made of other academic practitioners (p. 442). However, those who argue that academics should abandon academia for full-time activism represent a vastly different position. As such, Jenni introduced the philosopher Paul Nizan (in Schalk 1973), who claimed that intellectuals support oppression by refusing to participate in politics, because they don't want to sacrifice their comfort, security, and order. According to Nizan, academics should abandon their class and join the downtrodden in radical action, leaving behind their silence and abstractions, using their intellectual powers to transform society (Jenni 2001: 449). Instead, however, Jenni argued that "we should combine indirect service with direct work for the suffering. ... The prestige of an academic position confers credibility and power, making one's voice more resonant in public forums. Thus, a more credible response to evil is to use an academic position as a base for direct social service" (ibid.: 452).

A few Israeli leading academics have also expressed a strong stance about the complexity of the position of the intellectual, often an academic, confronted with contradictory loyalties in the realm of politics: the welfare of his nation/community/social-professional faction versus his commitment to universal values of morality and justice. The historian Yehoshua Arieli contemplated whether the display of commitment to one's nation is dominant in the collective consciousness among citizens of states that emerged under exceptional circumstances of national liberation. He claimed that conflict of obligations is typical to the Israeli case, the outcome of the Zionist revolution. Nevertheless, he felt a responsibility to express a critical position against the claim of Jewish historical right to the land of Israel, including territories inhabiting a majority of Palestinians. That claim, he concluded, contains a great deal of blindness and moral insolvency that cannot withstand rational justification. He anticipated the Palestinians' growing resentment and their resort to terror that would follow an escalation of the Israeli aggressive reprisals (Arieli

1992, 2000). However, Arieli doubted academics' ability to conduct a concerted action of resistance, pinpointing that Martin Luther King, Mahatma Gandhi and other famous leaders of peace and justice did not emerge from among the ranks of the academy.

Jacob Talmon, another leading historian at the Hebrew University, expressed a similar position, warning PM Menachem Begin against the messianic conviction sanctioning the biblical promise of the Land of Israel regardless of the Palestinians' wishes (a long letter first published in the daily *Haaretz* under the title "The Homeland in Danger," 31 March 1980). He considered the triumph of 1967 and the following expansion of settlements in the occupied territories a potential disaster for the economic, political, security, and moral standing of Israeli society.

But the most vocal figure in Israeli academy was Yeshayahu Leibowitz (d. 1994), renowned chemist and philosopher at the Hebrew University, who became the mythological moral leader of Israeli students and faculty struggling against the continuing occupation of Palestinian lands. His position and frequent public appearances were particularly impactful because of his identity as an orthodox Jew attracting mostly secular liberal audiences. He has often been compared to the biblical prophets who spoke truth to power. As I will later describe, he was invited to speak in AD KAN's meetings and rallies. To this day, advocates of peace and army moral rejectionists who refuse to serve in the occupied territories refer to him as a moral model in their writings and lectures. He seems to share a similar standing with the British E. P. Thompson and the American linguist Noam Chomsky, charismatic scholars who came out of the sheltered corridors of the academy clamoring for action in the real world, attracting a cohort of loyal followers among their students and colleagues.

However, the commentators and activists mentioned above have not consistently addressed the more problematic circumstances in the modern era that have engaged, willingly or reluctantly, a cohort or a segment of national academies in political participation. Social scientists made some general analytical observations about the role and practice of intellectuals displaying their unique positions in public affairs. For example, they noticed a differentiation between the socio-humanists versus the professionals—the "soft" versus the "hard" sciences practitioners.

I present now a few of the better documented cases of intellectuals'/academics' comportment during acute national political eventualities.

The American Scene

Probably the most stinging condemnation of the society of intellectuals, particularly academics, was vented in *The Last Intellectuals: American Culture in the Age of Academe* (Jacoby 1987). A historian at UCLA, Russell Jacoby claimed that since the late 1950s, the habitat, manners, idiom, and publishing venues of intellectuals have been transformed with the expansion of American academia, the retreat from the city squares and the public arena, to the comfortable, safe sanctuaries of campus life. The younger generation of intellectuals had become "almost exclusively professors: campuses are their homes; colleagues their audience; monographs and specialized journals their media" (ibid.: 6). He recalled the sorry tale of McCarthyism's successful purge and the silencing of academic radicals. The academy did not fight McCarthyism. However, he argued, younger professors called upon their innovative spirit in assailing the interpretations dominant in their disciplines by establishing a credible body of radical, feminist, Marxist, or neo-Marxist scholarship. In a scorning mood, he contended that genre is largely technical and unreadable, except by specialists (ibid.: 141).

Schalk, the historian mentioned earlier, suggested a somewhat different view, comparing the intellectuals'/academics' engagement during the traumatic wars that involved France in Algeria to the United States in Vietnam. The students had preceded their elders in opposing the continuing war. However, the entry of intellectuals/academics into the political arena started with Noam Chomsky's February 1967 NYRB article, "The Responsibility of Intellectuals." The following demonstrations and petitions engaged a growing number of major universities' faculty, authors, poets, essayists, and artists, such as the 1967 "Call to Resist Illegitimate Authority" against President Johnson with four thousand signatories, two-thirds of whom were academics. That followed the formation of an antiwar organization called "Resist."

Chomsky, who was arrested during the march on the Pentagon in October 1967, indicted intellectuals who declined to fulfill their responsibility and pointed at eminent academics who had moved into politics but displayed a kind of "hypocritical moralism" that masked and apologized for aggression (e.g., Arthur Schlesinger and Henry Kissinger). However, Schalk claimed, since the end of the Vietnam War, a mood of disengagement returned to dominate American academia—which is also true for other intellectual classes in advanced industrial nations (1991: 170). In a later presentation, Schalk reckoned: "Highly intelligent men and women have concluded that society has evolved to the point where any action in the public sphere would simply be isolated and ignored acts of moral witness, may be the central factor in producing the end of engagement, and hence the end of the intellectual" (1997: 282).

Among the anthropologists, I mention Franz Boas, the founder of modern American anthropology, presented by Lesser (1981: 21–22) as a *citizen-scientist* "who applied the work of anthropology to problems of society, and was an activist on academic and political issues—in both ways serving as a model for anthropology as a humanitarian science." A pacifist, he publicly opposed World War I from the beginning, considering it an imperialist war and denouncing President Wilson in the press. However, he was later condemned by anthropological organizations for publishing a letter in a nonprofessional journal accusing a few (unnamed) anthropologists of serving as government agents. Nevertheless, Boas has remained the mythological professional and moral leader of present-day American anthropology. I could personally verify Boas's reputation during my visit to a British Columbia museum dedicated to the Potlatch ritual masks and other sacred objects. The Canadian government confiscated these objects in the 1920s, assuming the Potlatch communal rituals affected a waste of wealth and curtailed economic development (the Potlatch ban was repealed in 1951). To my surprise, on exhibit were displayed copies of a letter Franz Boas addressed to the Canadian federal authorities strongly condemning this brutal abuse of human rights and cultural traditions. I was deeply moved by that revelation of the credo of anthropology and suddenly also proud of an unknown feeling of "tribal" affiliation with this great man, a German Jew.

The Franz Boas "scandal" proved a difficult issue in later years, a subject for debates and formal American Anthropologists Association organization (AAA) resolutions concerning the norms of ethnographic ethics. Namely, these resolutions raised the problem of social scientists' involvement in counterinsurgency campaigns offering their knowledge on cultural and social norms, manners, and associations observed during research conducted overseas. Though counterinsurgency operations are needed to secure the lives of American combatants in foreign enemy lands, assisting them seemed to violate relationships of trust with the people with whom anthropologists work (e.g., Gonzalez, 2004).

By and large, the tribe of American anthropologists kept away from political issues not relevant to their professional work. That position was tackled during the 1967 AAA meeting and a subsequent symposium that sponsored a petition concerning the moral and political issues of the Vietnam War. However, the organizers were aware that a large minority of the association's members had passionately dissented from the resolution "because they believed that the politicalization of a scientific association could only result in its rapid demise" (Fried, Harris, and Murphy 1968: xi). The editors of that symposium's records commented on the anthropologists' retreat from an articulate position about the Vietnam War, claiming instead that they had attained the sanctuary of political neutrality.

The issue of American anthropologists' engagement in activist agendas working for racial, gender, ethnic, or economic equality, as well as interlocking in wider political disputes, was exhaustively reviewed by Price (2004), who researched the lingering impact of the era of McCarthyism. Hoover's FBI saw the prospect of free inquiry by intellectuals as a threat to national security and the American way of life. American anthropologists were among Senator McCarthy's suspects from the very beginning of his witch hunt, as evidenced in the extensive archival research of FBI and government documents released to Price under the Freedom of Information Act. The FBI's intrusive surveillance of liberal and moderate anthropologists such as Oscar Lewis, Margaret Mead, Ashley Montagu, Cora Du Bois, and others establishes the extent to which the US secret police meddled in the academic and private lives of intellectuals who promoted local social issues and international perspectives. A generation of social anthropologists, the author claims, learned to not think under the rubrics of Marxist critique, while many in the discipline learned to ignore anthropology's natural, and ethically required, activist roles. Moreover, Price revealed the assistance of anthropologists and other academics who were willing to become FBI informants and sources, among them George Murdock, who voiced concern that Oscar Lewis was a communist.

Among the more visible cases of official reaction against ostensibly threatening anthropologists is the story of Kathleen Gough, who spoke out against President Kennedy's "reckless" nuclear gambit and suggested that Cuba's revolutionary role in fighting imperialism was laudable. Although an academic of reputation, she did not receive a recommended raise of salary and was told her upcoming tenure application at Brandeis would not be approved (ibid.: 314–15). Price suggested that McCarthyism's impact on anthropology should not be measured in the number of individuals who lost their jobs; more accurately, it should be measured through the extent to which it broadcasted messages of fear and self-censorship to those who might otherwise have generated radical critiques or taken action for social justice. He also indicted the AAA's refusal to assist members attacked under McCarthyism by proclaiming that such actions would be considered political and hence inappropriate for a professional organization (ibid.: 351). And finally, his verdict of today:

> Few American anthropologists engage in activities designed to threaten the status quo of American or international patterns of inequality in the level of past anthropologists. ... Instead, the discipline is awash with postmodern reflectionists, many of whom skillfully critique the manifestations of hegemonic power in subjects both ideographic and universal but few of whom actually confront the political-economic power bases that generate and support these structural exhaust features of the contemporary world. (ibid.: 349)

Another publicized case is that of David Graeber, known as an anarchist activist (Graeber 2004). An assistant and associate professor of anthropology at Yale University (1998–2005), Graeber had protested against the third summit of the Americas in Quebec City in 2001 and the 2002 World Economic Forum in New York. He was a leading figure in the Occupy Wall Street movement. In 2005, Yale decided not to renew Graeber's contract, preventing his eligibility for tenure. The decision sparked an academic controversy.

No doubt, anthropologists are deeply engaged with the welfare of their subjects in various parts of the globe. However, only rarely have they organized their colleagues to express an effective public response to critical political issues at home or abroad. The 2016 BDS[1] vote among the AAA membership aimed to boycott Israeli academia represents a rare case (see chapter 14).

The German-Austrian Case

Although my family left Europe in the 1920s unaffected by later developments in Europe, the Holocaust nevertheless gradually became an important element in the educational and national ethos of my generation. There is no need to retell in detail the smooth if not enthusiastic integration of the German and Austrian university academies, leading scholars included, into the Nazi ideological and organizational system (e.g., Weinreich 1946; Grunberger 1971: 304–23). In a panoramic presentation—*The Decline of the German Mandarins* (1969)—Fritz Ringer reconstructed the history of German academics (whom he called "mandarins," recalling the elevated class of Chinese literati) from 1890 to 1933, an era that raised many internationally renowned scholars—among them distinguished sociologists (e.g., Simmel, Tönnies, and Weber, "who did not abandon all rationality for the sake of community and culture"). However, when the 1914 war broke out, "German academics of all political persuasion spoke almost exclusively of their optimism and enthusiasm. Indeed, they greeted the war with a sense of relief" (1969: 180). Although the mandarins seemed frightened with the new fanaticism of the late 1920s, they did little to safeguard the clarity of thought and oppose the "revolution." The National Socialists easily established their total control of the German universities. Nearly 1,700 faculty members were dismissed, among them 313 full professors (ibid.: 440). Ringer concluded, "Many German intellectuals now defined their position as 'inner emigration' and sought a retreat in esoteric scholarship—the Mandarins' empire was in ruins" (ibid.: 443).

The almost mythical figure of "engagement" remains the celebrated philosopher Martin Heidegger, who supported the Nazi movement since 1931. He was appointed rector of Freiburg University with the intention to "revolutionize" the institution, and he gave propaganda lectures across Germany, ending them with the standard "Heil Hitler" and responding in conversation on politics that "one must get involved" (Lilla [2016] 2001).

Depressingly, the German and Austrian establishment of physical and cultural anthropologists was actively involved in the Nazi machine. As recorded by Gingrich (2005) in his opening presentation, "From a presentist perspective, the vast majority of sociocultural anthropologists in Germany were more or less active supporters of the Nazi regime" (p. 111). In 1938, the Berlin Society for Anthropology, Ethnography, and Prehistory excluded all its remaining Jewish members, among them Franz Boas in the United States. The German delegation to the peacetime conference of the International Union of Anthropology and Ethnological Sciences in Copenhagen in August 1938 included the infamous Josef Mengele, who performed deadly human experiments on prisoners at the Auschwitz concentration camp.

Gingrich (professor of anthropology at the University of Vienna) differentiates three categories of accomplices of historical responsibility:

> First, some anthropologists made successful contribution toward the professional destruction or physical elimination of other persons, by denouncing them, by recommending that they lose their jobs, and so

forth. Second, some anthropologists carried out applied research for Nazi purposes—that in cases of responsibility in the narrow sense would benefit from the Nazi killing machine or contribute to it. Third, some anthropologists produced explicit propaganda for the Nazi regime and elaborated its ideology by using or abusing their academic or professional authority. (2005: 128)

Though his background was American, it must have been a challenging task for a leading figure in postwar Austrian anthropology to record the history of wartime academics in Vienna who shared their German colleagues' comportment. However, when I enjoyed generous hospitality at the Vienna Institute of Cultural Studies (IFK) in 2014, the issue of wartime history was never raised in my presence. At that time, I had never visited concentration camps in Poland, Germany, and elsewhere, but by "default" I visited the Steinhof psychiatric hospital in Vienna. In the company of an American friend interested in modern architecture, we planned a visit to the Otto Wagner–famous Art Nouveau church situated on the beautiful park grounds of that hospital in the outskirts of town. No doubt the Wagner church, built (1904–7) for the mentally ill, is probably the most unusual and exceptionally attractive church I have seen in many years of visiting churches and attending services worldwide.

But I was totally unprepared for a small museum on the same hospital premises that left a far more impressive footprint in my Vienna memories. We discovered that the hospital was also the main site of the Nazi program of euthanasia and enforced sterilization of mentally ill and other handicapped children and adults. I made another trip to the site to read the records of the respected medical specialists who participated in these atrocities and who mostly regained their positions after the war. On leaving the site, an ethical "consolation" came to mind: on graduation, anthropologists do not take a sort of Hippocratic Oath to uphold specific ethical standards during fieldwork and later in authoring their ethnographic texts …

By "accident" I met Professor Georg Pfeffer, head of the department of ethnology at the Free University of Berlin, who approached me during a meeting at the European anthropologists (EASA) conference in Prague in 1992. We developed a close friendship that initiated an invitation to a semester of teaching in Berlin (2002), and we have continued our correspondence to this day. Georg rarely missed a chance to express his bitter feelings about his father's cohort of academics and their collaboration with the Nazi regime. We shared our views and worries about present-day social and political realities in both countries. My stay in Berlin was a tantalizing experience. As I experienced the openness of colleagues and students in discussing the past and present, it was beyond my comprehension that this was the site where humanity and its acclaimed researchers, anthropologists included, had been transformed into barbarity.

The French Case

Ruminating about German and Austrian academics' conduct during the Nazi era calls to mind Alan Riding's minute examination of French intellectuals, writers, and artists' comportment during the German occupation (*And the Show Went On*, 2011). Though not concentrating on French academics, Riding highlighted the Musée de l'Homme network of professionals, among them a few ethnologists, who were ready to fight and die "at a time when most of the French were coming to terms with the occupation, they were almost alone on their belief in the *idea* of resistance" (ibid.: 116). They met every week, published a clandestine newspaper—called *Résistance*. Twenty-eight of their members lost their lives—seven were executed and others killed fighting in the resistance. But on the whole, as Riding's book title clearly indicates, the majority of the French "mandarins" conveniently collaborated with the occupation. They did not decline subsidies from the German embassy, and they enjoyed a wide circulation of their writings; attended and conducted successful theater, opera, ballet, cabaret, and film performances, art exhibitions, and receptions at the embassy; and accepted invitations to Germany: "Visitors arriving from the unoccupied zone were often surprised by and disapproving over how normal Paris seemed" (ibid.: 55). "Most Parisians accepted the reality of the occupation and were following Pétain's counsel that collaboration with Germany was best for France" (ibid.: 71).

And the Show Went On presents an unflattering portrayal of French literati strata, intellectuals of various professional, academic, and arts sectors. However, from my own faraway familiarity with the case under examination, I am impressed by the courageous behavior of the Musée de l'Homme network dominated by unknown young ethnologists who had no previous experience in party politics or insurgency. As commented on by Riding, their study of human behavior through the ages had led them to spend years far from France. The author thus seemed to suggest that they represented a professional viewpoint of a wider cultural perspective. Anyhow, in the first front-page editorial of the *Résistance*, their improbable leader, the linguist Boris Vildé, urged people to form dissent groups and concluded, "We promise we have only one ambition: to see a pure and free France reborn" (ibid.: 112). Although not a university campus, the Musée de l'Homme embodies an institution closest to an academic anthropological research environment. Moreover, the *Résistance* group's recruitment and opening activities were reminiscent of AD KAN's early days.

However, in contrast to the era of the Nazi occupation, the war in Algeria engaged a large cohort of leading French intellectuals/academics who have come out against the war, among them Jean-Paul Sartre, François Mauriac, and Simone de Beauvoir. Their impact reached its peak in a series of 1957 public demonstrations, and in March 1958 Sartre published in *Les Temps Modernes* his powerful antiwar call "We Are All Assassins." However, as in the United States following the Vietnam War, the intellectual-academic French scene has remained mute and apparently removed from the memories of past national tragedies since the end of the Algerian War (Schalk 1991).

The Peruvian, Shining Path Case

An unexpected personal experience with the consequences of academics' revolutionary agenda engaged me a decade after the start of the intifada, though outside the Western Hemisphere. During 1998–2002, I served as consultant with the Netherlands-Israel Development Research Project in the Central Highlands of Peru exploring patterns of immigration to North America and Europe. The program involved researchers from Peru and the Netherlands. We were situated in Huancayo, the central city of the Mantaro Valley surrounded by many farming communities on lower and upper levels of the surrounding hills.

Throughout that study, we encountered the tragic impact of the Shining Path (Sendero Luminoso), the radical Maoist movement active during the 1980s. The revolutionary organization intended to eradicate social inequalities in Peruvian society, support the poor peasantry, galvanize and liberate the body of first-generation Indian students, Quechua-Spanish speakers in particular (e.g., Strong 1993; D. S. Palmer 1994). It was instigated by Abimal Guzmán, the illegitimate son of a middle-class merchant, a charismatic professor of philosophy considered a distinguished intellectual. Guzmán recruited a cohort of dedicated disciples, close colleagues, and students at the San Cristobal of Huamanga University in Ayacucho. Guzmán, who advocated armed battle against the regime, exuded the image of a teacher; in all public appearances and posters, he is dressed in a suit, wearing glasses, a book in hand. The leader-teacher represented education incarnate and, therefore, truth incarnate, virtue incarnate. At the university, Sendero professors had encouraged students to write their theses on the power structure of peasant (i.e., Indian) communities in areas potentially appropriate for starting the armed struggle.

The movement gained control of the students' councils in a few other universities, Lima included. The Shining Path expanded its membership during the 1980s, especially in the countryside. They built a brutal anti-government guerrilla force aimed at obliterating the capitalist order. This radical agenda was based on a simplified and accessible version of the Marxist theory. Under the supreme authority of Guzmán, mostly young academics and their followers carried out the mission, resulting in violent attacks on the state apparatus and the church. The group also mounted a direct assault eliminating the communal leadership and administrative strata of local and regional organizations (assumed to maintain the social order and its old power relationships), claiming over thirty thousand lives.

The movement's regime of vindictive authoritative control gradually lost its popularity among the lower classes of rural and urban citizenship. The Shining Path eventually fell apart with the capture of Guzmán in 1992 along with over thirty-six hundred guerrillas.

We met with a few survivors of that era's brutal events; for example, a nurse who was called at midnight to attend a car accident's victims but found it was a false alarm. On her return home, she discovered her husband, the village communal secretary, shot by hooded visitors. However, we also met with young men who seemed to have been among the former recruits or supporters of the movement. They represented an active cohort of better-educated villagers who anticipated our team's support for their initiatives to modernize their communities.

What can one learn from the Peruvian case about the prospects and consequences of a protest movement led by academics intended to change a set of social, economic, cultural, and political circumstances? No doubt, Peru represents an ethnically, culturally, and politically heterogeneous and fragmented society. The Sendero leadership and its major base of recruits came from the lower ranks of Peruvian society, mostly first-generation university students of peasantry extraction whose prospects for satisfactory employment in close or more remote urban localities seemed very slim. That intrinsic element negates the ordinary structure of academic representation in Western societies, Israel included, where most faculty and students are recruited from the more privileged social sectors.

I am not expanding on the exposition of protest-revolutionary movements founded by intellectuals in other non-Western societies who intended to transform the social-cultural structure of inequality, especially Pol Pot's brutal regime in Cambodia. Like Guzmán in Peru, Pol Pot enjoyed of better education (also in Paris) and taught French literature in a Cambodian college. However, his revolutionary style of Marxism (the Khmer Rouge) resulted in the worst genocide—of his own people—since the Nazi era. Thus, the academic participants and entrepreneurs introduced above intended to erase inequality and promote citizens' engagement in politics. Although they successfully attained an effective position of power, they eventually terminated their mission disastrously, sacrificing numerous innocent lives. They left a scary legacy remembered with other colossal human horror chronicles of the twentieth century.

The South African Case

Naturally, the South African case raises one's curiosity about the comportment of its leading academics during the apartheid era. As is well known, an oppressive regime left them no freedom for the open expression of anti-apartheid positions. David Webster, a senior anthropologist at the University of Witwatersrand and an anti-apartheid activist, was assassinated by a clandestine agency of the apartheid state. Though not all submitted to the pressure, the apartheid ideology had supporters among those least expected to join that system of racial administration. Robert Gordon's "How Good People Become Absurd" (2018) presented the profile of J. P. van S. Bruwer, a leading South African anthropologist who supported the apartheid regime in theory and practice.

In *Complicities: The Intellectual and Apartheid* (2000), Mark Sanders displayed a more comprehensive exploration of South African academics' support of the Afrikaner government's racial ideology. He concentrated on N. P. van Wyk Louw, professor in South African language, literature, culture, and history, who defended apartheid as a response not merely to the South African "race problem" but to "problems of Europe." Pivotal to Louw's argument was the notion that imposing a separation of white and black national groups would foster the "full development" of each and prevent a single group from dominating the others. It followed for him that racial separation was an "ethically just" response to the problem of racial domination (2000: 58). Louw, like other nationalists of his time, began as an advocate for the Afrikaner, particularly the proletarianized Afrikaans worker. When apartheid is the horizon for judgment, Sanders concluded, "one seems bound to consider Louw a 'failed' intellectual, one who ultimately put loyalty to the volk ahead of a critique of racism." The early Afrikaner nationalist imagined himself becoming free of Anglo–South African hegemony. This was the acceptable, anti-colonialist face of Afrikaner nationalism, which also led other intellectuals to a definition of the identity of the *volk* in relation to the "mass" of black Africans. Sanders discussed a few other South African academics, including University of Pretoria sociologist Geoffrey Cronjé, who co-authored a classic in apartheid writing.

Max Gluckman, my mentor and leader of the Manchester School of Anthropology, a South African citizen who conducted his research among African tribes, was barred from entering South African territories for his activism against colonialism and racial inequality. Ironically considered a communist, with a history of political activity in South Africa, Gluckman did not reveal to his students that facet of his persona during and after the training dedicated to their professional conversion from sociological abstractions to ethnographic engagement.

The Apartheid System Revisited
(South Africa versus Israel)

Related to the South African case, and to the recent BDS controversy at the AAA condemning Israeli academia for collaboration with an apartheid regime (see chapter 13), I was intrigued by the South African Benjamin Pogrund's *Drawing Fire: Investigating the Accusations of Apartheid in Israel* (2014). No doubt, the image of apartheid has been the most powerful claim and advertising symbol employed by the BDS propagators calling for an international boycott of Israel, its academics included. Pogrund, born in Cape Town, was with the *Randy Daily Mail* newspaper in Johannesburg for twenty-six years and pioneered the reporting of black politics and black existence under apartheid in the daily press. He was jailed for a few years for exposing abusive conditions in prisons for blacks and political prisoners, and was denied a passport for five years. As a result, he immigrated to Britain, where he continued as editor and foreign reporter for the British press. He authored three books dedicated to the life of South African leading black figures, his close friend Mandela among them. He immigrated again in 1997, to Israel, to found a center in Jerusalem devoted to dialogue between Jews, Muslims, Christians, Israelis, and Palestinians.

His recent *Drawing Fire* offers a panoramic review of the history and conditions that led to the founding of South Africa and Israel, the existential conditions of blacks throughout the apartheid regime in South Africa, and the position of the Arab minority within the Israeli Green Line borders. It inquires and compares the life circumstances of Palestinians in the territories under Israeli occupation, analyzes the critical reports on Israeli politics, and finally, looks to the future of Israel-Palestine coexistence.

Pogrund has been an unusual eyewitness to the social-political realities in both South African and Israeli societies. Now an Israeli citizen, he does not hide his reservations about the darker features of the Israelis' treatment of the Palestinian inhabitants beyond the Green Line borders or his worries about the inevitable consequences of the continuing occupation. A longstanding, candid, and trustworthy reporter on daily life experiences of blacks and whites under the "authentic" apartheid regime, and having paid the harsh price for fighting against that brutal system, he took on the task of educating his readers about the ideology and practice he observed in South Africa—the very system that BDS supporters and other critics indiscriminately compare with the Israel/Palestinian case.

Pogrund elaborated a long list of discriminatory laws, daily practices so brutal and degrading that most outsiders have rarely comprehended the full extent of their impact on people of color in South Africa. No need to delve into that repertoire of racist ideology meant to separate ethnic-cultural human groups in most daily fields of human interaction: economic, political, residential, medical, educational, legal, transport, sport, marriage, and sex—as well as restrictions to freedom of movement, freedom of speech, freedom of association (e.g., party politics, national elections, trade unions), etc. However, Pogrund explored that list as it applied to the Israeli Arab minority within the Green Line borders who make up about 20 percent of the population of eight million. Formally, they enjoy equal rights of citizenship with Jews, and are entitled to the same freedoms, facilities, and governmental, communal, and personal support. No doubt, he claimed that "Israel is a hotbed of discrimination, but Arabs are not the only victims" (p. 55). There are Western

(Ashkenazi Jews) versus Middle Eastern Jews (Mizrahim), Orthodox versus secular Jews, and other socio-economic-geographic-ethnic-gender divisions. In any case, the discrimination of Israeli Arabs is not remotely comparable in theory and practice with blacks under apartheid.

But as for the Palestinians in the occupied territories, Pogrund argued that the situation is more complex, having drastically declined since the start of uprisings, with restrictions to Palestinians' travel into Israeli areas and the expansion of Jewish settlements in the West Bank. He is clearly critical of the West Bank occupation regime, a case of colonialism and hence an international offense casting a pall over the image of the State of Israel: "But to claim that this is the same racist rule as apartheid in South Africa is without substance or truth" (2014: 150). He continues wrestling with the realities of occupation and its changing circumstances over time: the checkpoints, detentions, separate roads, security barriers, economic and water exploitation, and the rest that are not ideological goals but consequences. These realities are submerged in the messianic mission to control much of the West Bank. Perhaps this brings Israelis closer to South Africa's white Afrikaners. Pogrund recalls his South African political representation and personal experience as forewarning to Israel, because "it proved to be not only morally reprehensible but also realistically untenable" (2014: 151). For the time being, however, he concludes, it is not apartheid, and use of the label is inappropriate and wrong. Moreover, it creates confusion because it distracts attention from the occupation.

No doubt a most reliable witness of both national histories on two continents, and who decided to choose Israel for his final destination, Pogrund has been deeply concerned with the occupation. It is a reality that has taken on a life of its own, leading to unending conflict and dire humanitarian ramifications for both Israelis and Palestinians. In a phone call with Pogrund, who resides in Jerusalem, he informed me of the severe methods that kept South African academics from acting out against the system. For example, faculty and students who engaged in political activities were denied passports, forcing them to give up plans for graduate studies or participation in professional forums outside of South Africa. Consequently, South African scholars looked elsewhere for job opportunities even in the early stages of apartheid. During that conversation, it seemed discourteous to interrogate Pogrund about his present-day mood as a resident of Jerusalem, the simmering focus of the Israeli/Palestinian conflict ready to explode without warning, and in view of the stagnant political "status quo" with no freeze on the expansion of settlements in the West Bank. I am reminded of the opening sentence to his book's preface: "Living in South Africa was easy in moral terms [it was good versus evil]. Living in Israel is difficult" (2014: xiii).

However, a neutral observer (if there is one) might have commented on the AAA supporters of the BDS boycott of Israeli academia on the allegation of apartheid representing a constituency of critics who have rarely shown a strong stance against massive assaults of human rights elsewhere: for example, discrimination of minorities and brutality directed against citizens in their own country, or military attacks of other countries orchestrated by their own and other Western governments. No doubt, the Middle East's present-day colossal political chaos and human atrocities have been much affected by the disastrous American/Anglo invasion of Iraq. Another blind spot for these critics is the Chinese occupation and destruction of culture in Tibet. It seems the boycott of the Israeli academic scene is far less costly than the price of giving up China as a venue for visits, research projects, and professional conferences.

Though not an academic in formal terms, Pogrund acted as a participant observer in both South Africa and Israel. Few anthropologists could claim similar know-how and personal engagement in their respective field-sites.

Conclusion

The list of national cases presented above portrayed sociopolitical circumstances that entangled intellectuals-academics as participants in the arena of ideology and practice impacting the lives of other fellow citizens. However, it does not suggest a comprehensive picture of that phenomenon. But the cases convincingly attest to the varied cohort of "intellectuals" who do not represent a uniform category of chosen people instinctively recruited to "challenge the underlying values of society" and defend the code of tenets defined in the argot of "universal human rights."

It seems "normative" to criticize those individuals who display a visible position of complicity in support of society's underlying values, or to praise those who explore and challenge these values. But little attention is given to the large, quiet audience that preserves a low profile during the era of conflict. We empathize with Vogelgesang's (1974: 14) exposition of American leftist intellectuals during the Vietnam era: "Intellectuals are men and women of ideas who explore and challenge the underlying values of society. There is a normative function: to prescribe what ought to be." However, we tend to remember and keep record of those on both margins of the debate and struggle. That observation was exposed by Mark Lilla in *The Reckless Mind: Intellectuals in Politics* ([2016] 2001), reviewing the story of many West European intellectuals who welcomed with open arms Fascist and Communist regimes and portrayed Western liberal democracy in diabolical terms as the real home of tyranny. They tried to convince the public that modern tyrants were liberators. Lilla ended that accusing account with a warning: "Whoever takes it upon himself to write an honest intellectual history of twentieth-century Europe will need a strong stomach" (p. 198).

In conclusion, the prevalent perception of academics marks them as highly knowledgeable and critical about the world around them close and remote. However, they have no precedence for participating in the dynamics of national politics compared with other citizens in a democratic society. They may join national politics as party members and parliament delegates, but they do so as individuals sharing and competing with other compatriots coming from various social strata. They often use their skills and knowledge to express their opinions and suggestions in academic and public forums, and they earn prestige but not power in the real sense of the term. No doubt, a few academics have gained immense influence in world affairs as moral or ideological leaders—it is sufficient to mention Karl Marx—but recalling Mannheim's assertion (1968), not as members of an academic class representing social-political solidarity or experiencing a cohort's ambience of *communitas* in anthropological terms (Turner 1969).

In any case, the above presentation of intellectuals-academics' engagement or absence in the public forum does not affect in any way—comparison or value judgment—the following account of the Israeli case as observed before, during, and after the first Palestinian uprising.

Note

1. BDS—Boycott, Divestment, Sanctions—a Palestinian-led campaign promoting various forms of boycott against Israel.

4

Israeli Academics' Political Involvement Prior to the First Intifada

Naturally, one wonders about the role of Israeli academia—teachers and students—compared with university life in the Western hemisphere. Earlier, we introduced Professors Arieli, Talmon, and Leibowitz, leading figures in Israeli academia, who expressed their moral convictions about the intellectual's responsibility in the public forum. However, by and large, AD KAN participants had neither prior experience nor an example in Euro-American academia by which to model the initiation of a faculty-led protest organization on campus. As a student and later a university teacher, and as a guest in other academic institutions and at conferences, I never observed or attended discussions involving academics' actual engagement in national affairs.

Altogether, Israeli universities have a short history. The first, the Hebrew University, was founded in Jerusalem in 1924; Tel Aviv and Bar-Ilan (religious) Universities were started in the 1960s; Haifa and Beer Sheba (Ben-Gurion) Universities were started in the early 1970s. The Technion engineering school in Haifa preceded the Hebrew University (1912). During the early pre-state years of the Hebrew University, a small group called Brit Shalom (Covenant of Peace)—whose leading figures included university president Yehuda L. Magnes, Professors Hugo Bergman, Martin Buber, Ernest Simon, Gershom Scholem, and a few others—began actively preaching for a peaceful political coexistence in a binational state of Jews and Arabs in Palestine. Though famous for its eminent members, their agenda had little impact on academic and political life.

Indeed, as noted by Anita Shapira (1997), historian of Israel's founding years, the creation of Hebrew universities in Palestine was not a priority for the visionaries and pioneers of Zionism. On the contrary, transforming Jewish Diaspora livelihood and working life revolving around manual labor, agriculture in particular, has been its major goal and expectation away from the "Shtetel" (segregated Jewish East European community). It was also time to separate from the tradition of Jewish-texts expertise as major accomplishment, of men in particular.

During the first post-state decade, a notion of harmony seemed to typify the academy's view and support of the government's political programs and administrative policies led by the charismatic founder David Ben-Gurion. Moreover, Ben-Gurion considered himself a friend if not actually a member of the society of intellectuals and developed close relationships with prominent scholars and other celebrated literati. However, that harmonious era ended abruptly when a group of more than sixty of Jerusalem's leading academics, representing the departments of history, philosophy, sociology, literature, law, and Jewish studies, confronted PM Ben-Gurion's authoritarian conduct in a security blunder known as the Lavon Affair (a failed Israeli covert operation in Egypt intentionally linked to Pinchas Lavon, the minister of defense). In January 1961, they put forth a public statement that labeled Ben-Gurion's crusade against an inquiry committee as a serious challenge to democracy. No doubt, their public intervention had an impact on an ongoing process that led to Ben-Gurion's political demise.

Years later, a few Tel Aviv academics were involved in the aftermath of the traumatic 1973 war with the emerging political party Shinui (Change) that merged with the DASH Party ("Democratic Movement for Change"), which was led by Jerusalem's eminent archeologist Professor Yigael Yadin. This party helped bring down the continuing rule of the Labor Party, but it actually facilitated a takeover by the right-wing Herut (later the Likud Party). The DASH Party soon disappeared, leaving a bitter sense of failure and loss of faith in the prospects of "honest, peace-loving intellectuals'" ability to shape present-day public life in its various dimensions. It was a grim warning that academics are probably inept at successfully playing in the national political arena.

Leading scholars in the Jerusalem sociology vanguard seemed to represent that ideal of academic disengagement in their lifestyle, emulating Talcott Parsons's theoretical perspective (e.g., *The Social*

System, 1951). Abstract and maintaining a value-free disposition, that paradigm evoked the notion of moral neutrality.

As for Israeli students, they never seemed to take a special separate position in Israeli public life compared with their generation's cohorts in other Western countries. Israeli universities were all relieved of the students' revolt that engulfed many campuses in the United States and Europe during the 1960s. Presumably, the majority of Israeli students, aged twenty to twenty-two, who entered college after termination of their compulsory army service with the IDF (three years for men and two years for women) were too anxious to go ahead with their studies, proceed with professional careers, and often start family life. Moreover, many among them had taken a break before starting academic studies to engage in what became an Israeli rite of passage: a few months to a year traveling to South America or the Far East to conclude the two to three years of restrictive military life. It is no surprise then that Israeli students have not initiated social-political public activities, except for occasional protests about pragmatic issues: financial grievances or specific campus-departmental conflicts.

The above account has presented a brief review of the overall public-arena ambiance that seemed to prevail on Israeli campuses up to the sudden explosion of the Palestinian uprising nicknamed the "first intifada."

5

The Founding of AD KAN

> *Never doubt that a small group of thoughtful, committed citizens can change the world, it is the only thing that ever has.*
> —Margaret Mead

That somewhat relaxed era of social-political disengagement on my part reached its last station at the end of 1987 with the start of the first Palestinian intifada. I do not recall the exact moment—an event or flicker of consciousness—that shattered my peace of mind and prompted me to write a short letter to the liberal Israeli daily newspaper *Haaretz* titled "The Time Is Ripe for Civil Disobedience in Israel" (24 December 1987). The letter opened with the accusation that "we are all partners to the occupation even though we might hate it with our deepest heart and soul's moral convictions." It went on in a more optimistic tone: "Past experiences tell us that we [leftists] are not weak. Alongside the uprising protest events we witness in the occupied territories, the time arrived for civil disobedience in Zion." However, the most poignant point in the few lines of that blatant communication was the clause "I shudder when I am reminded of the intellectuals in countries not to be named ... condemned by history." The most forbidden comparable images in Israeli public discourse have become a sort of a campy style of naming in disguise.

It was the first time I had ever identified myself as a member in the category of "intellectuals." It seemed a mark of identity usually associated with celebrated authors, leading philosophers, historians, and essayists. I also lacked at that time the standard definitions for the status and roles prescribed to intellectuals and taught in some sociological courses. Actually, my education appeared deficient; I was not well versed in the pillars of Western civilization, the "toolkit" of true intellectuals, from Greek philosophers to Hegel, Kant, Marx, and others. I was not in the habit of name-dropping to impress students, not even the more recent popular heroes among the "postmodern" social scholars, such as Foucault and Derrida. However, it seemed a fitting moment to put on that presumptuous mantle and approach others who felt they shared the status of intellectuals, signing my letter with the title of "Professor and President of the Israel Anthropological Association."

That letter raised a moving and totally unexpected response from a wide circle of readers. It dawned on me that I could not return to my ivory tower's relaxed schedule. Of particular importance was meeting with actor and director Sinai Peter, who invited me to join the Yesh Gvul (there is a limit/border) movement. This protest organization started during the 1982 Lebanon War and later extended its mission to call on IDF soldiers to refuse military service in the occupied territories. They thus implemented the call of Yeshayahu Leibowitz, the charismatic scientist and philosopher at the Hebrew University who believed that the military occupation of the Palestinian lands and people would be terminated once a few hundred Israeli soldiers refused to attend their military duty when called to serve beyond the Green Line. Yesh Gvul had gained much publicity, support, and condemnation, and its members who declined the order to join their units serving in the West Bank and Gaza incurred severe jail sentences. But a few hundred soldiers never deserted at the same time. Nevertheless, it remained a visible group of dedicated comrades, mostly enlisted among the reserve forces, who vocally demonstrated on behalf of those who were jailed.

However, although I empathized with their cause, I could not join Sinai Peter's friends. For one, I was no longer enlisted in active military duty with the reserve forces. But there was another reason to decline his invitation, an idea that started simmering in my mind: the movement of disobedience against the continuing occupation might gain a stronger impact if a growing number of protest groups would emerge in various national institutions and social-professional agencies, a phenomenon that seemed to gain momentum.

I was invited around the same time to join a group of academics, called the Twenty-First Year [of occupation], which mostly recruited faculty from the Jerusalem and Tel Aviv universities. Two of its founders drafted a covenant, a document of many pages suggesting a blueprint for a revolution to bring an end to the Israeli regime of occupation. Although I agreed with its ideological orientation, the group itself, nonetheless, seemed too elitist, reminding me of a cult of religious believers. Their covenant left no room for any sort of accommodation for and compromise with the realities that had developed since 1967, blaming only the Israelis for the situation on the ground. One could not expect that perspective to attract a wider Israeli audience beyond a small circle of an intellectual "priesthood." In fact, after a short period of activity, the Twenty-First Year organization disintegrated, and most members joined other protest groups. This was a time when nonparliamentary groups and protest formations suddenly emerged as part of a spontaneous wave of public resentment. Kaminer (1996) reviewed the circumstances, ideology, and practice of the various groups operating in the field of protest. He observed the gap between the radical rhetoric and activities that had soon disaffected participants among the Twenty-First Year's membership.

Soon, following conversations with a few close colleagues in the social sciences faculty and particularly with the late Leon Sheleff (a prolific sociologist, law scholar, and human-rights activist who emigrated from South Africa), we decided to advertise an open meeting with other concerned colleagues. Handwritten messages were placed at a few information boards on campus, and we were surprised to find the meeting room packed with twenty or more teachers, especially from the social sciences, the humanities, and mathematics departments, when we arrived at the social sciences faculty building meeting room. It was evident that many of our colleagues on campus were undergoing a moment of self-searching even though they had not previously engaged in political activities. They were experiencing acute guilt about their manner of academic disengagement, accustomed to going on with their daily affairs as if unconcerned about the surrounding political realities.

No doubt, the sudden uprising of the Palestinians against the occupation shuttered the "normalcy" of the situation as perceived by many Israelis. A common observation fostered an assumption that the Palestinians, who had integrated into the Israeli labor force—where they were regularly employed in the major fields of construction, farming, and other services—enjoyed a better socioeconomic situation compared with the pre-1967 days. I emulated that common perception when the contractor refurbishing my family's apartment employed mostly skilled and unskilled workers who came every morning from Gaza. We maintained amicable relationships with the

Gaza men, discussing various issues with them (they were surprised I did not believe in God!). But at this moment of sudden revolt, we were forced to confront the brutal reality behind that curtain of deception. The terms of the benevolent Israeli regime, and the mirage of the Palestinians' accommodation with that reality, were suddenly stripped of the shroud of national security and self-righteousness to reveal a blatant system of Israeli domination.

By the end of that first faculty gathering, followed by a few more weekly meetings with a growing attendance, we decided to organize a one-day conference inquiring into the various aspects of the continuing occupation. Soon, on 25 January 1988 (a month after the *Haaretz* letter), we inaugurated our project, calling on the faculty, students, and others to attend a long afternoon conference titled "AD KAN, the Destruction of Israeli Society as Consequence of the Occupation." The heading AD KAN (No More) was the product of the daily conversations with Leon Sheleff as we looked for an icon raising an association with the Yesh Gvul organization, short and direct. Again, we advertised the coming event with handwritten posters and worried that only a small number of attendees would show up. The list of speakers included eight experts representing the fields of sociology, political science, economy, and law, mostly from TAU but also two Israeli Arabs of professional reputation from other campuses.

Despite all gloomy expectations, we were astonished when the main hall at the law school that we were allowed to reserve for that extra-academic activity (also the site of the senate meetings) was packed with more than 250 faculty and students. It became clear that there were many teachers and students on campus anxious to engage in protest against the continuing occupation of Gaza and the West Bank. The opening remarks echoed the unfulfilled promise by Foreign Minister Abba Eban, which had facilitated my return to Israel twenty years earlier: "We shall be magnanimous in victory." Instead, I emphasized the heavy price we were paying for the settlements project in the occupied territories (which was yet small considering its expansion during the next decades), the reality of the military control of another people, the horrific hatred nurtured among the Palestinians, and the decline of world support for Israel's legitimate claims. Other speakers at the panel presented their perspectives of the continuing occupation as harmfully reflected in the various dimensions of life seen through specific professional mirrors.

Many among the attending audience signed up for future activities and contributed modest donations to cover expenses of the coming events. We now had the resources to communicate better with what seemed like an interested group on campus who supported the agenda of civic protest. A few days later (1 February 1988), we circulated the first official short letter calling on the academic staff to join future activities under the slogan AD KAN:

> In view of the deteriorating political and moral circumstances highlighted by the Palestinians' revolt, members of an institution dedicated to the promotion of science and culture cannot remain apathetic, sealed off in the academic ivory tower. Anyone interested is invited to contact the signers of the letter; Professors Meir Smorodinski (Exact Sciences) and Moshe Shokeid (Social Sciences).

The first public event enjoyed coverage in daily newspapers that emphasized the entry of academic voices into the public political arena. However, we were unprepared for the toll of becoming an attractive subject for sympathetic journalists, who called to inquire about the origins and plans of our organization—indicative of a wider public mood of political protest.

A few days later, a petition protesting against the government policies dealing with the unrest in the territories, signed by six hundred academics mostly from the Jerusalem and Tel Aviv campuses, was published in leading newspapers. A major two-page article by prominent writer Ronit Matalon presented interviews with a few of the signers (*Haaretz*, 2 February 1988). The Jerusalem representatives, including Professor S. N. Eisenstadt (the leading Israeli sociologist), seemed more restrained in their choice of terms concerning the role of academics in the public forum, while the Tel Aviv representatives were all associated with the emergent protest organization (not yet officially named AD KAN): Jonathan Shapiro (sociology), Ariella Friedman (psychology and social work), and Uri Maor (physics). Shapiro, known for his work on Israeli political parties, complained about the politicians' skill in coopting the academics. The physicist Maor anticipated the coming end of the Israeli ambience of social consensus that would tear off the curtain of empty slogans reiterated by the politicians. He went on to describe the participants: "We are mostly 40/50 years old, a beaten generation in the political sense, victims of the 1973 war and its aftermath." Ariella Friedman was reported as the speaker in the last conference at TAU; in it she interrupted her presentation, unable to control her tears while expressing her feelings about the Israeli military rule and the suffering of the Palestinians. She expressed her inability to continue tolerating the scene of the "invisible" Palestinians and her urgent need to meet with them. She believed the emergent protest organizations might carry an important impact, a phenomenon she observed in the United States during the students' revolt against the Vietnam War. I was reported as writer of the call for civil disobedience; I admitted I did not know how successful our venture might prove to be, but was ready to endure its failure and the potential loss of personal reputations. The reporter compared the "Tel Aviv vibrant and emotionally charged organizational atmosphere ... with the more poised Jerusalem academic perspective as expressed by Prof. Eisenstadt's position."

The *Chronicle of Higher Education* published a long article by reporter Herbert Watzman from Jerusalem (17 February 1988) titled "Professors in Israel Organize to Oppose West Bank Politics." Relating to the petition signed by six hundred academics from all campuses, he interviewed the Jerusalem professors David Kretzmer (law) and Shlomo Avineri (political science) about the terms of political protest. However, he quoted me at length, claiming that "in Israel the faculty is probably more to the Left than the student body, different from the American case where protest tended to originate among the students. ... However, I believe it is a remnant of a Jewish tradition respecting representatives of higher education. ... It's important that both inside and outside the country, people will know that the universities are opposed to what is going on."

The next public event (29 February 1988), a demonstration on campus called "Against the Continuing Occupation and the Lack of a Creative Vision towards a Peaceful Solution," enlisted eight AD KAN academics and four student leaders as speakers, including the Arab Students Association representative. It drew a large audience of supporters and viewers. In introducing the speakers, I emphasized that they represented reluctant performers; after all, they usually escaped public attention and were instead engrossed in daily stresses and other routine matters on campus. But now they all strutted into the public arena, aware of the heavy blood-price we would pay without an end to the tragic situation orchestrated by our nonsensical national leaders.

But the next public event (17 March 1988) became a critical moment in the development of the movement—an event titled "Testimonies from the Territories." The term "territories," applied to the occupied Palestinian lands, was used instead of the biblical geographical names, such as Judea and Samaria for the West Bank, as called by the Jewish settlers and their supporters. Respected Palestinian representatives—a physician, a teacher-chair of the association of Palestinian authors, and a lawyer from Gaza—were invited to inform the audience about the circumstances of daily life in their communities. Again, it was a very successful gathering, representing a moment of public exposure to the dire consequences of Israeli control, as spokesmen for the people under the Israeli rule appeared for the first time on campus as respectable professionals. Dignified and eloquent, they revealed a picture not familiar among Israelis who had hitherto met Palestinians mostly as laborers engaged in low-class manual occupations.

The introduction to that event reminded the audience about the damaging international media coverage of the Israeli regime's occupation evils, which had been previously concealed by the local media. We wanted to present firsthand evidence and preserve the university as an island of free information and ethical behavior. It was not a story of a small PLO terrorist minority, as we were told in the past. We confronted a momentous popular civil revolt embracing Palestinian society. Our posters on campus were taken off as soon as they were pasted on the information boards, not by reluctant students or outside visitors but most probably by the university maintenance staff. While Rehavam Ze'evi (minister of tourism, known colloquially as Gandi) could express in a conference on campus his right-wing ideology advocating a transfer of the Palestinians, a lecturer who flaunted a leftist poster was treated brutally by the security personnel. We had anticipated the university leadership to act against the silencing of information on campus. The introduction ended with the imagery: "To stay *beseder*—do obediently the expected—is a safe strategy when the foxes dominate the streets. But we all know that the hour of the foxes is due to disappear sooner or later, and those who are silent today do actually join the foxes."

One cannot forget the unexpected experience a few hours later, after midnight, when an urgent phone call informed me that our guest speaker, the lawyer Abu Shaaban, was detained by the Israeli military on his return home to Gaza. That traumatic moment realized our claims about the illegitimate Israeli regime of occupation and radically changed our position from a conceptual lecture-hall humanitarian one to an actual engagement with the Palestinians' struggle for freedom. Abu Shaaban, a respectable and articulate lawyer, was punished for joining our agenda that was peacefully displayed on the premises of an Israeli university campus. He was apparently penalized for his courage to speak out about the legal conditions of his people in Gaza under "our" Israeli rule. I could not go back to sleep before communicating with a few active members in the group to decide our next steps. It was an urgent responsibility to do whatever was in our capacity to free the man who was paying the price for accepting our invitation. Moreover, was it not also the security authorities' subtle message to Shaaban's leftist hosts in academia to stay away from any association with informed Palestinian interlocutors?

The next afternoon we were ready to demonstrate in front of the Minister of Defense Rabin's residence in a Tel Aviv neighborhood close to the TAU campus. The core membership and supporters showed up equipped with posters protesting the arrest of an innocent Palestinian. A few journalists were also invited to cover the quiet event. A few days later (21 March 1988) we organized a public forum on campus with Israeli and Palestinian lawyers to discuss the Israeli policy of incarceration without trial. When Abu Shaaban was released shortly afterward, we believed our efforts played a part in the "happy end" of that traumatic episode. That experience, however, also served as a "rite of passage" confirming our "coming of age" as a recognized player in the field of protest organizations contesting the continuing regime of occupation. It was also the moment of inaugurating the label AD KAN, the title of our first conference, as the official name of the organization.

6

Opening the Sealed Box of AD KAN

I intend to tell a story kept inside a decaying box in my office at the Tel Aviv University department of sociology and anthropology. The box contains preserved documents relating to AD KAN, the university protest movement against the continuing occupation of the Palestinian West Bank and Gaza. Founded during the start of the first intifada in December 1987, the organization dissolved in 1995 following the signing of the Oslo peace accords. That carton was delivered to my office sometime in 2005, when Ora Slonim, the dedicated unofficial secretary of AD KAN, retired from the social sciences faculty administration. Once opened, I retrieved fading fliers and posters, announcements of group meetings, public lectures, public protests on campus or elsewhere in Tel Aviv and other places, communications with the university administration, newspapers clips, the list of members and supporters of the organization, lists of money donations and bank records—all coated with a heavy layer of dust.

The box lying on the floor of my office next to the entrance has been an upsetting reminder of a period of tense emotions, an unusual experience of *communitas* (in Victor Turner's terms) with my colleagues: the sensation that we were "academics in arms," our shared notion of high hopes, and finally our feelings of abysmal failure and the loss of a mission with the fiasco of the Oslo Accords. That notion of loss culminated with the sudden death of Leon Sheleff, my closest partner in that exceptional sociopolitical experience. I called on the inner core of AD KAN veterans to discuss a way to preserve that modest archive or find an interested student to write a thesis in any academic venue based on the story of AD KAN. We met at Ariella Friedman's home, the gathering reminiscent of the long-forgotten days of the first intifada. But no suggestion presented itself, and I lost interest in saving that treasure trove of memorabilia and searching for an enthusiastic redeemer.

Why open it now and tell its story? I have always claimed that I am against the notion of nostalgia, refusing to attend reunion gatherings of old schoolmates and "erasing" my own birthday from special attention. Am I developing a hidden yearning for a cherished era in my Israeli university life? I believe it is a wish to let go of the pain of a lost dream. A desire to reconcile with the sad realization that I am unable to help change the political reality I bitterly resent—the continuing Israeli occupation of the West Bank with no resolution in the foreseeable future rather than the founding of an independent Palestinian state alongside Israel. It is the recognition of an unresolved enigma: how can a nation that many observers consider a Western society, respected for its advanced science and technology, instituted on the premises of secular liberal ideals, be led by right-wingers whose socio-cultural-ideological profiles are far remote from the elementary norms of the society constructed by the dreamers and founders of the state of Israel (the fruit of Theodor Herzl's Zionist vision)?[1]

Obviously, I am not the only Israeli to experience the loss of his/her "world of yesterday" (borrowing Stefan Zweig's title), the one that existed or was only envisioned. However, as I became more deeply engaged with the fading documents in my possession, it donned on me that I could speak for a generation of men and women who shared that five-year journey, who tried to unlock the gates of the academic tower and get involved in the public arena. We joined together, temporarily relaxing the norms of professional moral-ideological neutrality as we tried to act out—"to speak truth to power"—though we lacked prior experience on the stage of political action.

On opening that neglected box—covered with the long black cloth poster that said "AD KAN" in white letters that we used to display on the podium of hall lectures/panels or in the front row of protesters during demonstrations—I felt the urge to relate this story: my unexpected introduction into the scene of political protest in the main square and in the halls of the Tel Aviv university campus. However, beyond the exposure of a personal experience and its frustrating aftereffects, I try now to comprehend the circumstances and the consequences that befall "innocent" academics who attempt to come out of the ivory tower's comfortable shelter and take part in the "real" world surrounding their safe haven.

As expected from an anthropologist who never considered himself a storyteller, I approach my present task relying on the recovered "treasure box" as a substitute for fieldnotes collected during ordinary fieldwork projects. Naturally, I also looked for other informants' records from the protest groups that emerged during the period of AD KAN activity. Two academic sources are of particular interest. First, Kaminer (1996) recorded the history of the Israeli peace movement during the first intifada. He presented the list of about twenty voluntary organizations that were active at that time, their specific agenda, and their sociocultural background, AD KAN included. He described AD KAN as a radical group of academics compared with other contemporary protest movements:

> One development signified an auspicious change in the protest scene in Israeli academia—the establishment of the AD KAN ("No Further" [Kaminer's translation]) group of professors and lecturers at Tel Aviv University. AD KAN was established during the first days of the Intifada and distanced itself, from its very inception, from the traditional liberal Zionist approach previously dominant on Israeli campuses. For all practical purposes, AD KAN adopted the main points of the program of the militant wing of the peace movement, including the demand for Palestinian self-determination and recognition of the PLO as the representative of the Palestinians. For a faculty organization, AD KAN was exceptionally active: it disseminated information on the occupation, organized numerous demonstrations and seminars, and participated in an organized fashion in the activities of other protest organizations. ... AD KAN did become the dominant political force among the faculty at Tel Aviv University; it had many highly prestigious members of the faculty in its ranks and had broad support among "junior" faculty—including many of the non-tenures teaching staff. Thus, it also enhanced the prestige of the militant wing of the protest movement, which could show that it had serious support among the academic intelligentsia which hitherto had given almost exclusive support to Peace Now. (1996: 147–48)

Peace Now, a veteran mainstream liberal movement, coexisted with AD KAN. It called for a peaceful resolution with the Palestinians but was careful to articulate a clear approach toward that destination: "It was not willing to go out on a limb and demand recognition of the PLO and the establishment of a Palestinian state" (ibid.: 100).

Kaminer concentrated his more detailed report on three protest groups among the older and new voluntary organizations supporting the Palestinians or opposing the Israeli government's policies, representing various political, professional, and civil segments in the leftist wing of Israeli society.

Another article by Sasson-Levy and Rapoport (2002), presented from a feminist perspective, reported on the Twenty-First Year, a peace movement organization who opposed the occupation and whose membership's social background was close to AD KAN's. However, compared with records of protest organizations reported above and in later chapters, the following account of AD KAN seems more comprehensive; it consists of my insider knowledge and close relationships with the active membership as coordinator of most activities (except for short periods of academic engagements abroad).

Before I continue to report the story of AD KAN, its activities, and the changing context of Israeli realities, it seems fitting to recall an anthropological paradigm of ethnographic research in the contemporary social arena. I am referring to the intriguing query suggested in Hannerz's *Anthropology's World* (2010) and in the more specifically pertinent application for our case, Sanjek's *Ethnography in Today's World* (2013: 83): what does our designation of "the ethnographic present" mean? The implication for the following presentation is to allow us to observe the flow of present-day events free of the requisites of a planned field-site research project, particularly in one's home society. Consequently, unlike earlier anthropological engagements (mine and others'), the field of the current involvement is in a state of unceasing, almost daily flux, and not of a fully perceived and concluded social reality framed in a "normative" ethnographic text. It integrates impromptu situations I have observed in past and recent encounters, events, and communications that seem related to the ongoing discourse. That "open-ended" exposition also involves a consideration of other scholars' treatises and commentaries on the studied conflict, from the Israeli vista in particular.

Note

1. See, for example, Gans's 2008 presentation of the history of Zionism.

7

The Operation of a Protest Organization

The core group of AD KAN activists included about thirty, mostly senior, members of the teaching staff from different faculties: the social sciences, the humanities, the schools of law, education, business administration, and mathematics; one prominent representative was from the physics department. We had another small circle of supporters on campus, scholars of reputation whom we could call on to participate in specific events but who were not engaged in the daily "blue-collar" tasks, such as circulating information, distributing posters, attending regular weekly meetings, etc. A few of the Twenty-First Year movement joined us soon after that organization lost its impetus (including the philosopher Anat Biletzki and the linguist Tanya Reinhart) as well as a few veteran Marxist historians who were associated with left-wing parties but who now joined our group of political "novices."

AD KAN membership by and large was recruited from the "western bank" site of faculty buildings on campus hosting the "soft" sciences, versus the "eastern bank" site, which hosts mostly the exact/natural sciences; biology, physics, engineering, and medicine. Was it a state of mind or the daily "hard laboratory work" separating between these two major constituencies in our shared academic environment? But what made the mathematicians closer to the historians, sociologists, philosophers, lawyers, literary scholars, and linguists, distinguishing them from the neighboring practitioners on campus (except for the uniquely active physicist Professor Uri Maor and biologist Professor Joseph Neumann)? As reviewed in chapter 3, that major division was observed long ago by scholars who studied the role of intellectuals in modern society, comparing those engaged in human conduct/affairs with those participating in the applied professions (e.g., Merton, Brym, Reiff). The mathematicians, however, must have introduced a hybrid category on the campus map ...

True, our core group represented only a small fraction of the senior and junior faculty on campus and no more than 5 percent of the senate membership (as of September 1989). Nevertheless, we enjoyed significant visibility and a growing number of supporters who regularly attended AD KAN events. The professional standing of the core membership seemed too notable to be ignored by the university leadership (the rector and his deputy in particular), who allowed us the use of central halls for conferences and the central public square for demonstrations. They also called on the security unit to safeguard these activities, which raised intense antagonism among a minority of right-wing supporters on campus, but mostly visitors from outside. The security personnel were evidently unhappy with their responsibility that often negated their personal political inclinations, but they grudgingly honored their duty. I believe my "anthropological manners" facilitated a smooth relationship with that reluctant constituency on campus.

A document from an early stage in these activities illustrated the organizational structure, a graphic design of the links of communication and a list of membership of the various organs: chief operator; public relations and communication committee; events committee; publications committee; international relationships committee; students committee; finance committee; organization committee; campus agencies relations committee; other (protest) groups connections committee. The list of thirty-seven members included mostly senior faculty, a few serving on more than one committee. A daily newspaper report (*Al Hmishmar* 24 January 1989) disseminated information about the meeting of the representatives from a few protest movements—Peace Now, Yesh Gvul, the Twenty-First Year, AD KAN, and other leftist groups and public figures—to discuss cooperation to end the occupation and influence public opinion and support peace negotiations with the PLO.

Copies of letters forwarded by Sasha Weitman, a close colleague at the sociology department and a dedicated AD KAN participant, revealed his correspondence with Clifford Geertz, the most prominent American cultural anthropologist of the late twentieth century. Sasha requested his support of AD KAN's efforts to release Abu Shaaban, the Gaza lawyer arrested after participating at the movement's conference. Geertz graciously cooperated, sending a letter to the Israeli Consulate in New York imploring them to release Abu Shaaban, a step toward alleviating the tense political situation in Israel. Grateful for Geertz's prompt response, Sasha sent back a letter (1 May 1988) expanding on the stressful situation in Israel. However, to my astonishment, immediately after the first sentence, Sasha included in brackets the following comment:

> (Incidentally, AD KAN was formed following the publication in one of the daily papers of an angry letter at the beginning of the Intifada, by Moshe Shokeid, one of your professional confreres and my colleague in the department, calling on the Israeli public to "rise up in rebellion" against the occupation and the brutal repression. The morning after, and much to his surprise, Moshe found himself at the head of a faculty-led groundswell committed "to do something" about the situation. It is like that well-known Parisian personality in 1879 who, when asked why he was running so hard after the angry revolutionary crowd, answered "Why, because I am their leader, that's why!")

I had no previous knowledge about Sasha's intention to contact Geertz. Sasha, who immigrated to Israel a few years earlier, leaving behind a comfortable career in the United States, was deeply engaged in the group's activities, hopeful that its growing impact on Israeli politics would be reminiscent of the antiwar campaign on American campuses calling to end the Vietnam War. I do not remember discussing that story with Geertz during his 1990 stay in Jerusalem, nor do I recall mentioning it to him a decade later while spending a year (2000) at the Princeton Institute (IAS) enjoying a spell of relaxation in that haven of academic life. However, spotting Sasha's portrayal of the stage of protest magnified by his humorous literary flair (also as researcher of the French Revolution) helped me believe it all really happened, painfully retrieving the mood of that moment twenty-five years back. Records from that time contained other copies of letters addressed by close colleagues from overseas and forwarded to Israeli diplomatic sites.

AD KAN presented itself in a short, simply narrated flyer distributed, in particular, during public meetings:

> AD KAN, The University Peace Movement, an organization of academic faculty at Tel Aviv University whose members maintain different viewpoints. We got together following the serious situation Israeli society had fallen into after 20 years of occupation, the revolt in the territories and the government's [inept] response. That hectic situation entails horrific dangers both to the state of Israel and to the Palestinian

people. The continuing occupation is causing the deterioration of moral values and defies the democratic character of Israeli society. The policy of oppression and the "tough fist" displayed in its punishing methods only escalate the grave situation. The one way to escape that reality is via direct negotiations between Israel and the Palestinians. Both parties will give up unrealistic expectations and will accommodate with difficult compromises. We act in the hope of changing the Israeli government's positions with the following issues: 1. Acknowledgement of the Palestinians' right of self-determination and promising negotiations based on mutual recognition. 2. The representation of the Palestinian people will be decided by the Palestinians themselves. 3. Withdrawal of the dogma of "not speaking to the PLO under any circumstances." 4. Until the end of the occupation terminating the policy of the "tough fist," follow the Geneva code including the cancelation of deportations [of individuals to Lebanon] as well as of the administrative incarcerations, avoid collective punishment, prevent violation of private property and demolishing Palestinians homes. Implementing shared basic legal norms and allowing free political activity in the territories. AD KAN

A few years later (June 1991), the same flyer was rewritten to expand its constituency as an association of teachers, workers, and students at Tel Aviv University. It more explicitly called on the Israeli government to accept UN Resolution 242 demanding an evacuation of the territories Israel occupied since 1967. It went on to accuse the government of obliterating any process of peacemaking to allow expansion of the settlements project in the occupied territories. The flyer indicated that AD KAN was not suggesting a detailed peace program except for a two-state solution that would promise a just accommodation of claims raised by the disputant parties, ensure security arrangements, reduce conventional arms buildup, and disarm the region of nuclear weapons.

The flyers and other communications were authored by a few core members, circulated in advance and discussed by the wider membership during the weekly meetings. These gave us an opportunity to add, omit, or change the contents and style before the texts were finally distributed on campus and elsewhere. However, it was a trying task to keep the discussions going and avoid the tense arguments that disrupt the ambience of friendly communication in the company of assertive academics of differing temperaments and strong personal opinions on most issues.

Our initial year of existence, 1988, seemed particularly active, with thirteen public events: these were mostly gatherings hosting distinguished speakers, academics from TAU and other campuses, authors, lawyers, journalists, public figures, Knesset members, high-ranking retired army officers, mayors, and Palestinian professionals and political leaders from Israel and the occupied territories. The few demonstrations were held on the campus central lawn during midday hours, which allowed us the use of a megaphone. Attracting one to two hundred participants and many spectators, these open-square gatherings were usually addressed by AD KAN members. The titles of the public meetings included the following: "Is There a Possibility of a Peace Accord with the Palestinians?"; "The Battle of Alger and the Palestinian Revolt" (a film screening followed by a discussion); "From the Intifada to Reconciliation with the Palestinians"; "Is There a Possibility of a Peace Settlement without the PLO?"; "Open the Universities in the Territories! Talk Peace—Don't Oppress"; "Talk to the PLO."

Specifically, the demonstrations targeted the closure of Palestinian colleges by order of a military decree, which was based on the assumption that these were the hotbeds for radical political and terrorist activities aimed against Israeli rule, institutions, and civilians. We also called on other protest groups to join us in demonstrating against the mass arrests without trial of Palestinian activists, gathering in front of the Negev Jail "Anzar 3." Apart from these publicly advertised events, we received permission for a silent vigil in front of a major hall on campus during a conference hosting Defense Minister Rabin, for which we produced posters protesting the failure to reach a political solution and how that failure threatened the security of Israel (4 April 1988).

As much as the leftist active constituency of senior academics was small, the right-wing membership of supporters on campus was much smaller, with only two vocal representatives: Professor Yuval Ne'eman, a physicist of international reputation, former president of the university, Knesset member, and minister of science, who was among the founders of a right-wing party (*Hatehiah*—resurrection) dedicated to the project of Jewish settlements in the occupied territories. Of a lesser public position was Professor Noah Milgram, a psychologist who complained in the media about the leftists on campus who apparently intimidated those who disagreed with their opinions. However, the few visible right-wingers made no effort to organize any countermovement in support of the government's policies or to coordinate a public debate deliberating academics' involvement in politics on campus. In retrospect, Professor Ne'eman's position, although he was not active on campus (and I never met him at the senate meetings), might have had some influence on the mood of disengagement among the faculty on the "eastern bank" of campus who seemed to remain aloof toward the growing division in Israeli national politics.

Only one event organized on campus (13 March 1988) by *Nativ*, a right-wing journal, titled "Eretz Israel" (the land of Israel), was devoted to discussions about recent incidents on the ground and the risks of an international conference over the Israel/Palestine political situation. At that time PM Yitzhak Shamir was preparing to leave for the Madrid International Conference, designed to revive the Israel-Palestine peace process and engaging the Americans, the Soviets, and the Arab countries, including a Jordanian-Palestinian delegation. PM Shamir, who resented the meeting, finally agreed to participate under President's Bush administration pressure. Among the eight speakers, politicians, and other professionals, Professor Ne'eman was the only participant from TAU ranks.

A few days earlier, an AD KAN Students rally promised PM Shamir his greatest hour participating at the international conference in Madrid. They wished him the opportunity to join the historical moments in the records of PMs Ben-Gurion and Begin who made important strategic compromises. The idea of supporting a separate group named AD KAN Students was intended to avoid the development of a hierarchical "division of labor," letting the younger members fill in the less attractive tasks of organizational life.

The core group of twenty to thirty AD KAN members continued meeting on a weekly basis to discuss present developments and plan forthcoming public events. We managed to keep up the organization's momentum despite the frequent departure of core members who left on sabbaticals or conferences abroad. During 1989, we coordinated six major events, for which posters remain in the box of AD KAN memorabilia. Conferences were titled "A Palestinian State or Continuing Occupation"; "Don't Say We Didn't Know—Two Years to the Intifada"; "Education and the Occupied Territories"; "Destruction and Killing Our Life Routine" (a demonstration on campus); and "Academy and Politics—the Intifada and Our Lives" (a week of sit-in and class workshops with AD KAN and other professionals).

Among the guest speakers was Dr. Ahmad Tibi, the most visible Israeli Arab politician in the public arena, witty and eloquent, who served as political advisor to PLO leader Yasser Arafat (and a decade later, since 1999 to this day, is serving as a Knesset member as head of the Arab Ta'al Party); Professor Sari Nusseibeh, president of Al-Quds University in the West Bank village of Abu Dis, bordering Jerusalem, and scion of a distinguished Jerusalem family; lecturers from Birzeit University near Ramallah (a major Palestinian city);

and visitors representing international organizations (the European Parliament, etc.).

A report in *Haaretz* (7 March 1989) about an AD KAN conference quoted the outspoken, charismatic Emeritus Professor Yeshayahu Leibowitz (eminent Hebrew University chemist and philosopher mentioned earlier), where he repeated his belief that a few hundred soldiers refusing to serve in the territories would force the government to change its political orientation. He warned the audience that with the continuing regime of occupation enforced through military control, "Israel would become a fascist country with concentration camps not only exclusive for the Palestinians, but also for Jews like you [in the room]. You will enter there like beaten dogs since you are law-abiding citizens."

A most demonstrative action was the decision (initiated by the sociologist Avishai Ehrlich) to produce a blue button with the logo in black "AD KAN! Speak to the PLO." This was a symbolic gesture that advertised our identity on the campus premises. It was the first time I had ever adorned a piece of jewelry (not even a wedding ring), and it was embarrassing at first to display a sign of personal identity compared, for example, with a skullcap for Orthodox Jews or a rainbow button for assertive gay people. Actually, except for the skullcaps, one could rarely observe Israeli academics at that time wearing any type of ornament, displaying a tattoo, or donning any other indication of a specific personal inclination. It seemed like the most radical public gesture I could comply with ...

Considering the possible resentment by some faculty and students, it was only expected that the senior tenured faculty would wear these buttons in the packed halls of the larger introductory courses and in the smaller seminar sessions. Incidentally, while going through the ethnographic fieldnotes from my gay synagogue research in New York recorded in February 1989, I recently found an observation made at that time reminiscent of the situation experienced at home in Israel. I was speaking to a man who represented a group advocating the urgent need for the American government to help victims of AIDS, and he wore a black button with "Silence = Death" inscribed in red. As I recorded in my notepad, "At that moment it struck me, how similar are the protest groups in their strategies and symbols being reminded of the home button 'AD KAN! Speak to the PLO.' For a minute, it seemed I am back in an AD KAN activity calling to acknowledge the dangerous political reality; to stop the occupation and speak to the enemy." Anyhow, many years later, a few of the AD KAN buttons are still on my desk at home, four centimeters in diameter, the "provocative" message attractive in black ink on the light blue background. These modest articles of AD KAN memorabilia serve as reminder of the days one felt partner to a momentous happening that might lead to a profound change in the history of a country and nation, fulfilling at last Abba Eban's promise: "We shall be magnanimous in victory."

Besides the grim voices critical of the Israeli government's lack of courage to communicate with the PLO and stop the expansion of settlements, and the tough measures exerted by the regime of occupation, an atmosphere of optimism and comradery engulfed the group's intimate weekly meetings as well as during public events. For example, our guest speaker Professor Sari Nusseibeh was quoted in a report in *Haaretz* (12 December 1989) saying that he believed the United States would find a way to bring the Israelis along to talk to the PLO leadership, recruiting the PLO as participants in a broader delegation representing the Palestinians. The Americans might engage the PLO in any other disguise because they know the PLO is the only force able to attract the wide support of the Palestinian people. As for the intifada, he claimed it might continue over the coming months as part of a process leading to the birth of a Palestinian state. The Israelis, he concluded, could see the Palestinian revolt as a reflection of a similar process that took place during the founding of their own state. The presence of Sari Nusseibeh, the most distinguished Palestinian representative who expressed our shared intellectual and political beliefs, helped convince the membership that they were not a group of hopeless dreamers.

No doubt, it was not easy to develop close personal relationships with Palestinian academics. I found a copy of a letter sent to one of the speakers, a social scientist from Birzeit University, thanking for his participation and expressed a wish to keep in touch and help if needed, to which I attached an article about my experiences as a student in Manchester, the school he also attended for a degree. He never responded. Did he ever receive that message? Did he prefer to avoid frequent communication with a representative of the regime of occupation? Our experience with Gaza lawyer Abu Shaaban taught us about the potential consequences for those on the other side of the conflict who took a risk and participated in our activities. As reported earlier, I discovered only recently that Shaaban was punished by an extremist Palestinian group for his "cooperation" with the enemy.

Although the campus academic leadership did not identify with our activities and instead maintained an impression of restrained neutrality, we nevertheless enjoyed its tacit cooperation. A friendly acquaintance with Professor Yair Orgler of the business administration school, who served as vice rector at that time, facilitated communication with the campus administration. It was his task to allow extra academic activities on campus, and he never refused our requests for classrooms or permission for open-space activities that often demanded security arrangements. The participation of celebrated academic and cultural figures in AD KAN's advertised events must have boosted the organization's prestige on campus. In this context, I mention a letter sent to Yizhar Smilanski, among the most distinguished authors of the "Independence generation," thanking him for accepting our invitation to take part in one of our conferences. The letter also described the special character of our organization whose members were not known in the public arena and were not on the lists of political parties. I ended the communication with, "It is the first time I am proud of membership in that type of an association deserving being entitled academic" (9 August 1988).

It was only the small association of students, the Custodians of the Land of Israel, supported by outsiders, who tried to promote an anti-leftist movement opposing AD KAN activities on campus. They showed up at AD KAN events in a marching line, never more than ten attendees, raising the national flag and angrily shouting offensive accusations. Throughout our activities, the security personnel had to separate that small group of aggressive protagonists protesting against the "unpatriotic messages and the traitorous figures" of AD KAN and their guest speakers. The invitation of Palestinian speakers known for their open or assumed political support of the PLO made them even more aggressive. The appearance of our buttons calling to negotiate with the PLO invigorated their aggressive reaction, which included a campaign advertised on campus to remove "Arafat's agents" from the university ranks, naming ten of AD KAN's known members. These anonymous hate messages were directed to our personal mailboxes. One of these bullies, Avishai Raviv, was later identified as having been recruited by the government secret security agency to serve as an informant about right-wing extremist organizations. These noisy protesters also complained that the leftists on campus had been "terrorizing" anyone who disagreed with their political orientation, lowering exam marks and intimidating untenured lecturers.

The AD KAN box includes correspondence with the campus leadership complaining about the failure to deal more effectively with the hostile Custodians of the Land of Israel. A few daily newspapers also reported on that type of anonymous verbal harassment on campus (*Haaretz, Al Hamishmar,* and *Davar*; 24 November 1989). But the university leadership preferred to tolerate it under the norm of freedom of speech. However, a permission to hold a conference the Custodians scheduled on campus for January 1990 was canceled by the dean of students because of its public call to fire AD KAN's faculty, naming them as traitors, agents of the PLO. The university authorities preferred to refrain from more serious sanctions, and we avoided filing a formal complaint with an outside legal agency. In retrospect, these aggressive right-wing activists left no effective marks on campus.

Illustration 7.1. *AD KAN members protesting the continuing occupation and the construction of Jewish settlements beyond the Green Line (from left: Avishai Ehrlich, Moshe Shokeid, Ariella Friedman, Ruth Berman, Israel Gershoni), ca. 1989. Author's private collection.*

Illustration 7.2. Button with logo *"AD KAN! Speak to the PLO."* Author's private collection.

Illustration 7.3. *"AD KAN, the University's Peace Movement Calling [PM] Rabin! Instead of More Knives Cut off Now: Two States,"* a poster inviting faculty and students to attend a demonstration on campus, March 1993. Author's private collection.

8

The Media Coverage

As I have mentioned, the media was attracted to the protest movement emerging in academia. My stash of documents includes a few copies of the newspapers' more specific coverage of AD KAN activities. *Jerusalem Post* reporter Lea Levavi (28 February 1988) quoted the distinguished history professor Amos Funkenstein, who, at an AD KAN demonstration, claimed that "Israel's treatment of the Arabs in the administered territories is reminiscent of how the Germans treated the Jews in 1936" (a perspective rarely conveyed in the public forum). I was reported as organizer, and I was not embarrassed in my response that only two hundred persons and not thousands had come to demonstrate: "History will remember the few, and later thousands will claim to have worn our buttons in favor of talking to the PLO."

Haaretz journalist Nurit Amitai opened her report with a photo showing AD KAN protestors holding posters calling for an end to the imposed closure of academic institutions in the territories. TAU historians and professors Shula Volkov and Israel Gershoni commented that academics by and large prefer to stay away from political engagement, but their habitual silence is of special value and generates great public impact when they break that silence at situations of public urgency. The commentary indicated the presence of protestors mostly from the humanities and social sciences, and also quoted me explaining the lesser representation from the "pure" sciences as being related to their manner of work, which binds them to their laboratories, while "our [social sciences and humanities] work [is] based on the ongoing experiences among other people, thus, requiring the sensitivity to comprehend their feelings, and therefore we are more engaged." The mathematician Meir Smorodinsky agreed that the field work required of academics from the social sciences and the humanities makes them more inclined to engage in the public forum compared with other academic practitioners.

It seems I was convinced that the end of the occupation would happen soon; I expressed as much in letters published in various venues, such as in the weekly *Coteret Rashit* (8 March 1988) where I pointed at the Israelis' withdrawal during the days of the intifada from Jerusalem's Old City sites, markets, and restaurants, expressing their longing with popular songs of love for Jerusalem. But the right-wing politicians, stuck in their dreams and fears, remained unaware of the reality on the ground when the common people were ready to compromise and give up occupied territories for the sake of peace. No doubt, my conclusions based on wishful hopes and semi-anthropological observations neglected the growing power of the West Bank and the Gaza Strip settlements' constituencies and their political allies.

An extended report by Giora Noyman in the Tel Aviv local newspaper *Ha'ir* offered a review of the protest groups that emerged with the first intifada (2 February 1988). It was embarrassing to find a photo of myself among the representatives of a few other protest groups, along with an interview about the founding of AD KAN, in which I was quoted:

> Until now we were mostly busy with our research, but the day had come for us to understand that if we keep on silent, we'll not be able to see ourselves in the mirror. ... When the term starts soon, the students might discover that their teachers have been radicalized. ... One month later it will be evident that what is considered today a traitor's position would become the norm for everybody.

I proffered the reporter an assessment that six hundred academics out of about three thousand faculty members in Israeli academia were involved in protest activities (affiliated with AD KAN and other groups). In the *New York Times* (Sunday, 15 May 1988), Anthony Lewis wrote a critical article called "The Price of Occupation," which described the erosion of Israel's moral standards and mentioned in particular the case of Abu Shaaban, the lawyer from Gaza arrested on his return home after participating in a colloquium organized by Tel Aviv University faculty members. The *Jerusalem Post* weekend Metro supplement (Daniel Robbins, 1 April 1988) reported on unrest at TAU campus, quoting me claiming that new members were signing up almost every day and reporting on the recent protest against the arrest of the Gaza lawyer: "We see this as a severe blow to freedom of speech and academic freedom. It contradicts the basic norms acceptable in Israel."

Six months after the publication of the first call for "civil disobedience," another letter was sent to *Haaretz* reporting on the emergence of a protest movement on campus. The letter related the agenda of endorsing negotiations with the PLO, opposing the expansion of settlements in the occupied territories, and condemning the policy of mass administrative detentions of Palestinians without trial in temporary sites that might develop into concentration camps. However, it was returned with no explanation. Was it too extreme in its stinging vocabulary? A few months later, demonstrating in front of the Anzar prison in the Negev following the killing and injuring of a few inmates, I was quoted saying that "we were told to avoid comparisons [with Germany] and we did. In the meantime, however, women and children are not incarcerated, but why wait? Horrible things wouldn't have happened had peaceful citizens been informed on time!" (Ayelet Mazor, *Hadashot*, 8 August 1988).

In a long weekend magazine interview in the leftist daily newspaper *Al Hamishmar* (9 September 1998), the reporter recorded me reflecting on the experience during a visit to Belfast, a place that one could use to foretell the future development of violent clashes inside Israel, the construction of dividing walls between ethnic neighborhoods, and the habitual frisking on city streets. He related the impressions of AD KAN's visit to the Anzar desert camp where the Israeli government was facilitating the emergence of a Palestinian leadership and the creation of a national myth, the sociological outcome of Israeli authorities' shortsighted brutal strategy of conflict management. It was also suggested that compared with the intractable and belligerent Irish parties, the Palestinians represent a "life-loving" people who are far more likely to accommodate a political compromise. As often before in journalists' accounts, the reporter raised the view that the majority of AD KAN members did not represent publicly "visible" personas or anyone affiliated with a political party in the Israeli arena. About the same time, we paid to list thirty AD KAN participants (27 July 1988) in *Haaretz* claiming support for the four faculty and students punished with jail sentences for refusing to carry out their reservist army service duty in the occupied territories.

Also around the same time, an article was published in *Haaretz* (25 October 1988) that responded to a spiteful piece by Heda Boshes, a journalist known for her critical-humorous writings, who ridiculed the proliferation of leftist organizations as "an indication of the competition and hatreds based on personal interests and the inability to agree on anything concerning principles, strategies and personalities." Challenging her made-up assertions, it argued that I was never "a leftist" and that joining a protest group on Tel Aviv campus was part of AD KAN's advertised strategy to promote the emergence of similar organizations in as many other institutions and social sectors in Israeli society. We believed these types of grassroots activities would enable the participation of many people who otherwise would have been reluctant to associate with a larger organization removed from their daily life. This more intimate type of social-communal organization would nourish the landscape for a more effective call for peace negotiations. History tells us that the famous protest movements have evolved on the shoulders and the impetus of smaller social organizations. Does anybody wait for a Messiah to appear on a cloud from nowhere? Charismatic leaders also need some groundwork to facilitate their coming. Moreover, small groups are far more equipped to work together than larger political parties are. And finally, the membership of these groups would happily give up their separate organizations to join a mass movement. They do not need the small-group activity for the sake of sociability or for some kind of social prestige. Actually, their association with that extra activity is often unbecoming and even stigmatizing in certain institutions. The article ended by accusing Boshes, who was famous as a critical reviewer, for contributing to the atmosphere of indifference among those safely disengaged while observing the continuing deterioration of Israeli society.

In 11 November 1988, we paid to advertise another list of signers in *Haaretz* under the call "University Lecturers for Peace with the Palestinians." It went as following:

> We, academic staff at Tel Aviv University and the Open University call on the Israeli government to
> - Recognize the Palestinians' right for their own state
> - To announce its readiness to enter negotiations based on mutual recognition of whatever representation chosen by the Palestinians, the PLO included, in order to decide on the future of the West Bank and the Gaza strip
> - To avoid deportations, administrative detentions and punishment without trial
> - To end evasions of human rights; torture, humiliation and the gross use of governmental authority in treatment of the Palestinian population.

That list was signed by 110 faculty members. One hundred people signed another petition published in *Haaretz* around the same time (17 January 1989) under the title "Don't Touch the Protest," which stood against the investigations, intimidation, and legal actions aimed at the Yesh Gvul membership. The signers included a majority of AD KAN membership but also many other known academics, intellectuals, and artists. Efforts were made early on to integrate supporters from other campuses into a widespread University Peace Movement under the AD KAN moniker rather than have it remain solely a Tel Aviv campus organization. Successful contacts evolved between the AD KAN membership at TAU and the more active academics at the Hebrew and Open Universities.

On 11 November 1988, with the TAU and the Open University lecturers' call for peace, *Haaretz* published an article I titled "The Blood Wedding" ("Chatunat ha'damim"). The term *damim* carries a double meaning in Hebrew: money and blood. The article condemned the new right-wing government coalition based on its collaboration with a few religious parties. The religious parties joined the coalition, lured by the generous monetary rewards promised to the orthodox Yeshiva schools and the society of unemployed adult men who spend their days in the perpetual study of Jewish theology, exempt of military service. That expanding constituency in Israeli society was free of economic and security responsibilities, though not ideologically committed to the vision of regaining the Land of Israel. Nevertheless, it backed the right-wing agenda that included the expansion of settlements in the occupied territories. The unholy wedding of interests, resulting in the diversion of massive funds from national social services and basic education, promises that the next wars will be conducted on the shoulders of the silent majority whose sons and daughters bear the utmost price of spilling their blood on the altar of that exchange. Naturally, that political-monetary combination does not reckon with the blood of the Palestinians unfortunately trapped in this right-wing vision.

There are no records of the exact time or contents of the TV interview in which I participated in 1988 or early 1989, which probed about the protest activities of Israeli academics. However, the interviewer inquired whether I could testify about a similar number of peaceful supporters among the Palestinian academic constituency. The answer to that standard question was one I repeated on several occasions: It is not our business to verify a balance of publicly identified peace-loving academics on both sides, which is irrelevant to the reality of occupation of land and the subjugation of other people by my government. It is a moral and practical issue of utmost importance to the survival of Israeli society. However, the media (leftist in particular) seemed continuously interested in our activities, as indicated in the following chapters.

Reading the above media coverage twenty-five years later leads me through a web of contradictory feelings: from embarrassment about my presentation as a seemingly forceful persona, so remote from my self-perception, to feelings of surprise and pride about the group of colleagues who made a similar great detour from their habitual manners and interests. The following chapter reveals a portrayal of my mood at the time of the events described here that sadly also seems similar to my impressions about present-day Israeli political reality.

9

The Moving Scene Observed from Afar and Near

Early in February 1989, I left for a spring sabbatical at NYU. A letter I sent to Avishai Ehrlich, a close colleague at the sociology department and a leading AD KAN activist, reflected my frame of mind those days. I relayed my experience being interviewed by local reporters, aware we activists could not afford to evade venues for public information, and expressed distress over PM Shamir's intransigent positions. It was Israeli leaders' luck, or rather the tragedy, that the Palestinians did not capitalize enough on the intifada. I ended the letter expressing pleasure at escaping Israeli realities on the way to a lecture in archeology and later to a fringe theater performance, but that is … a momentous mirage. I added at the bottom of the page under the signature, "Warm regards to our friends [AD KAN members], the most soothing piece of reality I remember from our university life."

I sent a letter to *Haaretz* from New York titled "Tears in New York" (4 April 1989), in which I described the distressing experience of attending a conference at Columbia University titled "The Road to Peace" (March 1989). I reported on the Israeli delegation of leftists, considered in the Israeli public arena marginal personas, who could not gain the sympathy of their audience (of nearly one thousand participants), who were listening to celebrated cultural and political figures representing the Palestinians. The situation was destined to serve as a platform for criticism of Israel as a colonial power. I expressed my sadness on discovering the change of atmosphere in the city, where until recently one could have felt free of the stigma of identifying as an Israeli. Most painfully was the absence of American

Jews and non-Jews who years ago volunteered to publicly support Israel against the aggression and real danger Israel was exposed to by its Arab neighbors and their supporters. Listening to the eloquent speakers portraying a "real Israel" that avoids recognizing the legitimate wishes of self-determination of another nation and refuses to use the term "intifada" in its media made me want to explode in tears and anger, imagining the stone-faced Prime Minister Shamir. A "terrorist" in his past life as a member of the most extremist Jewish movement against the British mandate in Palestine, Shamir somehow retained that blindness and stubbornness without considering any accommodation to the present reality, a recurring folly that history had already proved not only with the British rule in Palestine. I ended my story by recounting that I could not endure that "ritual" of self-blaming observed in my temporary New York retreat, and walked out of the convention hall.

About the same time, another upsetting experience left its sour mark on me while attending a guest lecture by Judith Butler, a leading voice in US academia, at CUNY Graduate Center titled "Jewish Ethics under Pressure." Though I was acquainted with Butler's work in the field of feminism and sexuality and whom I pleasantly encountered on her visit to Tel Aviv, I was surprised by and took offense to her lecture, which actually presented her anti-Israeli national politics position. It was not her political agenda that irritated me but rather the unethical announcement of her talk, which did not indicate the specific subject of her presentation. Moreover, she started her talk by claiming that she was not a Zionist although her Jewish parents had sent her to a youth summer camp in Israel. Is one a Zionist simply because of his/her birth certificate, passport, or residence in Israel? The hall was packed with hundreds of young students. No doubt, seated in a back row, it would have been an impossible mission to try to respond to that icon of oration, visibly stubborn in her self-righteousness. I soon walked out before enduring her list of the unethical manifestations and illegal actions displayed by the Zionist in the hall ...

Long before the successful presence of the BDS movement in US academic institutions in the 2010s, the winds of change had begun to eradicate the previous standing of the Zionist project. This change sowed the seeds for forces that would undermine the legitimacy of Israeli control of Palestinian land and question the reality of its endurance as a democratic state. My letters from New York expressed desperation arising from the Israeli leaders defined as the "Hayatulas whose intractability transforms Zionism into a foulmouthed term."

In 1988, my study of Israeli immigrants in the United States was published. However, as mentioned earlier, I gave up at this moment plans to issue a Hebrew version, having lost the motivation that first triggered this research engagement—the assumption that it was of crucial importance to the future of Israeli society. The ethnographic description of the stigmatized *Yordim* was basically sympathetic. Yet, I now felt a stronger empathy toward these compatriots of mine who probably made the smart choice to escape the responsibilities and growing moral worries of concerned Israeli citizens. That sentiment has not left me since then—I contemplate at aggravating moments the missed options of joining the Israeli academics who took the route of emigration.

As already indicated, AD KAN continued its activities despite the periodic absences of its core organizational officeholders. Letters signed while I was in New York by Professors Jonathan Shapiro, Meir Smorodinsky, and Israel Gershoni were addressed to Prime Minister Shamir, Defense Minister Rabin, and Education Minister Yitzhak Navon, asking them to meet with a small delegation to discuss the enforced closure of the academic institutions in the territories. The letters included a draft of a petition signed by two thousand teachers and students during a "protest week" held at all major Israeli academic institutions. The petition against the closure of all Palestinian colleges and high schools exposed the futility of that policy. The policy was antithetical to human rights and Jewish ethics, and it did not contribute to improved security in the country; it only incited hatred and violence. The letter ended with the phrase: "We are ashamed; in our name—the 'people of the book,' you wage war against schools—named in Hebrew homes of books [*beit-sefer*, the basic term for an educational institution]." But only one response could be found in the box, signed by PM Rabin, explaining that these institutions were closed because they had become centers of the intifada, promoting vile incitement and violence. It went on to recount the futile efforts to reopen these sites of learning, and condemned those Palestinians who exploit young people and destroy their opportunities to return to normal educational circumstances. This was undoubtedly a respectful response, but it included no invitation to meet with the representatives of AD KAN. It seems to be the only official response.

Even more disappointing, though, was a letter signed by Professor Israel Gershoni directed to the TAU rector requesting a meeting of an AD KAN delegation with members of the Tel Aviv University board of trustees, who were arriving for their annual business meeting in May 1989. A short, handwritten reply on the original copy of Gershoni's letter, signed by the rector or his unidentified assistant, explained abruptly:

1. The schedule of the trustees' meetings is the University President's office responsibility.
2. That schedule is prepared six months in advance.
3. AD KAN is not an academic group designed for academic goals normally dealt with by the relevant university bodies.

I was unaware of this episode at the time, and I never discussed it with Gershoni (a leading scholar in Middle East history), who was, although younger and not yet a "full professor," too self-assured to put up with an insult. My own relationship with the rector at that time (coming from the exact sciences) was somewhat ambivalent. I used to comment humorously that he treated me like a "mistress met at a back street": he was friendly and expressed his appreciation when we occasionally met at the end of day in the parking lot, but he was never supportive at official meetings, nor did he show up at AD KAN activities. His approach was indicative of the careful attitude displayed by the campus leadership, who pretended to uphold a neutral political position (except for the vice rector, with whom I had a friendlier personal relationship).

On 23 November 1989, we got the official document confirming the legal registration of our organization as a nonprofit association with the Interior Ministry: AD KAN the University Peace Movement. My home address became its official reference site, and its objective was detailed in that "birth certificate": "To promote activities in university campuses oriented to strengthen the consciousness of peace in Israel."

At the next public event, announcing that "coming-of-age" inauguration certificate, I informed our membership that Rabbi Arthur Hertzberg, among the admired leaders of American Jewry and whom I met in a recent visit to New York, had asked to join AD KAN.

Three daily newspapers widely reported a protest event on campus in November 1989. Sociology professor Jonathan Shapiro was quoted as saying that world leaders must tell themselves that the Israelis behave in a ludicrous manner, moving soon toward self-destruction, while American Jews keep a distance as they observe the growing of antisemitism around the globe. I was quoted delivering an obituary for an Israeli soldier (Yariv Bar-Yosef) who committed suicide after acknowledging his part in the killing of an innocent Palestinian. He was, the obituary claimed, an innocent victim of the intifada, one of many on both sides of the continuing occupation of the Palestinian territories. A photo displayed AD KAN protestors standing in the front line with posters calling on Defense Minister Rabin to stop the killings and instead talk to the PLO. Identified in the center of the photo was psychologist and core activist Ariella Friedman, an impressive young blond woman holding a large poster with the inscription, "How many more bones shall we break and how many children would go blind? It is time to speak to the PLO! AD KAN." Journalists were attracted to Ariella's posture and often photographed her in other demonstrations.

An article written sometime earlier titled "The Last Will of Sergeant Yariv Bar-Yosef," emphasized that his suicide offered us an important lesson:

> Civilians and soldiers, including those of a privileged social background, higher education and good manners, are not immune to the degrading consequences of the escalation of collective violence. No need to be an Arab, German, Cambodian, etc., to be able to kill innocent people or stay aloof in view of unrestrained brutality. The message is inscribed on the walls: Yariv was not a state minister or a leader in Israel, but his act of suicide would become a formative myth in Israeli culture. He could not accommodate with his loss of humanity—his suicide left the message imprinted with his blood.

Sadly, Yariv Bar-Yosef's tragic story faded long ago from public memory. These days, however, public opinion is deeply divided over the case of a soldier, Elor Azaria, who shot an already-neutralized and wounded Palestinian during the "knives intifada" of 2015–2016.[1]

The last weekend of 1989 caught me at a personally painful time. With my eleven-year-old son and Ora Slonim (AD KAN volunteer secretary), I attended an officially authorized Peace Now demonstration surrounding the walls of Jerusalem's Old City. European participants also attended. We prepared for a pleasant experience on a sunny day. However, it soon turned into a violent event when the police patrolling on horseback started to urge the protesters to disperse. The three of us were sitting on a garden stone when, without provocation, I was suddenly beaten with a club. As we ran off toward the next entry gate to the Old City, we were gassed, and Ora was injured by a rubber bullet. As later reported on the news, a few overseas visitors were seriously injured by the water cannons and other means used to disperse the demonstration. We were shocked and humiliated at how our national guardians defending "peace and order" in an allegedly democratic society brutally mistreated peaceful citizens.

I wrote a letter to the minister of police expressing my anger and demanding an inquiry into the brutal treatment of the peaceful participants of a lawful demonstration, claiming I could identify the policeman who had hit me. The minister, Haim Bar-Lev, responded a few days later, maintaining that the police force had acted as they were trained to; however, he would inquire into the likelihood that individuals behaved against the rules of conduct. Sometime later, I was invited to attend an inquiry committee to identify the photo of the policeman who had attacked me. The case got some publicity following an article in *Haaretz* titled "For the First Time I Was Beaten with a Club" (5 January 1990). It exposed the irony of standing in front of the walls of the city that generations of Jews had dreamed about and prayed for, and expressed the rage of being physically harassed in view of my young son by Jewish police forces ordered by a visionless government.

To this day, I dare not ask my son how that experience impacted him. One can imagine how Palestinians have been treated on similar occasions. I was not informed about the outcome of the inquiry and tend to believe that it did not affect the career of the indicted policeman. However, I received a long letter of support from Rabbi Yermyau Milgrom, a member of the association Clergy for Peace, congratulating me on the courage to publicly expose the ugly face of the police force and complaining about the automatic backing they receive from the official media. He claimed that the police intervened during the demonstration not because it became violent but because the Palestinian participants voiced radical nationalistic slogans. He endured a similar experience a few years earlier when he protested against the visit of the notorious racist rabbi and Knesset member Meir Kahane (later assassinated in New York) to Um El-Fahem, a major Israeli Arab town. Milgrom was beaten by the police and gave evidence of this treatment, but the two policemen who attacked him were soon promoted. In conclusion, he suggested that we must build a free radio station reminiscent of Abie Nathan's Voice of Peace, which would not be censored by official agencies unlike the present government-authorized and -funded radio stations. I never met Rabbi Milgrom, and I had no energy to look more carefully into his suggestion.

A few days later (10 January 1990), I was invited to represent AD KAN at a Peace Now public event. A major point in that talk (of which a handwritten address remains in my files) was an assertion that, against the popular stereotype, the campus is indeed a reflection of Israeli society. At the beginning of AD KAN, our events were packed, defying all expectation, and the media loved us and other emerging protest groups. Gradually, we came to observe the unwavering commitment of colleagues who were unable to return to their regular routine, even though the bulk of supporters went back to life as usual. The wider crowd of protestors probably kept moaning at meetings with close friends, but otherwise they joined the majority of Israeli citizens who remain apathetic. That mood of apathy dominates in spite of the many warnings that the harsh treatment of Palestinians observed in the territories would gradually trickle down into Israeli daily life. Whoever feels free to use force in the territories will also exert his power within Israel, as we could clearly see during the last Peace Now demonstration in Jerusalem. The process of dehumanizing "irritating" people and the freedom to beat them cannot be compartmentalized for long.

Two recent events that took place on campus at the same afternoon hour, the same hall, on two consecutive days provided evidence of growing public indifference: the first dealt with the closure of the Palestinian academic institutions, and the second focused on the freedom of press. The first was miserably attended, while the second was packed with students and other participants. No doubt the first event seemed more suitable for an academic crowd, but the second was far more engaging. That is equally true for the TAU senate, which refused to discuss the same disturbing and unappetizing subject (an affair related below).

The speech at the Peace Now event went on to mention the unwritten code among most writers about the occupation: avoid comparison with the "country that has no name," where a civilized citizenship remains unconcerned observing the gradual erosion of human rights of another people. I quoted the historian Richard Grunberger, who explained that the unchallenged Nazis' brutality against the Jews was not conceived as a real event among the majority of Germans because the Jews were "astronomically remote and not real people" (1971: 466). But when the fire got close to home, it was too late to escape the consequences. The policemen who harassed me and others in Jerusalem proved how one can treat humans, his own compatriots included, as worthless intruders. While the membership of the declining protest groups was being radicalized, the majority remained silent, assuming it would all end somehow, taken care of by the forces of time, God, President George H. W. Bush, the Arabs' "stupidity," etc. But unfortunately, we would pay dearly for that primitive logic.

One is inclined to consider the relevance of Hannah Arendt's famous epitaph "the banality of evil" to our report on how "good people" bend the reality of injustice and brutality. That condition of human behavior has been glaringly displayed in the following case observed on the campus's major stage, reminding one of Gordon's (2018) headline depicting South African scholars who supported the apartheid regime: "How Good People Become Absurd."

Note

1. Elor Azaria, an IDF soldier, in March 2016 shot again a Palestinian assailant who had stabbed another soldier but was already fatally wounded and "neutralized." Azaria was arrested, and his act sparked widespread public debate. He was sentenced to eighteen months in prison and released after serving nine months.

10

The Senate Debacle

The second intifada year (1989) started with an unsuccessful initiative in the campus's major academic arena. Ten AD KAN senate members signed a petition calling on the senate body to denounce the military closure of the academic institutions in the occupied territories. We failed abysmally on the first attempt, in January, when fifty senate members voted against adding a discussion on that issue to the senate monthly meeting agenda, while only twenty-four voted for it. We raised the issue again a year later. This time, we supported it with a petition signed by 250 faculty members requesting that the senate endorse a decision calling on the government to open the colleges in the territories. The signers represented mostly "western bank" departments with very few from the "eastern side"—the exact sciences departments and schools.

It was my task to introduce the motion on the senate floor, and my short address might have irritated a few attendees. I confessed that I had rarely attended the senate meetings, as I was humiliated by invitations to discuss and vote on issues already decided by the central administration officeholders—such as the recent investment of British prime minister Margaret Thatcher and US president Ronald Reagan with honorary degrees, although both had degraded university life in their countries under their leadership. Also, I was not pleased by the habit of postponing decisions from one meeting to the next (under the norm of a two-hour session), thereby causing a change of constituency between sessions. I reiterated our plea to save the senate's honor and to mildly communicate a protest against the closure of the academic institutions, which had been carried out by the same regime we elected and that supports us (as a funded public institution). And finally, the aforementioned Professor Yeshayau Leibowitz (distinguished Jerusalem University scientist and philosopher), who was recently awarded a TAU honorary degree, opened his acceptance comments claiming that he felt alienated by and shameful of the Israeli academy that dishonored itself on this issue.

We were nearly successful this time (April 1990), with forty-two supportive votes versus forty in opposition, which enabled a discussion on the senate floor. However, we were defeated at the end of two sessions (with the changing population of attendants a possible cause). At a meeting the following May, forty-nine participants voted against the public announcement of a TAU senate petition condemning the closure of the academic institutions in the territories (only thirty-two had voted for it). Two events—a conference and a sit-in day of protest conducted on the campus central square with leading scholars, journalists, and artists—held a few weeks earlier did not seem to change the senate floor's reserved atmosphere or its members' wish to avoid intervention in "politics."

A report in the popular local newspaper *Ha'ir* (23 March 1990) presented a few protagonists, the sociologist Jonathan Shapiro and me, versus the right-wing psychologist Noah Milgram and the chair of the Likud Party's student association on campus. There is no need to repeat Shapiro's or my position expecting the academics' involvement, but we insisted on separating professional teaching forums and personal politics in the public arena. However, Milgram claimed that the leftists harass their colleagues among the faculty who oppose them and whom they define as idiots. The students' representative complained that openly right-wing students are punished by leftist professors who give them lower marks on their exams. But Milgram ended his complaint gleefully convinced that the leftists' great hour on campus was short lived: the growing number of mostly orthodox American Jews immigrating to Israel, the coming emigration of antisocialists from the Soviet Union, and the demographic expansion of the Mizrahim (versus the Ashkenazim) constituency, which was also mostly right wing, would eradicate the influence of the old "elitist" (also a code word for leftists) regime in the Knesset and elsewhere. (In retrospect, his prediction came true.)

The presence of about 80 senate members was not unusual, since many among the 335 (including those in the medical school, faculty representatives, and officeholders) at that time rarely or only irregularly showed up unless they had a personal interest in an issue on the meeting agenda. To be sure, the closure of Palestinian schools did not attract more or less than the ordinary attending crowd. An argument voiced during the senate debate by a leading international law scholar active in campus organizational affairs was visibly effective, in which he warned the participants that their meddling in political issues might provoke the government to intrude in academic affairs. Others with opposing positions claimed that we had no firsthand information about the Palestinian students' behavior, and some expressed personal worries about the faculty's responsibility for the security of their own compatriots, not to mention the potential public reaction, including that from their neighbors, against the academics' interference in political-security issues. It was a sad reaction from tenured full professors, most of them apparently of liberal convictions, citizens of a democratic country, who could turn into a morally apathetic flock of timid employees worried about their professional welfare.

Israeli universities are public institutions funded by the ministry of education, which is often headed by a right-wing coalition party member. Nevertheless, it seemed unimaginable at that time that Israeli universities would be punished and academic freedom be curtailed for that mild expression of protest. It was embarrassing when an unidentified participant turned to me angrily: "What do you want of me?" Obviously, AD KAN was not alone in facing a majority hesitant to oppose the authorities' harsh policy and the university leadership's reluctance to confront the government's uncompromising position. However, one could comprehend the Israelis' deeply rooted belief in the military authorities' loyalty to national security and the reliability of national information agencies, a conviction that might have affected citizens' critical perspective, tenured full professors included. Nevertheless, it was deeply disappointing to observe that escape from moral responsibility, as if our faculty was located in Tel Aviv's terrestrial sanctuary and had no connection to whatever took place beyond the fading Green Line. True, unlike residents of Berlin and Vienna, Tel Aviv citizens could live full lives without observing a Palestinian checked out, humiliated, or evicted from his land. It seemed as if our distinguished colleagues viewed the petition promoters as naughty boys and girls disturbing their peaceful routines.

A few months later, the schools in the occupied territories were reopened without the assistance of Israeli agents of science and culture. That experience, however, remained a trauma among AD KAN participants, but no less a lesson about "human nature" probably representing the ethos of "survival of the fittest." While recording the senate event, I found some consolation at the same time in reading the recent Hebrew translation of Zweig's *The World of Yesterday*, about the "happy" days before the colossal European tragedy. As usual, he lamented, the intellectuals remained indifferent and passive in their positions when the clouds were coming close. As evidence, he indicated, not a single leading persona of the day raised a serious warning in his or her writings. For better or worse, however, one could not claim that Israeli cultural icons (leading authors in particular) and reputable academics remained deaf and silent when confronting the reality of the continuing occupation and its abysmal consequences.

A report in *Ha'ir* (Kohba-Shlomo, 7 July 1990) under the title "The Rhinoceros" described the affair on the TAU senate floor. The article presented the major position of Professor Yoram Dinstein, the law scholar who argued against academics' intervention in politics, versus that of Professor Asa Kasher from the department of philosophy, who believed that involvement was part of academics' responsibility as the social elite. And last, it presented the position of university president Professor Moshe Mani, a physician, who wished to avoid a clash of feelings and more division on campus—like those found on the Knesset floor in Jerusalem—even though he was liberal in his worldview and supportive of the ongoing discussion. However, the reporter conceded one "compliment": that TAU had been the only national university to raise the issue of school closures, regardless of the consequences.

At the end of that saga, I wrote a summary recording the senate sessions (including the first in 1989), concluding with an unflattering observation about the mental disposition of those present during the discussions as well as the absentee senate members. They behaved in a manner reminiscent of academics elsewhere in recent history who kept away from "political" issues considered inappropriate for decent scholars engaged in pure science. The testimony predicted that the last senate session would be remembered in the records of our university as "Black May 2" (a poetic lamentation of the day).

A similar sad conclusion was expressed during the early phase of the intifada by Stanley Cohen, a leading criminologist at the Hebrew University (1988: 96):

Most of my academic colleagues have no sense of being on the edge of their society, of seeing it from the outside. As a result, they are reluctant to take a stand that might be interpreted as "disloyal" or "unpatriotic" or (worst of all) "anti-Zionist." So, even today, they defend an idealized version of Israeli history and culture as if it were reality.

In closing, it seems fitting to return to Arendt's "banality of evil," a verdict one might adjust to the "banality of conformity" in relation to the senate chronicles.

11

Raising the PLO Presence on Campus

We continued in 1990 with a schedule of three major events: a conference titled "How Long Would the Academy Keep Silent Confronting the Brutality of the Continuing Occupation?"; a sit-in demonstration on campus premises, protesting the third year of closed academic institutions in the occupied territories; and a conference titled "Three Years of the Intifada: Is There a Probability for Negotiations with the Palestinians?" The two eloquent speakers in "Three Years of the Intifada" were major figures in the arena of unofficial communication between the two national constituencies—Faisal Husseini, among the most distinguished Palestinian leaders and a close friend and partner in arms of PLO chair Yasser Arafat, and the Israeli leftist politician Yossi Beilin, among the architects of what would become the Oslo Accords. These events recruited hundreds of participants and were generously reviewed in the leftist media in particular. However, the visit of Husseini on campus stirred much tension, especially considering that he was the son of Abd al-Qadir al-Husseini, commander of the Arab forces during the invasion of 1948, and a relative of Haj Amin al-Husseini, the former grand mufti of Jerusalem (who had met with Hitler). Faisal Husseini who worked for the PLO, endured administrative incarceration as well as incarceration in Israeli jails. But he was also lauded as a pragmatist who taught himself to speak Hebrew (he died of a heart attack at age sixty in 2001).

Hosting Faisal Husseini in the large auditorium on campus was a major security issue. All 650 students, faculty, and invited guests who attended were checked by the security personnel hired to assist the university staff. They worked to keep at a distance about thirty angry protesters, a group composed of students and other right-wing supporters who were shouting and raising posters condemning the speakers and admonishing the audience for joining forces with the enemy. It was later discovered that the protesters had also damaged the tires of faculty cars displaying Peace Now stickers that were parked near the auditorium (see reports and photos in *Haaretz, Davar, Maariv, Yediot Ahronot, Hadashot, Al Hamishmar*, 30–31 December 1990).

Faisal Husseini presented a position calling for a compromise: He acknowledged the reality that the Palestinians would inevitably give up their vision of materializing their full rightful claims (such as return to the villages and towns they lost in 1948). But he insisted on an international peace conference that would offer guarantees for the implementation of the decisions concluded at this forum. Yossi Beilin, however, recommended instead a summit of direct negotiations between representatives of both nations leading to the immediate creation of a Palestinian state. The physicist Uri Maor, who chaired the event, was reported to have compared the aggressive protestors outside the hall with the fanatic warriors of the Middle Ages.

Four posters in the AD KAN archival box provide information on two conferences and two demonstrations conducted in 1991. The two conferences included "Is It Possible to Sign Peace Treaties with Arab Countries without the Palestinians?," hosting Mr. Hanna Siniora, a distinguished intellectual and editor of the major Palestinian newspaper, and two leading Labor Party Knesset members; and "Discussing Peace" with two Palestinian leaders (Faisal Husseini and Ziad Abuzayyad), popular Tel Aviv mayor Shlomo Lahat, and Motta Gur, an ex-IDF chief of staff. The demonstrations were titled "The Settlements Are Barrier to Aliya [immigration to Israel] and Peace," which featured Dedi Zucker, a leftist Meretz Party Knesset member and a continuing AD KAN supporter; and "Aliya and Peace Are Victims of the Settlements Mania," again featuring Zucker. Adding the Aliya issue to the agenda of protests revealed a message that AD KAN was a "Zionist" organization.

A summary of the event's "Discussing Peace" discourse (recorded in English by Professor Ruth Berman, a distinguished linguist), chaired by Uri Maor, displayed the different positions presented by the four speakers (30 December 1991). As had happened during an earlier AD KAN event with Faisal Husseini, an exchange of blows developed outside the meeting hall packed with about one thousand students and faculty. The fight was incited by members (mostly from outside the campus) of the extremist Kach movement, who called the organizers "traitors" and shouted "death to the Arabs." Husseini announced that the Palestinians were prepared for a transitional period of five years if they were given the right of self-determination. However, Tel Aviv mayor Shlomo Lahat, a member of the Likud Party, expressed his hope to see the establishment of a Palestinian state alongside Israel within a ten-year autonomy regime period as an interim solution, which would be negotiated with representatives the Palestinians chose for themselves, including from the PLO; but he also insisted on having Jerusalem undivided as Israel's capital. Husseini also stressed the need for Jerusalem to remain united but as an open city, hosting both Israeli capital and that of the new Palestinian state. General Gur, who led the unit that captured East Jerusalem in the 1967 war, declared his opposition to a Palestinian state and to talks with the PLO but insisted that Israelis and Palestinians can and must find means of coexistence. Abuzayyad, a leading politician who served time in prison for unlawfully entering Jerusalem, stressed that the city could not belong to one people; it should be politically divided but remain physically united. He recalled the dream of "reclaiming the whole of Palestine" that the Palestinians had entertained since 1948; now they were forced to accept a different reality based on the principle of two states for two peoples. Faisal Husseini stated his position presented above.

The Israeli speakers did not represent the "usual" leftist personas. They did not display AD KAN's basic ideological orientation. However, the "Discussing Peace" conference highlighted a major separation of aspirations between the Israeli and the Palestinian representatives. The two Palestinians accepted the prospects of two states but refused to give up the new state's municipal and political share in Jerusalem. The two Israelis remained adamant about an undivided Jerusalem under Israeli authority. Moreover, the ex-general was reluctant to recognize an independent neighboring state alongside Israel. It seemed a futile exchange of polite responses in the company of deeply estranged interlocutors. However, during the following interlude of public debate, the Israeli former chief of staff Gur was fervently criticized by comments from the floor.

As later analyzed in the press reports, both Israeli speakers surprised the audience with their unexpected positions. Mayor Lahat, a Likud member, expressed his approval of a Palestinian state, and General Gur, a Labor Party member, opposed that idea. Nevertheless, the atmosphere was civil between disputant parties anxious to reach a settlement based on some shared principles of rational engagement. The event offered an opportunity to openly discuss the issues at the center of the bitter conflict. Thus, it demonstrated AD KAN's essential wish to see the two parties start negotiations that might eventually lead to a settlement, however grudgingly accepted by both sides. It echoed peace activist Abie Nathan's repeated epitaph: "You don't make peace between friends." The event and the violence displayed outside the lecture hall received wide coverage in the daily newspapers (e.g., *Maariv* and *Hadashot*, 31 December 1991; *Haaretz*, 2 January 1992).

At an early stage, we invited Peace Now leadership to meet with the AD KAN core membership at the social sciences faculty premises, with the aim to discuss shared ideas and strategies to encounter the continuing Israeli military occupation. We believed that this meeting influenced Peace Now's decision to adopt AD KAN's strong position, calling for the recognition of the PLO as the Palestinians' legitimate national leadership and as the major partner for peace negotiations. For many years, Peace Now has been the foremost "apolitical" civil movement advocating for a peaceful accommodation with the Palestinians. Though it reiterated that it favored self-determination and was ready to give up land for peace, the movement appeared reluctant to come out publicly and demand recognition of the PLO and the establishment of a Palestinian state (e.g., Kaminer 1996).

That discourse with Peace Now delegates took place during the period when meeting with PLO representatives was considered a punishable act. Abie Nathan, founder of the Voice of Peace radio channel, received an eighteen-month prison sentence in September 1991 for his continued meetings with PLO head Yasser Arafat. Prior to his arrest, sixty AD KAN members had already advertised a protest directed toward right-wing Knesset speaker Dov Shilanski supporting Abie Nathan's request to repeal the ruling that made meeting with the PLO a punishable offense. Ten core members also joined a list of signers representing leading artists, authors, and other public figures who announced their wish to join Abie in a meeting with PLO representatives (*Haaretz*, 6 June 1991). An unpublished letter of mine expressed bitterness about the ruling and Abie's arrest, asking: how could a democratic regime disallow personal communication that does not involve revealing national security information? Israeli leaders communicated with Hitler's inheritors without first purifying them in a ritual bath or examining their love of Jews through a court authorized lie-detector device. That undemocratic ruling is typical of regimes I do not mention by name.

An AD KAN delegation "visited" Abie, demonstrating outside the prison site. That October, we sent a letter to President Chaim Herzog asking him to meet with an AD KAN delegation of eight members representing major disciplines on campus to discuss the harsh punishment of Abie Nathan and request his pardon or a reduction of the eighteen-month sentence. A polite official response explained that the president could not deal with appeals unless the accused issues the request. However, following Abie's release after six months in prison (his sentence was eventually shortened by the president), he invited AD KAN's core members for a festive dinner at his home residence in Tel Aviv.

The Gulf War that started in August 1990 changed the public discourse for a while. During the weeks leading up to the war, a few AD KAN members published their opinions in major newspapers about the impending conflict. They mostly objected to Israel's direct involvement but advocated the potential opportunities for regional transformations that might lead to a new Middle East order: a peace accord with the neighboring Arab countries and, at last, a resolution to the Israeli-Palestinian conflict (e.g., Leon Sheleff, *Jerusalem Post*, 20 December 1990; *Davar*, 8 January 1991; Tanya Reinhart, *Yediot Ahronot*, 10 December 1990; Avishai Ehrlich, *Davar*, 6 January 1991). Ten AD KAN core members signed a short letter sent to all daily newspapers (December 1990) calling on the Israeli government to immediately recognize the Palestinians' right to self-determination and suggesting the initiation of negotiations with the PLO about borders and other vital issues involving the Palestinian delegation. Another letter on behalf of AD KAN (February 1991) was sent to all newspapers requesting an immediate end to the Gulf War military closure of the Palestinian territories forbidding Palestinians entry to Israel (the major source of employment and income for many thousands).

About the same time, a large poster in *Haaretz*, signed by thirty-five AD KAN members, called on the security agencies to release Professor Sari Nusseibeh, president of Al-Quds University and a PLO activist, from his sudden administrative detention. We claimed that the government had taken advantage of the Gulf War tensions to punish the Palestinian leadership and keep them away from the forthcoming new regional order. On his release, Nusseibeh sent us an evocative letter with the opening paragraph:

> I cannot find the proper words to express my gratitude for the interest you have taken in my case and the solidarity which you have expressed. Inside a prison cell, such support is invaluable. Above all, it reinforces one's faith in what is human in a situation that seems shockingly inhuman.

He went on to describe the fabricated accusations and poor evidence brought against him. No doubt, Sari Nusseibeh exemplified an exceptionally admirable and gracious persona.

The next two years, described in the following "last stage," revealed an effort to continue the protest, raising a somewhat less focused agenda for public discourse.

12

Toward the Last Stage

During 1992 and 1993 six major public events—conferences and public protests—took place with the following titles: "The Settlements and the National Financial Balance"; "The Conquerors' Silence" (with a film documenting an IDF soldier's diary); "A Salute to Emile Habibi," an Israeli Arab citizen who got the Israel Prize for literature; "AD KAN Calls on Rabin [now PM]—Instead of More Knives Cut off Now: Two States"; "Gaza and Alger," at which the famous Alger film was screened in addition to a report by an Israeli journalist (Gideon Levi) informing from Gaza; and "Why Do the Right-Wingers Incite against the Arab Knesset Members?" The speakers included two representatives of the Knesset Arab parties. These are the last announcements and posters in the AD KAN box that date from before the Oslo Accords. Thus, the field of activity remained very similar, though with a detour into the reality of Jewish-Arab relations within Israeli society.

The event celebrating Emile Habibi, who had recently been honored with the Israel Prize for Arab literature, seemed unusual for the AD KAN agenda. Habibi, a Christian Arab who stayed on in Haifa after the 1948 war, was active in politics and served as Knesset member of communist parties before he became fully engaged in literary work. It was the first time an Israeli Arab citizen was honored at that major ceremony, conducted on the annual Day of Independence, and shown on television with the PM and other leading national figures. Acceptance of the prize signified his strong commitment to peaceful Arab-Jewish coexistence. AD KAN's decision to honor him was triggered by Professor Yuval Ne'eman, the most visible right-wing academic on TAU campus, who demonstratively returned his own Israel Prize award (for physics) as protest against honoring Habibi, who was rumored to maintain contact with PLO members.

Defying all norms of civil conduct, the right-wingers stormed into the ceremony event hall and screamed insults in front of the PM, the minister of education, and other national dignitaries as Professor Ne'eman threw his own prize at Habibi. They were pushed away by the offended audience. Naturally, one wonders about the state of mind of an internationally renowned scientist and campus leader who orchestrated such a surreal political demonstration. However, in his speech on campus (5 June 1992), Habibi admitted that he would have visited PLO leader Arafat in the hospital following an operation had the Israeli authorities allowed him to.

Habibi's appearance was also protested by a small, young, noisy group of members of the Kach movement, led by the same familiar figures observed in many other loudmouthed right-wing events around the country, who screamed "death to the Arabs." The meeting was interrupted when the security personnel searched the hall after an anonymous phone call warned about a hidden bomb. At any rate, Habibi relayed these hateful events to *Haaretz* (6 June 1992), concluding that there was no alternative except a historical compromise between the two peoples sharing the same homeland. Professor Sasson Somekh, the keynote speaker at "A Salute to Emile Habibi," was not among AD KAN's active members, but he was a leading scholar of Arabic literature on campus who served on the Israel Prize committee that awarded the honor to Habibi. In retrospect, honoring Habibi in the major TAU assembly hall symbolized AD KAN's academic, political, and social ethos.

On 9 September 1993, PM Rabin and PLO chairman Arafat signed the Oslo Accords, their mutual recognition of two independent national entities. The Israeli government eradicated at last the rule forbidding association with PLO members and acknowledged the organization as the legitimate representative of the Palestinian people. For all practical purposes, AD KAN's mission and hopes were fulfilled.

Ten days later, I sent a letter to *Haaretz* titled "Soul-Searching of the Little Citizen—Member of a Protest Group," which I intended to honor and congratulate AD KAN members and all other protest movement participants who devoted their time, resources, and reputation, convinced that there was no other way but negotiating peace with the PLO. It expressed astonishment at the quick turn of affairs since the days when we were ridiculed and harassed for disturbing the peaceful routine of campus life and antagonizing public consensus, wearing our provocative buttons pleading "Speak to the PLO." It mentioned the painful hours we were defeated at the senate meetings and the embarrassing experience of being considered a nutty minority. On such a happy day, I noted, we should remember the small protest groups that emerged since the early days of the intifada, identified by poetic names, representing various groups of professionals and others. They proved that the "little citizen" is not powerless against the regime's control and dominant public opinion. They deserved public gratitude for maintaining the vision of a better future beyond the destructive regime of occupation that inevitably corrupted basic values of a civilized society. It ended promising we would return to our normal pace of daily professional life and leave the politicians to fulfill their promise with the Palestinians. We would not take part in the forums celebrating and explaining the benefits of peace. Our gratification was embedded in the knowledge that we were on the right side of history, even when scorned by mainstream society.

Observing the signing of the Oslo agreements celebrated with handshakes on the White House lawn and the Nobel Peace Prize awarded to the three partners (Arafat, Rabin, and Shimon Peres), we felt our mission was accomplished. It was time to give up the routine AD KAN meetings and return to our regular professional life. In mid-December 1995, a last communication informed the core membership about our organization committee's inability to coordinate a conference dealing with the future of the peace agreements (for example, the major national political personas were now too busy with the hectic peace consultations in the aftermath of Rabin's 4 November 1995 assassination). The message conveyed that we could not continue with our activities as we did when protest groups were the only entrepreneurs of peacemaking. Although we were not ordinary political activists, our goal had finally been achieved. The State of Israel was now fully engaged in a process of negotiation and testing peace accords with the Palestinians.

No doubt, we could not imagine that the assassination of PM Rabin would soon be followed by Peres's (Rabin's partner on the Israel/Palestinian reconciliation process) May 1996 election loss to Benjamin Netanyahu, head of the Likud Party, and the ensuing collapse of the Oslo Accords. However, thus came to an end the era of AD KAN's regular activities. The next two chapters narrate my colleagues' and my response to the demise of the peace promise and the loss of hope for the cessation of the binational conflict in the foreseeable future.

13

The Aftermath: "When Prophecy Fails"

When peace seemed jeopardized by the assassination of PM Rabin and victory of the Likud Party with Benjamin Netanyahu's election as prime minister on 18 June 1996, we lost the energy and the conviction to try again to transform the reality of conflict. With a sense of deep frustration and despair with the ongoing confrontation between Jewish settlers and Palestinians (in Hebron in particular) and the failure of the Oslo Accords, I sent a personal letter a few months later to *New York Times* columnist Thomas Friedman (3 October 1996), whom I considered a fair and thoughtful analyst of Israeli politics and whom I once met on campus. My letter followed reports by his colleagues, William Safire and Abe Rosenthal, who seemed seriously mistaken in favorably endorsing PM Netanyahu. A few excerpts from that letter:

> It is no pleasure for me to admit I have no faith in the future designed by my elected Prime Minister and regret I cannot endorse him as your eminent colleagues do. After all, I live in Tel Aviv and my two sons are soon due to serve in the Israeli army and may be assigned to defend the small group of fanatics, including not a few from Brooklyn, who see themselves as custodians of my ancestors' graves in Hebron [the site of the graves of the Patriarchs]. A site never visited, not because I am secular or because I have no respect for my co-religionists' sentiments … I simply believe that Judaism and Jews can survive without the cult of graves and without the senseless provocation of 300 Jewish fanatics surrounded by 150,000 Palestinians [residents of Hebron]. After all, the late Lubavitch Rebee, the "Messiah" from Crown Heights [in Brooklyn], had never been to Hebron or even Jerusalem. … Modern Israeli leaders as

others in the mainstream of Jewish history were ruled by pragmatism no less than by religious dogma. Rabbi Yohanan Ben-Zakai, the founder of Yavneh (the historical/mythical basis of Jewish learning and survival for 2,000 years) escaped Jerusalem as a traitor in the eyes of the fanatics who eventually witnessed the destruction of the Temple and the dispersion of the Jewish nation. Ben-Gurion, the architect of contemporary Israel was also a pragmatist. But pragmatism has never been the ideology of Likud, new or old. ... However, history is on our side, I only hope it will not take too much life, pain and destruction before your eminent colleagues as well as many of my countrymen who voted for Netanyahu will realize the price of their folly defending ancient graves instead of human life, Israeli and Arab alike.

Friedman's response (5 November 1996) ended with, "All I can say is that things cannot be all bad as long as people like you are out there. Keep the faith." Twenty years have passed since that exchange of messages. Sadly, it seems to me, one needs a mind restoration in order to "keep the faith."

As detailed in a later chapter, I visited Hebron for the first time twenty-one years later (2018) in the company of Breaking the Silence, the most visible recent protest organization, established in 2004 and recruiting discharged and reservist IDF personnel who recount and publicize their distressing experiences while serving in the occupied territories. The record of that visit, observing in vivo the scene described to Thomas Friedman without firsthand experience, confirmed the worst imagined reality perpetrated in the name of the ancestors. Actually, I did not enter the revered tomb, observing instead the circumstances of occupation—the absurdity and malevolence of those scheming to redeem the land and graves of the Patriarchs (see chapter 15).

One more poster in the box announcing in 1999 what was probably the very last organized AD KAN conference raised the same old subject: "A Palestinian State or Continuing Occupation?" So, the last public accord in a saga of ten years returned to the starting point of AD KAN's activities. However, AD KAN's story officially ended with the notice announcing its erasure from the interior ministry's list of nonprofit organizations (No. 58-015851-7) as of 4 April 2001.

In sum, the collection of flyers left in the AD KAN "treasure box" reports on thirty major public events organized during the first intifada starting in January 1988 and ending in May 1993 (close to the conclusion of the first Oslo Accord in September 1993). That "crop" of organized AD KAN events does not include the participation of its membership and supporters in collaboration with other protest movements, Peace Now in particular—for example, taking part in the Hyde Park Peace Chain held on Saturday, 6 June 1991, which bonded the congregation of attending protest groups along the Tel Aviv Haifa Road north of town. The jovial event included stage performances, speeches, and public discussions on the prospects of a peace accord.

However, my last personal communication was voiced twenty years later (June 2013): the homily delivered on the tenth anniversary of the death of Leon Sheleff, an admirable colleague during the days of AD KAN who passed away suddenly after presenting a public lecture in Jerusalem on the specialty of the Jewish people. As mentioned already, it was mostly Leon's response to my "rebellion" letter to *Haaretz* that initiated the emergence of AD KAN. I often contemplated that, had not Sheleff passed away, we might have linked again with some sort of political activity on campus. As a scholar of law who emigrated from South Africa during the apartheid era, he sustained, with his unwavering stand and legal convictions, my own self-confidence and belief that we were not fighting a quixotic battle. At a later stage and after retirement, I discovered that one could not regroup a likeminded cohort of colleagues and students to share common views and act together to retrieve the spirit of AD KAN. Or, was it my own loss of stamina to restart an already lost battle?

The major theme at the memorial gathering (at the law school hall that hosted many AD KAN conferences) concentrated on an enigma: the first intifada witnessed a small but strong group of prominent academics on campus who devoted their time, energy, and reputation to the vision of a peaceful accommodation with the Palestinians, while the disappointing present-day reality featured the almost complete silence on most fronts of protest. Now retired, I reported on the sad scene witnessed the year prior (2012) when the small group that inherited AD KAN (named HaKampus Lo Shotek [the campus is not silent]), consisting mostly of students and lacking high-ranking faculty members, held its event outside the university gates while surrounded by a much larger and aggressive crowd of right-wingers. Never had AD KAN events been driven out of the campus premises, a clear sign of the loss of status and influence on the university arena. What happened? Why had a new and effective younger cadre of scholars not yet emerged to carry on the flag of protest against the continuing occupation and its obvious destructive consequences in Israeli life, as well as in view of the deteriorating position of Israel around the world? Is there hope for a new wave of potent protest among the present generation in academia?

At that moment of reminiscing, the BDS boycott on Israeli academia seemed yet a remote threat on the horizon. The above complaint was coming from a deep personal sense of disillusionment. Actually, two years earlier, my article titled "Why Israeli Academia Would Be Boycotted?," identifying the possible scenario of a harsh international reaction to the unsolved Israeli-Palestinian conflict, was published in *Haaretz* (30 June 2010) . The trigger was an announcement made by Education Minister Gideon Sa'ar, who considered punishing Israeli academics who advertised their criticism of the Israeli government's treatment of the Palestinians and supported the voices calling to boycott Israeli establishments. The article explained that I would no longer participate in the American Anthropological Association's annual meetings dealing with the Israel/Palestinian conflict by trying to introduce the Israeli political-ideological narrative. That was a response to the minister's position: his government had escaped from a civil-democratic code of demeanor and chose a path suitable to totalitarian regimes. However, it was not a surprise to discover the article fully translated into English in the Israel-Academia-Monitor.com (a search mechanism to find anti-Israel academics), identifying my university affiliation and informing donors to Israeli universities about the misuse of their contributions: "Moshe Shokeid in *Haaretz* as an example to how old and deeply rooted is anti-Israel activism in the academia."

Was not this public announcement a late-hour satisfaction on my part for being noticed by "the enemy" instead of talking to the already converted constituency of the *Haaretz* readers? In any case, it seemed no less a chilling reminder of the failed efforts to change the reality and image of Israeli society.

Though I had given up active participation in organized protest activities, I found in later years an outlet for my growing frustration in three semi-academic venues: occasional articles expressing exasperation with daily social and political realities, mostly directed to the opinion section of the liberal newspaper *Haaretz*; a book of letters directed to the late Theodor Herzl, the founder of modern Zionism (*Herzl Doesn't Live Here Anymore,* 2005); and a few speaking engagements in public forums dedicated to the Israeli/Palestinian conflict.

The following summarizes six addresses I delivered in mostly academic venues. The first is from 1996: a public debate on campus about military service of young soldiers and reservists in the occupied territories. The panel included Shulamit Aloni—a charismatic political leader, founder of the leftist party Meretz, Knesset member, and minister of education—as well as a few other academics on campus. Against the position expressed by other participants, I claimed that although we were resisting military service with the IDF in the occupied territories, we nevertheless lacked the moral authority to impose that position on younger people, my sons included, who were destined to join the military ranks. It is a personal choice that involves a serious price of detention and social stigma in present-day Israeli society. The panel was also an opportunity for me to suggest the futility of demonstrations, arrayed on Tel Aviv Rabin Square and other major city squares, against Jewish settlements in the occupied territories while the supporters of the settlements appeared en masse on the settlements' grounds. The thousands who opposed the government's policy of expansion in the West Bank should have revealed their revulsion on the scene of that continuing violation against a future peace accord and given up the "tribal" rituals in Rabin Square at the center of Tel Aviv.

A paper presented at the Israel Anthropological Association meeting in March 1999 discussed the dual role of the anthropologist as researcher and citizen as well as the limits of empathy and obligation in ethnographic study. It opened with the current issues of reflexivity in anthropological writings and the problematic situations that might arise from the ethnographer's commitment to his informants. In that context, I relayed a debate I had with Ted Swedenburg, an American ethnographer who confessed he had not told the truth in support of his Palestinian subjects (see later in this chapter). It also raised the dilemma of Israeli anthropologists' engagement in present-day political conflicts in their own society. I mentioned the few who got deeply involved in the political arena at an early stage, Henry Rosenfeld and Jeffrey Halper in particular, while the majority remained passive, maintaining the traditional academic position of neutrality.

The complaint was also directed at the dominant professional genre of critical sociology and anthropology, whose mission is to look back and angrily criticize research done years earlier—claiming, for example, a paternalistic perspective displayed in the studies of immigration conducted during the 1950s–60s. Nicknamed "institutional sociologists," the researchers in this genre were condemned for collaborating with the state to integrate the newcomers regardless of their wishes and cultural/ethnic traditions (see Shokeid 2001). That rage against an old presumed research misconception engaged a few younger scholars and their students while allowing them to keep a distance from urgent social and political issues, specifically the reality of the continuing control of the Palestinian people and its impact on Israeli society.

The fashionable present-day "postmodern" discourse about the pros and cons of different types and locations of research projects, the diverse styles of ethnographic writing, and the lone anthropologist's unique experiences at fieldwork might have all hindered the development of an Israeli sociological-anthropological collective display of *communitas* as well as a concerted professional response to local social-political predicaments.

A lecture I presented a few years later (27 June 2002) while spending a teaching term at the Free University Institute of Ethnology in Berlin was titled "An Israeli Anthropologist as an Ordinary Peacenik: A Report on the Banality of Violence." The address centered on the role that Israeli intellectuals had played during the first intifada. However, it was relating to the present-day reality of the second intifada, known as the Al-Aqsa Intifada—which started with PM Ariel Sharon's visit to the Temple Mount (September 2000)—that had evoked the continuing volatile circumstances in Israel. Naturally, it was a sensitive moment to report in Berlin about the perplexity of the situation, when AD KAN faculty members tried to recruit Israeli citizens to join a protest group against the continuing Israeli control of the Palestinians. It was apparent that the audience had been reminded of the situation in Germany during the Nazi era when the majority of the population, the intellectuals included, remained silent.

I was open in my presentation about the irritation the subject might raise among some listeners and admitted that the annoyance was also felt in Israel whenever one compared the circumstances to the Nazi era. One could not forget Professor Yeshayahu Leibowitz who warned all along, during the euphoric days of the 1967 victory, about the danger that the occupation might corrupt and destroy Israeli society. The presentation reiterated the story of AD KAN, its achievements and failures, as well as the later public mode of accommodation with the killing of PM Rabin and the hopeless encounter between PM Sharon and PLO chairman Arafat. However, the account did not absolve Arafat of his part in the collapse of the Oslo Accords.

In Berlin, the stage of my darkest dreams, I presented firsthand observations and sad conclusions about the obstacles confronting academics in their efforts to recruit a wider constituency to intervene in sociopolitical events. Nevertheless, it was also a moment of satisfaction to reflect on the short period of AD KAN and other protest groups' concerted action, which proved how alliances connecting similar social congregations and representing different courses of professional engagement could have a potential impact. The Berlin talk ended with the familiar dilemma: academics are "professionals" who are supposed to keep a distance and preserve moral neutrality while examining social-ideological conflicts, but at the same time they are expected as "intellectuals" and citizens to voice their opinion when observing injustices and scenes of brutality. And as a last note, I quoted the prophet Hosea, who depicted the state of mind of "the man of spirit" (the intellectual in our terms) as "crazy": "meshuga hish haruach" (Hosea 9:7). Going against the winds of time and its normative conceptions, the intellectual seems a weird character among the mainstream. Thus, the intellectuals—who suspect the authority of the biblical promise to Abraham and divest their sentiments from the horrible records of violence and humiliation Jews have endured among the nations, but who seem to desire accommodation with the Palestinians fighting against the Jewish state—must be "crazy" in the eyes of the West Bank Jewish settlers and their right-wing supporters.

Incidentally, on a Saturday morning walk in a nearby park, a day after writing the previous paragraph, I listened to a September 1993 radio interview with Yossi Sarid, ex-chair of the leftist Meretz party and a minister of education in PM Rabin's coalition government, who had passed away a week earlier (5 December 2015). It was a moving reminder of an extraordinary chapter in Israeli history. Yossi Sarid, known for his eloquence and "straight talk," was discussing the hopes and risks awaiting Israel with the recognition of the PLO as a legitimate representative of the Palestinians and admiring PM Rabin's honesty and the immense courage he demonstrated with the coming signing of the Oslo peace accord. These were the most hopeful days of AD KAN's membership. Sarid's words in 1993 represented both the optimistic vision and the tragic end of a story one could title "When Prophesy Fails."

After the disastrous events following Rabin's assassination and the collapse of the Oslo agreements, Sarid continued his engagement in politics and fostered his later career as a highly visible writer and speaker until his sudden death. However, the interview rebroadcast as a memorial tribute to a leader of the party I supported for many years was also a reminder that the above "historical" text is not the fruit of a wild personal imagination. Since the Oslo debacle, in contrast to Sarid's reaction but similar to those of most of AD KAN's members, I retreated from active participation in the public forum, concentrating instead on research ventures at a new field-site: gay life in New York, a subject and location far removed from my professional engagement with Israeli issues.

No doubt, choosing a somewhat unconventional ethnographic study as a mainstream anthropologist was a gratifying experience. However, was it any less of an escape from Israel's depressing realities and the feeling of failure to "change the world," the title of that text? In contrast with the earlier fieldwork sites, my identity as "participant observer" in the company of a gay synagogue congregants and among members of other gay organizations was mostly obscured. I developed close friendships with men and women sharing a similar sociocultural background, who were combating the pains and stigma of their sexuality and gender identity in American mainstream society.

I turn now to another event, one that took place during a sabbatical leave at NYU in 2005, where I participated in a panel following PM Sharon's dramatic withdrawal from the Gaza Strip and the erasure of Israeli settlements founded on that territory. It seemed utterly unexpected when Sharon, the founder of many Jewish settlements in the occupied territories, led the disengagement from Gaza. Sharon's dramatic change of course was reminiscent of those of other leaders who dominated the stage in recent history (de Gaulle in particular), proving that, for better or worse, our destiny depends much on the power and vision of great, mediocre, or evil individuals. However, I argued, since there is little chance to see Sharon stay in office long enough in order to complete the de Gaulle task of disengagement from the West Bank, we confront the question: who would inherit it? If Netanyahu were to replace Sharon, I preferred to keep silent about the prospects, unless the impossible might strike again. (Years later, it seems that initial pessimistic assessment relating to Netanyahu was quite accurate—no "miracle" had struck again!)

During the panel I compared the advent and consequences of the West Bank Israeli settlements project with Hurricane Katrina that had recently devastated New Orleans (August 2005). The argument pointed at the major losers of the colossal investment of national resources in the occupied territories who were the lower classes of Israeli society, residents of the periphery's towns and the poorer suburbs of metropolitan cities. But different from the disenfranchised Katrina victims who had little impact on the American power structure, the Israeli lower classes vote largely against "themselves," supporting right-wing parties—the hotbed of nationalistic policies and investments, the West Bank settlements in particular. However, at that historical moment of the Gaza evacuation, the golem (a clay giant of Jewish folklore that came to life, destroying its progenitor) that had hijacked the Zionist ideology and practice lost one of its major cancerous extensions. Nevertheless, one is deeply worried about Netanyhau, waiting for the next national elections, who has employed the services of Arthur Finkelstein, the American election campaigns expert, a virtuoso able to install in power Caligula's or Nero's pets.

I suggested that we should screen pictures on television directed at the Israeli victims, comparing their neglected neighborhoods with images exposing the affluence of the West Bank Jewish settlements financed by public agencies. My presentation ended exclaiming:

> I may sound emotional and probably pathetic, but if a continuing withdrawal from the West Bank and efforts of peacemaking would not be the course of close history, I'll visit the graves of my parents and tell them I advised my sons to pack and return to the Diaspora. I am not waiting for the arrival of the Messiah but instead for the return of Herzl [founder of the Zionist movement].

Actually, the same year I published my collection of letters directed to Herzl, *Herzl Doesn't Live Here Anymore*. (Clearly my distrust of Netanyahu started when I first identified him operating in the public arena.)

A year later (2006), I was invited to speak at the SFAA's (Society for Applied Anthropology) annual meeting in Vancouver on a panel titled "A Peace of Compromise: Is a Just Solution Possible for Palestine and Israel?" My contribution intended to expose the failure on both sides of the conflict. A different set of complaints from those usually directed toward Israeli leaders, it blamed equally the Palestinians' stance of waiting for "justice" and their refusal to compromise and accommodate the physical and political present reality. Could a rational observer anticipate the prospects of "justice," meaning the return of land and homes lost since 1948, without a total annihilation of the Israeli state?

I began my presentation by recounting a disturbing encounter with Arab students at Manchester University shortly before the 1967 war. Nearly forty years ago, a few days before the outbreak of the 1967 hostilities, a meeting between Jewish students and an Israeli delegate who would report on the crisis was advertised on campus. When the meeting occurred, however, the hall was also packed with Arab students who seemed gleeful about the expected outset of an armed conflict. The Israeli delegate made a poor presentation of content and style; he appeared uncertain and poorly expressive. The Jewish students seemed resigned to a coming disaster. At that tense moment, I intervened, addressing the jubilant Arab attendees. Forty years later I cannot forget that repugnant scene and my short sudden oratory: "You are pushing us to war, but remember, a war is a game: you can win, you can lose, but if you lose don't ask for the prize!" They pointed their fingers at me and teased, "Go on! Go on!" A few days later, they avoided me on campus trails. Sadly, my interlocutors apparently represented the privileged educated strata of Arab society.

Incidentally, Vancouver embodied a stage where "justice" was never fully accomplished, given the suffering and losses of the local aboriginal population belatedly called the "First Nations." However, on that occasion I did not mention my moving experience (relayed in chapter 3) at the Potlatch Collection Repatriation Museum, which hosted four hundred pieces of ritual regalia confiscated by the Canadian government in 1921 and returned to local communities in 1967. Most moving, however, was the copy of a letter on exhibit signed by Professor Franz Boas, addressed to the Canadian authorities protesting the brutal suppression of British Columbia aboriginal peoples.

But I reminded the audience of the Arab brethren who betrayed the Palestinians by keeping the refugees in camps and depriving them of citizenship in the neighboring countries. Is the Israeli-Palestinian conflict among those insoluble situations destined to perpetuate throughout world history? I ended my gloomy presentation with the hope of the unexpected, refurbishing Martin Luther King's famous epitaph: "I have a dream, that one day a de Gaulle wearing a yarmulke and a Mahatma Gandhi wearing a kufiya will sit to the table and construct a reasonable compromise that would allow both Palestinians and Israelis to live side by side in peace." And quoting Herzl: "If you really crave for, this is not a fairy tale." (PM Rabin and Chairman Arafat had lost that chance …)

I was later invited to participate in a similar forum, the Under the Radar panel, at the American Anthropological Association's 2008 annual meeting. The title that year, "Reflections on Peace and Justice: Restoring Multiple Narratives and Framework of Compromise," seemed to repeat the theme of the SFAA Vancouver meeting. Indeed, the Israeli-Palestinian conflict seemed to foster a growing visibility and interest among a group of engaged anthropologists. They displayed a genuine wish to explore the circumstances and prospects of a peaceful settlement on a site close to the concerns and worries of Jewish anthropologists. Moreover, Israeli anthropologists represented a relatively significant cohort of non-American members compared with other non-American nationals on the AAA ranks. Naturally, I repeated personal experiences from AD KAN and the Manchester days: hopes and disappointments in the leaders on both sides. However, I added an anthropological interpretation to explain Chairman Arafat's last confusing stand at the implementation of the Oslo Accords. That late interpretation was based on my earlier research in Jaffa, where I had studied the impact of the code of honor in local politics among Arab residents. It suggested that Arafat could not reconcile himself to the destiny of an Arab leader, a man of honor who would give up bringing "justice" to his people, meaning a full-scale return to the towns and villages of pre-1948 Palestine.

Nearly ten years later, while I was reading Hacham's 2016 reconstruction of the first intifada and its aftermath (reported in chapter 2), I found that he suggested a similar thesis about the cultural ethos that had restrained Arafat from taking the last step, betraying his promise to liberate Palestine. That thesis reminded me of Walzer's *Just and Unjust Wars* (1977), which explored the diverse ways that different cultures perceive how morality underpins war and the methods of fighting. This perspective did not reduce the Israeli leaders' share in the continually declining circumstances that have jeopardized the conclusion of conflict. My address at the 2008 AAA forum ended in a pessimistic assessment about the situation that seemed insoluble at the time without a momentous catastrophic or charismatic turn of events.

As for the role of anthropologists concerned with that case and other conflicts, I pleaded that we should give up our inclination to absolve the underdogs from responsibility and support self-serving, guilt-ridden mantras of "justice." Preaching and waiting for "justice" emboldens the extremists on both sides. As much as we feel obligated to listen carefully to the various protagonists in our ethnographic studies, we should also listen to the conflicting narratives of both sides in that "intractable" conflict and advocate a mission of compromise for a better life in this world.

The last public presentation took place at the following year's AAA Under the Radar session (2009). Invited as a discussant, I commented mostly on a paper that presented the public discourse related to the Canadian Deborah Ellis's children's book and play *The Three Wishes*. The text brought together a collection of stories told by an equal number of Israeli and Palestinian children. This unusual dramatic staging confronted the audience of theatergoers with two national narratives told at the same performance—instead of the familiar presentation of one exclusive perspective of national history and daily experiences. It offered an opportunity to reveal other Palestinian and Israeli authors who employed a similar strategy of presenting a dual perspective to the conflict.

The first was celebrated author and leading PLO figure Ghassan Kanafani, whose evocative story *Returning to Haifa* (2000 [1969]) had recently been staged in a major Tel Aviv theater. The narrative presents the tragic events of the 1948 evacuation of the Palestinian residents of Haifa (a major port city). Trapped in the chaos of this hectic departure, an Arab family leaves behind their baby sleeping in his crib. The baby is found and raised lovingly by a Jewish immigrant couple who lost their own child in the European Holocaust. However, after the 1967 war and the opening of the border between the West Bank and Israel, the Arab couple, now successful residents of Ramallah (a main West Bank city) and parents to another son, are able to travel to Haifa and discover what happened to their lost baby. The meeting ends sadly when the child, now grown up and a soldier in the Israeli army, condemns his biological parents for fleeing without a fight. The humiliated father concludes that only a military confrontation might retrieve the lost Palestine, though it might lead to a confrontation between his sons: the Israeli Haifa patriot meeting his biological Palestinian brother from Ramallah on the battlefield.

From here I turned the presentation to Sami Michael, a leading Israeli author (born and raised in Iraq) who, nearly forty years later in his novel *Pigeons at Trafalgar Square* (2005), changed some details and added a sequel of sorts to Kanafani's Haifa-Ramallah encounter. His "refurbished" version described the adopted-Palestinian-baby-turned-successful-Israeli-businessman coming to terms with his biological roots and trying to reconcile the two opposing national identities. However, the new narrative, which exposes a wish to promote a peaceful solution to the dual identity, ends tragically. The two brothers who have crossed the dividing national-political fence die together when the Israeli brother is attacked on his way to visit his ailing biological mother by angry Palestinians, and the Palestinian brother is killed trying to save him from his vengeful assailants. In conclusion, both prominent Palestinian and Israeli novelists could see no light at the end of the tunnel promising a peaceful ending to the conflict tormenting their peoples.

The last interlocutor in that presentation was another leading Israeli author, David Grossman, who tackled the issue of the Israeli West Bank occupation in his acclaimed book *The Yellow Wind* (1988). Utilizing a semi-anthropological method, Grossman had spent a few months visiting and interviewing West Bank Palestinians, Jewish settlers, and Israeli administration officials dealing with West Bank residents, Palestinians in particular. Grossman concluded that both Israelis' and Palestinians' lives were being severely damaged by the occupation and the missed reconciliation between the two national visions.

In closing, I observed sadly that Kanafani's, Michael's, and Grossman's shared pessimistic verdict came close to home as two among them paid the ultimate price as part of the continuing conflict: Kanafani was killed in 1972, most probably by Israeli agents, as reprisal for the Japanese Red Army gunmen's massacre at Ben Gurion Airport (Tel Aviv) in service of the PLO sometime earlier. Grossman's son was killed in the 2006 Lebanon War. However, the discourse also exposed the continuing and courageous bearing of witness by a few dedicated Israeli journalists (especially Gideon Levy and Amira Hass), who have not wavered in informing the Israeli public about the severe daily consequences of the military control imposed on the Palestinian population in the West Bank and Gaza. Incidentally, the panel was conducted during a major eruption of violence on the border of Gaza (Hamas's shelling of the nearby town of Sderot, the abduction of an Israeli soldier, and the massive IDF retaliation), which added a tone of urgency to that academic setting.

The presentation pondered the potential impact of novelists and other literary critics on their audiences' political perceptions. Are they able to lead their protagonists in a new direction, promoting political "accommodation" rather than following the present tragic messianic hopes for "justice"? And last, what can anthropologists contribute to a peaceful management of that conflict when other agents representing the best talents of observation and writing seem to have failed?

An unexpected academic encounter with Israeli realities took place when I was invited to present the annual lecture in anthropology at Pomona College in Claremont, California (February 2012). The advertised lecture offered a discussion of some methodological issues related to my work among the gay community in New York. I was generously hosted, and I visited classes and met with students. However, on the morning of the scheduled presentation, I was forwarded an e-mail from Professor Daniel Segal of Pitzer College addressed to the faculty of the seven colleges of the Claremont consortium. It informed his colleagues that he would not attend my lecture although he "admired and [has] taught Shokeid's ethnography *A Gay Synagogue in New York*." However, he claimed that my work on Israelis and Palestinians "participates in a Zionist degradation and marginalization of Palestinians. He is speaking at Pomona at a moment when the State of Israel, under its extremist-right regime, is daily violating the human rights of our Palestinian sisters and brothers." And the last sentence: "Put simply, Professor Shokeid's representations of Palestinians are antithetical to what I believe—as an anthropologist, as a Jew, and as a person who seeks to live an ethical life in a complex and compromised world."

I was speechless at that pompous and vile accusation raised by a "good fellow Jew" (whom I never met or communicated with before), who, it appears, had never read an article or chapter of the accused publications dealing with his Palestinian sisters and brothers. In any case, I relinquished a suggestion to respond to Segal's accusation, avoiding any exchange with that display of academic self-righteousness. However, during the 2014 AAA meeting in Washington, Segal participated alongside other speakers at a crowded BDS session. The official position of the BDS claimed that the proposed boycott of Israeli academia was not aimed against individual professionals but was targeting Israeli *institutions*. Following the formal presentations, I took the opportunity to comment that I had already been personally boycotted by the honorable panel member. With no hesitation, Segal claimed that he did not stop me from presenting my lecture! It is beyond reliable speculation how many recipients of Segal's e-mail communiqué had actually avoided the Pomona presentation, but the experience gave me a nauseous feeling about that sort of anthropological morality.

Recording that distressing experience reminds me of earlier frustrating academic encounters, further consequences of my "problematic" national identity. I am reluctant to repeat in detail these events narrated years ago, before the position of Israeli anthropology became part of a public political debate. The first incident engaged a Dutch MA student, T. Van Teeffelen, who came to interview me in 1976 (during a sabbatical stay in Amsterdam) about the Manchester research project in Israel. Surprisingly, he subsequently wrote a thesis and later an article published in *Dialectical Anthropology* (1978) claiming that Israeli anthropologists studied only Jewish communities and neglected Israeli Arabs, exposing a romantic Zionist perspective (as symbolized, for example, in the titles of their ethnographies) and typical of the Manchester School of Anthropology, reflected its colonialist sins committed in Africa.

Invited by the editor of *Dialectical Anthropology* to respond to that highly distorted presentation of both Israeli and Manchester students, I wrote a detailed critique in terms of the sociology of knowledge, exploring the impact of the researcher's ideological-political commitments on his/her scientific writing. Although accepted for publication, the paper was rejected a few years later when the editor, renowned Stanley Diamond, belatedly explained that, on rereading its theoretical exposition, he concluded that it negated his own critical conception of the Zionist movement. I was stunned at that violation of basic academic ethics and civility (see Shokeid 1988/89). However, the late Eric Wolf, a member of the *DA* editorial board, graciously apologized to me for the editor's erratic behavior.

A similarly upsetting experience, mentioned earlier, took place a few years later when I came across an article published in *Cultural Anthropology* (1989) by Ted Swedenburg, an American anthropologist who studied memories of Palestinian participants in the 1936–39 revolt against the British Mandate aimed at the Jewish settlers. It was astonishing to read the author's admission that he had to "unlearn academic training in anthropology and history that compels one to unveil objective truth." Identifying with his subjects, Swedenburg decided to keep silent about the details of their participation in the revolt that must have included some unpleasant acts. I could empathize with the ethnographer's feelings of responsibility to protect his people from potential retaliation. But the self-presentation as rightfully concealing the truth seemed far removed from the ethics of reflexivity in anthropology.

My response was similar to the earlier critique of Van Teeffelen related to the sociology of knowledge. I avoided personal offense and allowed the editor of *Cultural Anthropology* to show Swedenburg the response before publication. Swedenburg responded with a much longer text that was published together with my contribution (1992), adding an uncivil attack of my work and persona. He used some out-of-context personal communication he circumvented via a close friend who contacted me pretending to be interested in my professional and social activities. For the sake of his "critique," he also revealed the name of the community of Moroccan Jews I studied in Israel.

I never finished reading that obscene piece of "academic" writing. The editor explained apologetically that whoever read that debate must certainly distinguish between the academic worth of the two testimonies. Actually, a few years ago, at the AAA meeting in Montreal, Swedenburg approached me in the company of a mutual friend and apologized for his unethical demeanor early in his career. However, it was an unforgettable lesson: never respond to ideologically committed interlocutors even under the guise of serious professional credentials. I implemented this lesson during the Pomona encounter and declined to respond to Daniel Segal's accusation.

My very last confrontation within the Israel/Palestine conflict, testing the management of a dual national and professional identity, occurred during the 2014–15 BDS debate. The 2014 AAA meeting in Washington ended with a vote to remove the motion of canceling the BDS agenda scheduled for the AAA resolution. The resolution called to refrain from formal collaboration with Israeli academic institutions—not including collaboration with individual academics. Following that insistent support for the BDS, the issue was postponed for a public debate (before a final vote) to take place during the 2015 meeting in Denver. In the meantime, sessions for and against the BDS were organized to be included in the 2015 program. An online discourse was opened with two letters exposing the contradicting positions by major representatives of both sides, followed by comments from interested individuals.

To prepare for the November 2015 vote, the AAA executive appointed a task force to visit the two sides of the conflict and prepare a document reporting on the situation on the ground. Eventually, out of the seven delegates, only three arrived for a ten-day visit to meet with Israeli and Palestinian academics (anthropologists included). I was invited to meet with the three delegates for dinner in the company of another Israeli graduate student. I spent an agreeable evening in conversation with one of them who was acquainted with my work, but our dialogue had little to do with the BDS agenda; however, he confessed to having a close Palestinian friend, a native of East Jerusalem. I did not reveal that intimate information to my colleagues. But one wonders how the three experts' visit during a short, busy trip produced a comprehensive review that seemed to validate the BDS claims about the Palestinians' situation under the circumstances of Israeli military control. That condemning review could as well be written without the impression and expense of a task-force fact-finding project.

Although deeply critical of the Israeli government and not proud of my colleagues' inability to demonstrate a concerted response to the long-standing tense political situation, I felt compelled to react to the BDS agenda highlighted on the AAA program, which was bluntly unrelated to a world of past and present injustices.

My short internet comment open to all AAA members exposed the BDS blueprint's false pretense; although apparently aimed against academic institutions, its plea in fact targeted individuals who were funded, me included, by their home university. The online comment avowed readiness to pay for the sins of my government and redeem the Palestinians for the sins of their own leaders—assuming the AAA membership seriously believed the BDS boycott might help relieve the suffering of the Palestinians. It ended with the following: "In view of the many regimes of injustice and brutality around the globe (the US included), the signing in support of the BDS agenda seems a painless act of patronage and self-righteousness commanding the cheapest terms of personal engagement."

At the 2015 AAA convention in Denver, I attended a sample of the more or less eloquent presentations introducing both sides of the debate. It seemed that there was no chance of changing the mood in the corridors and meeting rooms. No doubt, the BDS case was well organized, complete with volunteers who handed out informative material about its goals, sweetened with cookies. Those who approached me had no connection to anthropology and were probably paid for the task. The association's business session was packed as never before during my forty years AAA membership. Nearly fourteen hundred men and women showed up, compared with the usual attendance of no more than four hundred members, for the exceptionally interesting event. Particularly noticeable this time was the relative youth of the crowd. The vote, as expected, left no doubt about the atmosphere dominating the hall and the annexed corridors: more than one thousand voted in support of the motion to conduct a final e-mail ballot (accepting or rejecting the BDS motion) among the entire eleven thousand AAA membership, which would take place before the 2016 meeting in Minneapolis. On leaving Denver, it seemed beyond doubt that this would be my last annual "pilgrimage" to the AAA conventions.

Despite all predictions, the final vote (counting five thousand who took part in the ballot) ended with a thin margin (of thirty-nine) opposing the BDS proposition. I was not jubilant upon receiving the "happy news," however; the ballot outcome seemed to confirm the professional standing of Israeli anthropologists and the support of their colleagues among the veteran cohort of the AAA membership as well as among a less radical audience. It was not in any way an endorsement of Israeli politics or the result of official Israeli agencies' pathetic machinations to fight the BDS. And last, I could remain a member of an organization essential to my professional self.

In the meantime, however, every day brings fresh and alarming news about semi-democratic rulings introduced by a right-wing Israeli government. Particularly troubling is the Nationality Bill, a July 2018 Knesset adoption, as Basic Law, which specifies the nature of the State of Israel as the nation-state of the Jewish people (by sixty-five in favor, fifty-five against, and two abstentions). It was sharply criticized for depriving equal rights of non-Jewish minorities. Even worse is the continuing expansion of unauthorized settlements in the occupied territories, as well as the brutal acts by settlers' youth who roam the hills of the West Bank, relieving their gusting hormones and fanatic messianic beliefs by targeting the Palestinian residents of nearby villages. But no less horrifying is the violent retaliation by young Palestinians against innocent bystanders on the streets of Jerusalem and elsewhere fostering the occasional recurrence of the "knives intifada."

Confronting these uncanny manifestations, I am often invited to join petitions protesting against various undemocratic steps taken by the authorities, thus contributing the symbolic "value" of an academic title. But as already indicated, I doubt the extent to which these indignant displays carry any practical impact, except for the personal notion that one has a virtual community of people who share a distressing predicament, a sad transplant of a lost communal *communitas*.

It seems fitting to conclude the documentation of the AD KAN story with a recent unexpected reminder of that past moment in campus life and its present-day relevance. After a long period of "silence," as I had decided to stop using *Haaretz* to express my rage until the delusional beliefs and actions of Israeli governments (partly shared with our Palestinian interlocutors) would reveal their devastating consequences, I published an article there on 17 February 2016. It happened after a new right-wing group adopted the name AD KAN to advertise the "criminal acts" of leftist groups who supported the legal rights of Palestinians living under the settlers' abuse or revealing the army's use of unlawful measures in conflictual encounters. The title the editor had given to the Hebrew edition translated to "Raise Up My Educated Brothers," but the English edition seemed much harsher: "In Our Own Weimar Republic Academics Remain Silent." Both titles were taken from the text that repeated the eulogy at the memorial event for Leon Sheleff, which I related earlier. But now on a wider podium, I pointed at the new, vile AD KAN group enjoying the lush ground fertilized by PM Netanyahu and his supportive team, especially the religious right-wing minister of education Naftali Bennett. The editor even adorned the piece with Bennett's photo. The article alluded to the Weimar Republic days, when leading intellectuals remained unaware of the clouds hovering over the foundations of their country's democracy. It wrestled with the query and condemnation: why do Israeli academics remain silent in view of the political, cultural, and moral decline of their society?

The next day I was interviewed on a popular radio program (FM88), together with a right-wing retired IDF general. Naturally, my interlocuter dismissed the comparison with the German case, a continuing though fading taboo in Israeli public discourse. Equally assertive was my observation that we had lost hope for a peaceful settlement with the Palestinians and that public morality had declined in recent years.

Having reported on my mode of accommodation with the tantalizing outcome of the Oslo promise and the experiences confronting the compulsion to reveal my contentious national narrative, I will introduce in the next chapter core AD KAN members' memories of the first intifada days and their response to the aftermath of the failure of their peace venture.

14

Listening to AD KAN Veterans

Returning to the AD KAN case and context, I examine its membership's academic background, their choice of action during the first intifada, and their present-day notion of success and failure. Unsurprisingly, the participants represented a small section of TAU faculty, coming mostly from the social sciences, the humanities, law school, education, and mathematics. The natural sciences were almost totally removed from that academic-political endeavor. This academic representation confirmed the observations that social scientists made long ago about the roles and types of intellectuals. As indicated earlier, the membership seemed to equally represent men and women; most were relatively young, situated in higher academic positions, of advanced professional status, and inexperienced with political activism. They were ready to invest time and energy even though they were at the prime of their careers and anxious to develop an international reputation based on frequent participation in professional forums and publishing in Euro-American scholarly venues. At the same time, however, they were careful to avoid being labeled as "radicals," a designation that might have scared away a wider constituency of joiners and supporters. This is unlike, for example, the revolutionary style of the Twenty-First Year association, another organization targeting university participants for recruitment (see chapter 5).

Although they were a minority on campus, the participants nevertheless enjoyed considerable visibility and respect among the larger body of faculty and students. However, the group membership did not develop into a tight social circle, a semi-cult of followers who also socialized beyond the campus premises. Although it counted among its number a few popular teachers admired by many students, AD KAN had no charismatic personas attracting loyal disciples or presenting an authoritative ideological module of thought and action. It remained a voluntary association of equals dedicated to an issue removed from its members' ordinary daily activities and social obligations.

The role of "chief activator" (*mafhil rashi*) functioned as a sort of a mediator, navigating between the varied personal views and temperaments of a large group of reputable individuals displaying a wide spectrum of opinions, sentiments, and temperaments. We reached consensus through long, often hectic discussions, allowing everybody to express his/her point of view. It was a tricky task to maintain a civil atmosphere during ireful flares of personal communication or to conclude meetings with a consensus about a forthcoming activity or a text intended for public distribution, confirmed by a majority vote. We were puzzled yet gratified by our exceptional position as the only politically active campus group engaged in protest among leading Israeli academic institutions. And eventually, we felt we were successful partners to the process that facilitated the Oslo Accords.

However, we were not tempted to continue with that public mission on campus or develop personal political careers on the wider political stage. We canceled our registration with the interior ministry's list of nonprofit organizations. Actually, the majority of AD KAN participants soon retreated from any venue of public activity on campus and elsewhere unrelated to their academic work as teachers and researchers. Moreover, only a few of the veterans continued to socialize with their AD KAN mates beyond ordinary professional engagements. Upon reaching Israeli mandatory retirement age for academia (at sixty-eight), one is practically cast out from campus life. Many AD KAN participants gradually reached that "closing" phase of their role on campus. There is no "upper house" in the university constitution to enable emerita/emeritus professors to continue participating in campus affairs (except for a symbolic cadre of retirees representing the major faculties at the senate meetings).

However, I find no answer to the absence of active political dissent among the younger generation of academics at TAU and in other university arenas. And that is in spite of the growing dangers to Israeli democracy—an unavoidable result of the continuing military occupation and the control of another national population.

Trying to understand the mood of the days leading to the founding of AD KAN and the social circumstances that supported its activities, as well as inquire about present-day realities, I met recently (2016–17) with a few of its core membership, most retired but still academically active. Naturally, I missed those who left the country (e.g., Professor Anat Biletzki, philosophy), passed away, or were not available for other personal reasons.

First on that short list was Ariella Friedman, among the most dedicated AD KAN members, with whom I had an intimate conversation. Teaching at the departments of psychology and social work, she was engaged throughout her career with issues concerning personal and group welfare. Among her projects was bringing together Jewish and Arab students in a seminar to discuss the realities of sharing life in Israeli society. Ariella was easygoing, always ready to embrace a compromise during hectic discussions, and eager to openly express her feelings without disguise. We returned to the social-political atmosphere of the early days and later years during the first intifada. No doubt, she reminisced, we were affected by the dramatic explosion of the Palestinians' rage after two decades of their seeming acceptance of the Israeli regime and their apparent integration into Israeli economy. That sudden shocking reality roused a wave of astounded individuals in various institutions, organizations, and professions who felt that they could not remain silent. A long list of groups emerged that offered these individuals an outlet for their feelings of guilt and compassion toward the Palestinians—the "invisible" residents under Israel's ostensibly benevolent control. It was probably the zeitgeist, the spirit of the time, that moved us and our mostly "human sciences" colleagues to come together and join the panorama of protest.

"AD KAN was my home on campus," Ariella expressed, the phrase conveying a deep feeling of belonging and connection to the society identified under that banner of membership. One could define that expression in anthropological terms as a statement indicating the notion of *communitas* (Turner 1969): namely, the feelings of intimate relationships and comradery among a cohort of men and women who shared some extraordinary experiences that influenced personal and social transformations (such as rites of passage, army service, etc.).

The portrayal of "home" on campus revealed a contradiction in the usual description of social relationships in many academic units, often a stage of competition and disagreement on appointments, promotions, course syllabi, and professional status. AD KAN recruited its membership from a wide range of scientific interests, creating a community of scholars cutting across the borders of professional divisions and free from the usual frictions of academic circles. Although

AD KAN disbanded long ago and we have rarely met since, my recent meetings with certain of its members revived a warm bond I rarely experienced when meeting with other colleagues on campus, including those closer to my professional interests.

At my meeting with historian Benjamin Arbel (expert of Renaissance Italy), a somewhat younger member (though also recently retired), I was surprised to find that he brought along his own AD KAN archive, including the button. We had not met for nearly twenty years. Naturally, he was not the young man I remembered, the cheerful person contributing generously to the organization's tight budget. We spent a few hours meeting at my home, discussing various current issues, and expressing feelings of disappointment and despair about the present-day situation, so remote from the vision we nourished in the early 1990s.

He concluded by conveying a notion that had recently become familiar among my company of close friends: "Had I been younger I would have left the country!" Before departing, he recommended Sebastian Haffner's *A German's Story* (translated to Hebrew by AD KAN member Shula Volkov, a distinguished scholar of German history), a narrative that, he felt, exposed some similarities with recent political developments in Israel. Haffner's book represents a petrifying personal chronicle, written in 1939 but published in 2000 after the author's death. Haffner, a young man practicing law during the 1930s, left Nazi Germany in 1938 and returned in 1954, having become a prolific writer in England. In this early memoir, Haffner described in piercing detail Hitler's gradual takeover of his country's democracy, the growing state brutality, and the quick loss of elementary tenets of civil society among ordinary citizens who succumbed to the regime's ideological agenda. Moreover, he predicted the road leading to the destruction of Germany.

In a separate publication (*Anmerkungen Zu Hitler*, 1979), Haffner further explored Hitler's enigma: his ability to penetrate and control collective subconscious fears, his knack for orchestrating a continuing competition between his close lieutenants in power, the placement of concentration camps and other notorious sites outside of Germany, and, consequently, the ability or pretension of ordinary citizens to claim innocence and "not knowing."

One wonders: how much does that horror story reflect on some vestiges of present-day Israeli society? For better or worse we bear witness to the almost tenured PM Netanyahu, a shrewd politician, a master of populist propaganda, sensitive to his audiences' deep-rooted fears and desires. Thus, for example, he recently employed a new dramatic slogan—"ethnic cleansing of Jews" (11 September 2016)—referring to the international demand to evacuate unlawful Israeli settlements in the West Bank. During the 2015 national elections, he warned that "the Arabs are driving to the polls on buses" (thus, the Israeli Arab citizens were threatening the Jewish national electorate), thereby prompting Israeli voters and winning few more seats for the Likud Party, securing his continued hold on the office. A perceptive historian and sensitive observer, Arbel vented his anxieties of watching the successful strategy employed by PM Netanyahu as he courted the support of close interest groups, but also that of the less sophisticated constituencies magnetized by his inflammatory nationalistic messages.

I was planning to call on Uri Maor, the physicist and only active AD KAN member representing the "eastern bank" on campus. More than anyone else, Maor was connected with leading figures in the Palestinian diaspora leadership whom he met during his frequent trips on professional missions, and as such he offered us a better grasp of the mood among their number. He presumed that they were ready to negotiate with Israeli counterparts. Maor chaired the public events described above that hosted PLO leading representatives Faisal Husseini and others. He had called me a few months earlier in 2016, responding to my letter published in *Haaretz* that complained about the misuse of AD KAN's name for a right-wing group and lamented the political silence on campus. During that phone call, Uri told me he had married the nurse who took care of his late wife, herself a dedicated AD KAN participant. At her deathbed she expressed her wish for him to share the rest of his life with the woman who became part of their family. The nurse was an Arab woman who resided in a nearby Arab town. He relayed the pleasure of getting involved in that new environment. Unfortunately, a few weeks later, Uri passed away of a sudden heart failure. I lament missing our scheduled meeting. However, the last chapter of his family life seems to epitomize his deeply rooted conviction and dreams for a peaceful future, realizing a true harmony between Jews and Arabs sharing the same land.

I met with Ruth Berman, a leading linguist and member of the Israel Academy of Science, who was skilled in concluding subjects during AD KAN meetings. When we met, she expressed her amazement at the courage we displayed at the time: openly calling for negotiations with the PLO, publicly exposing that manifesto by wearing the AD KAN "Speak to the PLO" button, and inviting Palestinian leaders to address the Israeli public, among them Faisal

Husseini. Ruth emphasized the atmosphere of engagement that kept our weekly meetings fully attended for a few years—she herself had to commute a long distance from her home outside of Tel Aviv. Ruth played an important role in taking care of the group's announcements in English. However, Ruth thought we failed in remaining a "purely" academic society and not recruiting a strong cadre of students. At the same time, she understood that the Israeli student body was anxious to get on with their studies and family responsibilities after their army service. Ruth had no explanation for the present-day absence of political protest except for the notion of "despair" (*yeush*), the common explanation for the leftists' growing weakness in a society increasingly dominated by right-wingers.

Ovadia Ezra represented a younger generation within our ranks. A PhD candidate during his AD KAN membership, he is now among the senior teachers at TAU's philosophy department. However, our meeting carried a sad though moving aura, as Ovadia was enduring a condition of advanced cancer. He considered the AD KAN movement a unique congregation of prominent academics coming from various disciplinarian venues, representing morally oriented, honest individuals who could not remain silent in view of the injustices implicating them as Israeli citizens. However, he confessed, he was too timid at the time to take part in the discussions about the political announcements the group advertised. Instead, he took on various operational tasks such as distributing leaflets and calling on friends to join the organization and attend meetings. When I asked him about the present-day political silence on campus, Ovadia suggested that a profound change had occurred in the "character" of the younger faculty recruits among the "soft" sciences; he noted that they appeared far more individualistic, mostly concerned with their careers, and less engaged with communal and human-rights affairs. He expressed a deep pessimism about the future of Israeli society, its physical and moral entity, as a result of the growing constituency of right-wing parties. Sadly, Ovadia passed away a few months later.

Uri Yechiali, retired professor of operations research and statistics, was among the dedicated participants who came from the school of mathematics. In line with other interviewees, he seemed depressed about the current political situation and the atmosphere dominated by PM Netanyahu and his Likud Party. Yechiali quoted a parable he had apparently heard from an American observer: "What is in common between the United States and Israel? Ninety percent of the Americans are stupid and only 10 percent are smart. In Israel, 90 percent are smart and 10 percent are stupid. But both in the United

States and Israel the 10 percent dominate the country!" Comparing the vocal AD KAN days to the political silence on campus in recent years, he suggested that, at the time, we believed we could influence social-political processes and have an impact on them. But today, no one in a good state of mind seems to believe there is any option for effecting some real change in current national politics. Moreover, he seemed to think that university leaders are now more careful than ever to avoid disputes with the right-wing government agencies controlling their institutions' financial well-being.

We exchanged notes on the decision we made years ago, giving up the option of staying on in Europe or the United States. He completed his PhD thesis at Columbia University and returned to Israel against his supervisor's advice to take a teaching position in the United States. He hated the idea that his children would ask him to stay away when their friends would visit, ashamed of his foreign accent (an observation often reported during my study of the *Yordim* in New York). He concluded that he had a good life in Tel Aviv, but he was deeply worried about the unavoidable and massive explosion of conflict that would occur as a consequence of the continuing expansion of the settlements in the West Bank with no prospects of peace with the Palestinians.

David Gilat, also retired professor of mathematics, had a similar story of returning to Israel after seven years of graduate studies and the start of a tenure-track position at a leading US university. It seemed like the right time for him to go back before his young children could become fully "Americanized." There was the promise of a warm homecoming at the newly founded Tel Aviv University. As he experienced along with other AD KAN members, it was a shock during the 1987 intifada realizing that the Palestinians were not as content as commonly assumed, as they had improved their standard of living compared with the pre-1967 conditions under Jordanian and Egyptian regimes. "We [members at the mathematics department] were deeply disturbed, and spotting the note calling to attend a meeting at the Social Sciences Faculty, decided to see what was going on there, and we felt comfortable with that crowd." Moreover, the event that ended with the arbitrary detention of Gaza lawyer Abu Shaaban confirmed Gilat and his colleagues' dedication to AD KAN activities. As described above, the mathematicians formed the strongest group among the various AD KAN professional units.

To my question as to why a similar organization on campus had not emerged in recent years, David suggested some reasons that other interviewees had also conveyed: the experience following the collapse of peace negotiations was not as shocking as it had been during the first intifada, even with the eruption of intense violence, and mostly, there was a growing feeling of weakness among the leftists. In addition, for a long period of time, university budgets were severely reduced, and the load of teaching and administration was left to a smaller cadre of academic appointments. That growing workload left no time for extracurricular activities. However, David continued to attend political events advertised in various local forums and to support the leftist Meretz Party. In a similar mood expressed above by his colleague Yechiali, he concluded: "We have had a good life in the private domain, but the reality in the wider sociopolitical arena seems beyond our control." Twelve years since retirement, David was still actively engaged in academic life, teaching and conducting research.

I called on Sasha Weitman, whom I first met in mid-1970s in Stoney Brook when I visited him as TAU sociology department chair interviewing a candidate planning to soon join the Tel Aviv faculty. He was at that time a tenured teacher at New York State University at Stony Brook department of sociology. Observing his comfortable family lifestyle, I didn't feel right encouraging him to take a not-yet-tenured position and make a dramatic move to the hectic and far more modest living circumstances in Israel. I did not hide my feelings or reservations, but he was adamant about moving and soon arrived in Tel Aviv with his family of three young girls. He exemplified a model of quick absorption, soon fluently teaching in Hebrew and becoming a central figure in the sociology department's life.

We had not met in more than ten years, since we both retired from active campus life, and on the first phone call I mentioned the failed attempt to convince him to stay on in the United States. He responded sadly, "You were wrong at that time, but possibly right considering the present realities of Israeli society." Surprisingly, however, he didn't consider himself one of the core AD KAN members "who were far more politically sagacious." I wondered at that observation, as we had mostly been novices in politics and had avoided further intervention in campus and outside politics. None of the active members served as a faculty dean or took a prominent role in another major organization. In any case, from my viewpoint, he was among the most active members in confronting aggressive intruders, recruiting students and colleagues to support AD KAN activities (e.g., his communication with Clifford Geertz, mentioned earlier), etc. We returned at our meeting to his life history as a Holocaust survivor who at a young age changed identities as well as countries, from Poland to Italy, Morocco, and finally the United States.

It was an early dream of his to get to Israel and secure for himself and his children a "national identity" in the real sense of the term, without the adjective and its sociocultural corollary of "American Jew," etc. On arrival in Israel in 1975, he fell in love with the country, and for a few years he was extremely happy. It was the first Lebanon War (1982–84) that spoiled his love affair.[1] He was therefore content with the eruption of the intifada, observing the Palestinians taking a stand against their oppressors who seemed comfortable with the continuing military occupation and the Palestinians' silent submission. He shared those feelings with close students. Moreover, as a former student of Lewis Coser, the promoter of conflict theory (e.g., *The Functions of Social Conflict*, 1956), he considered the benefit of a conflict situation that would inevitably end in a settlement and accommodation. Consequently, he was excited about discovering the emergence of a peace movement active in his own department. He was very impressed by the political skills he observed among the members of the group he joined. However, he bitterly remembered his involvement in an aggressive row when he affronted a right-wing student who was tearing down AD KAN's posters. He was shocked and offended when the dean of the social sciences faculty seemed more sympathetic toward the "attacked" student.

When I asked him about the continuing political inactivity on campus, Sasha suggested that it was due to a loss of confidence among the Israeli public, many leftists included, in the Palestinians as reliable partners for peaceful relationships. He felt that the mood of suspicion originated around the days of the second intifada (the Al-Aqsa Intifada), which began in September 2000 and ended sometime in 2005, when many innocent people were killed by suicide bombers. His own daughter had luckily escaped a deadly explosion when she got off her bus one stop before it was blown up by a Palestinian suicide bomber.

I met with Israel Gershoni, among the most active AD KAN members and often taking on leadership responsibilities, a distinguished historian of Middle East studies specializing in the history of modern Egypt. Of a younger cohort, he was amused when I recounted the rector's impolite response to Gershoni's request to let an AD KAN delegation meet with visiting TAU trustees. Not yet a full professor at that time, Gershoni believed that his junior status was the reason he received such a dismissive reply. But life did not get much easier once he had attained professional reputation and academic promotion. He joined AD KAN because he believed it was an answer to his continuing frustration that Middle East academic departments taught and researched without engaging Arab colleagues, keeping away from the realities close to home in the occupied territories—an issue that could not be separated from the worldview of an "Orientalist." However, he paid a price for joining AD KAN, as it was considered playing politics, an engagement unsuitable for serious scholars, among his professional circle.

To contribute to the development of AD KAN's political orientation, he invited his close colleague Matti Steinberg, a leading expert on the Palestinian national movement (mentioned earlier), to teach us about the new trends transforming the PLO ideological course toward a possible accommodation with Israel, opening options for a dialogue instead of armed confrontation. Employed as a consultant to major security agencies, Steinberg was a reliable witness who offered strong support for our convictions and calls to recognize the PLO as a partner for peace talks.

Gershoni pinpointed the syndrome among academics anxious to gain public endorsement for their professional achievements, who are careful to risk loss of respect and honors by getting involved in sociopolitical conflicts. He acknowledged, however, that the protest on campus started among the social sciences faculty participants who had been more skillfully engaged in public issues as part of their habitual professional occupation.

To the question about the overall absence of current protest on campus, he identified a massive societal shift to right-wing positions that generate a more restrained atmosphere on campus. During the first intifada, a wider national constituency seemed anxious to reach a peaceful accommodation with the Palestinians. As Gershoni narrated an experience he had at the last senate meeting he attended before retirement, I was reminded of AD KAN's failed protest on the same stage twenty-five years earlier. Gershoni's recent complaint focused on TAU archeologists who took on an excavation project in Silwan, an Arab neighborhood on the outskirts of Jerusalem that is considered the ancient site of King David's city. They were supported by the right-wing organization EL-AD, and they had declined to involve the Palestinian Al-Quds University faculty members. Following a hectic discussion on the senate floor, only seven attendees voted to support his motion against the archeologists' terms of research, a greater defeat compared with our old experience. No doubt, he suggested, most senate members are liberal, but, as before, they prefer to maintain a calm ambience, particularly these days when TAU is lacking an independent financial endowment to secure its smooth operation. To that atmosphere of academic disengagement, Gershoni added the loss of communality in academic departments as part of a trend of growing individualism in professional interests. Therefore, there are less opportunities for political collaboration among close colleagues. In conclusion, he dismissed the possibility of repeating AD KAN's agenda and activities.

It took me some time to contact Avishai Ehrlich, but I finally got his present address in Tel Aviv. He was among the most active AD KAN members and was the creator of the memorably provocative buttons. He immediately recognized my voice on the first phone call, and we met for a long morning session at the TAU social sciences cafeteria, our old "home." Avishai had a somewhat different career compared with other colleagues in the group. He had been involved in much earlier political affairs while studying in London during the 1960s students' insurgency. He was close to leftist individuals and groups, including the socialist Israeli revolutionary organization Matzpen.[2] After his affiliation with the sociology department at TAU, he taught political sociology at various Israeli colleges. His know-how was valuable to AD KAN's political novices. Although I also graduated in England during the 1960s, I had no connection with the scene there that seemed so remote from the largely staid Israeli ambience before and immediately after the 1967 war.

As expected, Avishai did not think that one could compare our shared past with present-day social-cultural circumstances. In the days of AD KAN, he explained, the intellectual-academic elite enjoyed the elevated status they miss today. Academics these days, however, maintain prestige and eminence as representatives of a specific professional sector. Our protest movement was basically "white," its membership mostly Ashkenazim whose cultural sources and political orientation were rooted in the Western ethical-academic milieu. These days, those who would have been AD KAN members encourage their children to develop successful careers and relocate to more promising world sites.

He related a frustrating experience he had two years earlier, when he tried to organize a meeting of teachers and students at the TAU school of Jewish studies. The meeting was intended to discuss present-day social-cultural realities and possibly start a new academic, politically oriented movement (I had been unaware of that initiative as I was spending a term in Vienna at that time). The hall was packed with one hundred or more attendees, but the discourse soon deteriorated, displaying conflicting positions about the Ashkenazim-Mizrahim social-political schisms in Israeli society. That was the fruitless ending of his last effort to revive the days of AD KAN. He reckoned there was no option left for political action on campus.

Avishai described the current social-political scene as one dominated by the religious and settlers' sectors who maintain the fervent convictions and zeal lacking among the secular-liberal constituency. The growing influence of rabbis is symptomatic of that trend. We don't know what might have happened had PM Rabin survived, but his killing was not an unexpected accident. The activist disposition among the religious constituency reminded him of the pioneering secular Israeli society years ago, manifested today in the West Bank settlement movement. Moreover, the army, already short of suitable draftees, will inevitably increase the draft among the ultra-Orthodox. That development, he argued, is not as contradictory as it may seem; Zionism was never an utterly secular movement, and its agenda of a return to the Land of Israel was a result of the religious-national ethos rooted at its core. Ironically, Avishai concluded, these days have seen a step backward in the story of Israeli nation-building.

I met with Elana Shohamy, a leading language expert at the TAU school of education, on her return from a sabbatical in the United States, still under the spell of her American colleagues' shattering experience with Donald Trump's presidency. However, she turned nostalgic about the AD KAN days, when she found a group composed of faculty from various disciplines eager to dedicate time and energy toward eradicating the occupation regime. She discovered AD KAN soon after returning to Israel with two young children from an eighteen-year stay in the United States, yet not tenured at TAU. She was astonished to observe the participants' skills at organization, feeling somehow inept in their company. She was too timid to express an opinion and preferred to listen to participants better known for their ideological positions. As for now, she is recently retired but still engaged in research, teaching a team of assistants and often traveling abroad.

Elana's response to my query about present-day politics on campus started with the more common claims of despair on the part of most liberal residents (the "Tel-Avivians" as she named them) in view of growing right-wing influence among wider sectors of Israeli society. On campus, although most academics share a leftist viewpoint, politics are not part of daily discourse. There are small but impressive organizations outside the academy attending to the Palestinians' rights and welfare, but for the wider audience, the internet offers a virtual *communitas*. That makes a profound difference compared with the AD KAN days, when in order to share one's reaction to an acute social-political predicament with others, he/she needed face-to-face interaction.

In those days, Elana reflected, a widespread feeling persisted about the possibility of changing the reality of occupation and reaching a peaceful solution with the Palestinians. Today, however, no one believes that the evacuation of sites like Ariel (the major Jewish urban settlement in the West Bank) is a practical possibility. There is no effective organization opposing the West Bank settlements and the occupation regime that seem to have become a permanent reality. One consolation, she contemplated, is that the "two-countries solution" (Israel and Palestine) is still part of public deliberation inside and outside of Israel.

One of my last meetings was with Shlomo Sand, a somewhat younger AD KAN member and recently retired historian who is internationally renowned for such polemic books as *The Invention of the Jewish People* (2008) and *The Invention of the Land of Israel* (2012). He started his political engagement in Israel with Matzpen soon after 1967 but left when they fragmented two years later. He had no other political connections until he discovered AD KAN soon after he got his tenure position, a possibly delayed appointment due to his reputation as a "radical" leftist thinker. Most other core AD KAN members were already tenured and occupied senior positions. Sand perceived AD KAN participants as a group of liberal intellectuals whose "stomach turned over in turmoil" the minute they became aware of the young Palestinians' sudden rebellion against the occupation imposed by their own people. It was the end of a two-decade era of peaceful existence that started with the 1967 euphoria. Until the start of the intifada, there had been no organized eruption of violence to expose the Palestinians' mutiny against the apparently benevolent Israeli occupation.

When I posed my question about the absence of an organized Israeli academic response to the continuing occupation and its consequences for Israeli society, he emphasized in particular younger academics' "fear" about the prospects of appointment and promotion if their superiors were to consider them politically extremist. I was not aware of that potential element during my days as an active faculty member on campus, including time as a long-term representative on the social sciences faculty and the university committees of appointments and promotions. Sand assumed that the recent decline of student enrolment in the humanities and social sciences faculties impacted the scope of positions for younger scholars. And those recruited to the ranks might feel less secure, preferring to remain within a scholar's conventional habitual performance.

However, returning to the history of the 1990s, Sand expressed disappointment with PM Rabin, who failed to evacuate Hebron's Jewish settlers after Baruch Goldstein's massacre of Palestinians in the Cave of the Patriarchs.[3] Thus, Rabin revealed that there was no serious intention to implement the promise made to the Palestinians to halt the expansion of settlements. He blamed no less than PM Ehud Barak, who was partner to the failed Oslo agreements together with Ariel Sharon (head of the opposition at the time), who made his notorious visit to the Temple Mount that triggered the second intifada in 2000. The following horrific suicide bombings in central Israeli locations had a chilling effect on public morale and loss of confidence about the Palestinians' true motives in their quest of peace. That feeling of disappointment and panic also left its mark in the halls and corridors of the academy. Instead, the potential of protest found its expression in specialized civil organizations outside the institutional frameworks, serving the Palestinians' acute needs and protecting human rights under the regime of occupation (such as B'Tselem,[4] Checkpoint Watch,[5] and Physicians without Borders[6]), or focused protest groups operating inside Israel (such as Breaking the Silence, described later).

I last interviewed Dan Jacobson, an AD KAN member from the Social Sciences Faculty department of Labor Studies. Dani was among the very few in AD KAN's close circle engaged in national politics, as he was an active participant in the leftist Meretz party. As we sat down for coffee at the social sciences cafeteria for the first time in many years, he told me immediately, "We have failed!" He went on to explain that our endeavor at the time had not expanded its mission beyond the orbit of leftists in the local arena, and that we had not dedicated ourselves as "full-time" activists. For example, we continued following our professional goals, taking sabbaticals abroad rather than staying in peripheral Israeli towns to conduct educational programs among our less privileged countrymen (often Mizrahim, mostly supporting Likud and other right-wing parties). We performed our activities as sort of a part-time obligation while enjoying the company of our colleagues, meeting regularly in the same building we were having coffee. To my retort claiming that we were partners to the process that finally led to the Oslo Accords, Dani emphasized the international circumstances, the Americans' pressure in particular, strongly opposing PM Shamir's rejectionist attitude.

However, I queried, although we may have had little impact, why had no other group of academics taken on a similar mission at a later stage of the continuing conflict? Dani had a few suggestions. First, he labeled the experience "learned helplessness": a social psychology term for the syndrome identifying individuals and groups who give up performing a type of behavior or action that has repeatedly proven unsuccessful. Israeli leftists have lost hope that they can make a difference without an extraordinary internal or external development that might seriously risk the Israelis' present-day lives. Next, he suggested—reminiscent of Sand and others—that our generation enjoyed better and safer employment conditions in academia compared with the worsening circumstances for younger candidates looking for tenure-track positions. We were apparently able to risk antagonizing the campus administration and public opinion. Younger people today might be less willing to confront these hazards. His only daughter had actually been able to secure a position in an Israeli university. He is ambivalent about her potential participation in protest groups, considering his pessimistic view about the present trend of Israeli politics. But, he concluded, "we (AD KAN members) had a good life," and for the time being Israel seemed a safe haven in a stormy sea. In any case, he would not have considered moving out of Israel at any point, quoting a famous Israeli poet's epitaph: "A person is the product of his homeland's landscape." Dani said he could not imagine communicating in a foreign language as we do now.

In the meantime, Dani had since given up what he considered a "pathetic post-retirement ambition" to continue to pursue a professional career. He found an outlet in various volunteer activities for his energy and the feeling that he had become a forced partner to a dangerous regime. For example, he drives sick Palestinian children to Israeli hospitals for medical treatments (picking them up early in the morning at major checkpoints) and became a member of Save Israel Stop the Occupation (SISO), an organization calling on Israelis and Palestinians to break free of their historical demands and look for a solution based on present-day circumstances and options for a peace accord.

In conclusion, the interviews with core AD KAN members offer a complex picture of various perspectives on the past and present, though they often express the similar accounts of changes that Israeli and Palestinian societies, Israeli academia included, have gone through during the last twenty-five years. These claims often remind me of the public discourse voiced in Israeli "leftist" venues (for example, the *Haaretz* daily newspaper), which analyze the Israeli national political-ideological construction and the particular circumstances of university life. However, I end this reflexive portrayal of veterans' profiles returning to Ariella Friedman's nostalgic reminiscence, quoted above: "AD KAN was my home on campus." It was a transformative and moving experience for a group of men and women who have shared similar feelings of guilt and responded to a personal and collective trauma.

The next chapter expands on research methods and the issues raised by the veterans in view of a few reports and observations conducted among recent protest ventures in the Israeli arena.

Notes

1. In June 1982, the Israeli army invaded southern Lebanon after repeated attacks and counterattacks between the PLO and the IDF that caused civilian casualties on both sides of the border. The war resulted in the PLO's expulsion from Lebanon. Israel withdrew its forces from Lebanon in January 1985.
2. Matzpen, a radical socialist movement founded in 1962 calling for Jews and Arabs to recognize the Palestinians' national rights.
3. Baruch Goldstein was an American-Israeli physician and religious extremist who perpetrated the 1994 Cave of the Patriarchs massacre in Hebron. The attack left 29 Palestinians dead and 125 wounded. Goldstein was beaten to death by the survivors.
4. B'Tselem, the Israeli Information Center for Human Rights.
5. Checkpoint Watch, a volunteer organization dedicated to monitoring the behavior of soldiers and police at the border checkpoints where Palestinians enter or return from Israeli territories.
6. Physicians without Borders, an international human rights organization that includes Israeli participants.

15

Past and Present Israeli Protestors Reconsidered

My encounters with the AD KAN veterans exploring their experiences did not employ an inventive methodological or theoretical framework compared to Donna J. Perry's (2011) interviews with eighteen participants of Combatants for Peace (CFP), a movement formed in 2005 by Israelis and Palestinians: eight IDF reserve combat soldiers who refused to serve in the occupied territories and ten Palestinians who were serving time in Israeli jails for violent acts but who renounced violent resistance. An American, and a nurse in her professional background, Perry used "transcendent pluralism" as the theoretical framework to guide her study:

> The purpose of transcendent pluralism is to address problems of human devaluation through the identification and implementation of strategies by which people can respond to one another more fully as human beings and move toward fulfilling the human potential of living in dignity. This approach offers a method of inquiry from which to explore the cognitional processes within an individual decision … and within a particular community, cultural, and historical context. (pp. 11–12)

As claimed by Perry, that research approach to the interviews influenced the participants' ability to "enter interior self-reflection" and to feel comfortable communicating those reflections. Her background as a nurse had also been helpful in creating an atmosphere of therapeutic inquiry and trust (p. 169). In short, Perry suggested that the participants' decision to commit to nonviolent action and join the CFP involved a personal and interpersonal transformation.

Promoting a therapeutic message of reconciliation and joint Israeli-Palestinian amity, Perry advocated efforts to support mutual binational transformation. (The study was reviewed and approved by the Partners Healthcare Human Research Committee.)

The same CFP organization was reported in a later publication, *Conscientious Objectors in Israel* (2014), an ethnographic project conducted by American anthropologist Erica Weiss (presently teaching at TAU). For a few years, the author regularly attended public meetings with members of the group, who often addressed audiences of interested Israelis where they confessed experiences from their army service in the occupied territories that caused them to refuse their military obligations. The vast majority of self-identified conscientious objectors came from the upper crust of Israeli society, highly educated, "secular Ashkenazi Jews, whose original vision of Zionism imagined being able to balance between Jewish and liberal democratic ideals, have slowly found its world shrinking and closing in for them, from non-Jews to non-liberal political philosophies" (p. 53). More dramatically, "Israeli conscientious objectors went from being mainstream heroes to counterculture heroes" (p. 60). CFP testimonies divulge individual responsibility and guilt for actions the speaker took under orders. However, the ethnographer's observations reveal CFP testimonies about brutal treatment of Palestinians during military service in the occupied territories as performances that seek to persuade the audience to embrace the conscientious objectors' moral claims. Weiss's research also includes a group of younger objectors, men and women in their early twenties who had never served in the military; among them were many pacifists loosely associated with a feminist organization that favors demilitarizing Israeli society.

Relying also on other commentators on Israeli society (e.g., the Hebrew University sociologist, Kimmerling 2001), Weiss relates the conscientious objectors' disillusionment in part to the loss of influence of the Israeli secular left, whose worldview has been challenged by those who threaten their social dominance and moral values. A number of demographic and political developments have prevented this secular national promise from coming to fruition: for example, the expansion of the ultra-Orthodox sector, cultural trends among Middle Eastern Jews (Mizrahim) maintaining a kind of mild religiosity, and the problematic reality of Israeli Arabs as part of a de facto Jewish country. Finally, she writes, "the disillusionment my interlocutors of both generations experienced with military service went hand in hand with a growing disillusionment in Zionism" (p. 169). Obviously, these later studies mirror what has become a sort of lingua franca among a wide spectrum of Israeli "leftist/liberal" interlocutors, AD KAN veterans included.

Though not directly related to the subject of protest, I mention here a different research approach taken by Ochs (2011), an American anthropologist who conducted an ethnography of everyday life in two urban locations during the second intifada period (2003–4). Her observations, titled *Security and Suspicion*, tried to comprehend her Israeli subjects' response to the Palestinians' violent revolt (suicide bombers, etc.), as much affected by fear and desires for security even when political tensions did not so overtly dominate life (p. 28). That discourse of fear is reminiscent of AD KAN member Sasha Weitman's story about his daughter who got off the bus one stop before it exploded, killing and injuring many Israelis. No doubt, the atmosphere of fear, though probably not as overpowering in "daily life" as Ochs suggests, impacted public empathy toward the Palestinian cause, emboldened right-wing attitudes, and weakened protest activities.

My meetings with AD KAN's veterans employed the standard method of interpersonal communication used in earlier ethnographic studies, though I did not embark on a new field-site research project as did Perry, Weiss, and Ochs. I did not use a semi-clinical research apparatus, resembling a therapeutic technique, to conduct past and present observations and interviews. Moreover, I knew the participants well as colleagues on campus, and I had no intention of revealing their in-depth life histories prior to joining the movement, unless that was their desire. Furthermore, my report was not intended to expose a method to stimulate personal transformations supportive of nonviolent action and promote genuine peace in this troubled region. In conclusion, I shared with my subjects a similar social background, a common professional circle, and a national culture and history, circumstances that differ from those of most other early (e.g., Kaminer 1996) and later researchers of Israeli protest movements. Naturally, I cannot claim the position of "neutrality" and "objectivity," a premise that mainstream anthropologists who study "other" societies have also given up in recent years considering their observations and analytical conclusions.

The conversations with the veterans comparing the period of the first intifada with present-day circumstances naturally displayed evidence of critical transformations within Israeli society since then: the trauma and the aftermath of the assassination of PM Rabin and his replacement by Netanyahu; the growing power of right-wing and religious parties supported by recent immigrants from the former

Soviet Union, considered "antisocialists" (a disparaging image ascribed to leftist parties) and overtly nationalistic, as well as by a significant number of American Orthodox Jews attracted to the West Bank settlements; the continuing expansion of settlements and their population in the occupied territories (orchestrated by PM Sharon) as well as in the new Jewish neighborhoods in the outskirts of East Jerusalem; the demographic trends of high birthrates increasing the Orthodox and ultra-Orthodox sectors; and the continuing tendency of Mizrahi Israelis and residents of poorer peripheral locations to resent leftist parties assumed to represent the old-timer Ashkenazim, blamed for discriminating against the "Oriental" newcomers during the mass immigration of the 1950s and 1960s.

But they emphasized that the academy itself has changed, becoming "privatized," emphasizing the individual's safe professional environment, privileges, and ambitions, and allowing academics to avoid investment in collegial solidarity (in campus departmental units and other local professional forums). Faculty members fulfill their formal obligations of teaching, supervising, and attending to administrative chores, but they circumvent socio-professional volunteer activities in view of a reluctant audience in the close and wider arenas. To that argument, I add an observation that I have found evident in recent years: the attendance of faculty in departmental seminars and workshops not directly related to one's subject has shrunk over the years. The "staff seminar" at the TAU sociology and anthropology department was a major social event during the 1970s–90s, and most teachers and advanced students attended, regardless of the theme of presentation.

The veterans identified no less significant changes in the behavior of their Palestinian counterparts since their unarmed fight for freedom: the rise of Hamas in Gaza; the intensified aggressive methods of the Palestinians' "terror" response to the Israeli civil and military occupation; the use of live ammunition, suicide bombers, and knife stabbings, which replaced the first unarmed intifada's massive stone-throwing demonstrations, labor and markets boycotts, etc.

The veterans reflected on the ongoing decline of the Israeli left-wing parties that have lost much of their power, leaving the mostly secular, liberal, and better-educated sector, often referred to disparagingly the "old Ashkenazi elite," in a position of political isolation. Its own members often label this constituency as "residents of the State of Tel Aviv"—the "Tel-Avivians" in Elana Shohamy's terms—a socio-cultural-political niche separate from the national body. Unsurprisingly, the leftist and centrist parties competing for the same electorate are unable to act in concert and join forces. Moreover, the religious parties are comfortable partners to a rightist coalition government usually more tolerant and supportive of religious traditions. The ultra-Orthodox parties, in particular, are mostly eager for financial support to sponsor their educational system and subsidize many thousands of male students fully engaged in Yeshiva studies, free of military service and fathering growing families. Although the Palestinian issue has little importance in the agenda of most religious parties, they are inclined to support a worldview and actions that sanctify the possession of the Land of Israel as promised to the children of Abraham.

Last and unexpectedly, I met in August 2017 with Karen Wainer, an architect who helped organize a petition during the first year of the intifada (12 August 1988), signed and paid for by one hundred architects, mostly from Jerusalem. The petition warned against taking part in building projects in any Jewish settlements in the occupied territories. The message accused anyone engaging in the process of town planning or construction—in the roles of contractor, engineer, or architect—of promoting the continuing program of occupation and adversely affecting the lives of the people trapped under that regime. As she told me, the signers were mostly colleagues and friends at the Jerusalem Bezalel School of Architecture, other local institutions, and professional firms: "It was the family."

The organizers were in touch with the Twenty-First Year protest organization, which was active at the time in Jerusalem and Tel Aviv. The activists were thrilled when the petition came out, having assumed that architects elsewhere were not trying to resist state authorities. True, they were disappointed that a few of the leading figures in the profession refused to join their call. Nevertheless, among the signers was Arthur Goldreich, founder of Bezalel School of Architecture and famous anti-apartheid activist in South Africa, who gave shelter to Nelson Mandela and his colleagues on his farm.

However, this was the last public endeavor of that group initiative. Looking back at the intifada period and observing present-day political reality, Karen, who was born in South Africa to a family that left the apartheid regime, seemed deeply pessimistic. A trip she had taken a few months earlier, arranged by the Breaking the Silence organization (a recently founded protest group of IDF soldiers who publicly confess the acts of brutality they carried out during their active service), convinced her that the settlements project in the West Bank had become a fait accompli of continuing occupation. The settlements had turned into a geographical extension of the evaporated

Green Line border and an institutional replica of the pre-1967 Israeli communities.

To my question, "Why have we failed?" Karen used as an example the Twenty-First Year organization's leaders, who were engrossed in their polemical abstract style and detached from the wider Israeli public. They exhibited a sort of "elitism" that typifies most protest movements. In addition, "we" were not actively engaged in rejectionist activities, unlike, for example, the Checkpoint Watch group's dedicated women or Breaking the Silence's reservist soldiers. Signing a petition did not demand any labor, "and in reality," she admitted, architects have little impact on the system of territorial expansion. In an exasperated tone, Karen uttered, "Basically everyone wants to design a Pitsou Kedem villa ..."[1] However, she went on, "I continue attending all protest demonstrations for peace and against the occupation, though I know they have no effect. I meet the same people who feel the same ..."

Although the architects' one-time public initiative did not resemble most other protest movements emerging during the first intifada, it seemed to represent the zeitgeist of that time. Moreover, Karen's mood reflected the disenfranchisement that a significant cohort of Israelis often feel in a changing sociopolitical environment. The architects who organized the 1988 petition must have taken their model from other groups of committed professionals who acted during the first intifada (e.g., health practitioners, social workers, psychologists, the "purely academic" recruits of the Twenty-First Year and AD KAN). Their initiative came from a leading academic institution—Bezalel School of Architecture. However, compared with other protest groups, they did not develop a strong organizational structure that could maintain and generate continuing activities. As suggested, joining their call of dissent might have affected work opportunities among architects, a potential sacrifice not necessarily endured by other protesting professionals at that time. Nevertheless, the Jerusalem architects' ephemeral experiment with protest seemed to encapsulate the atmosphere of urgency engulfing a wider constituency of professionals and academics and deeply committed Israeli citizens during that critical moment.

As it turned out, my meeting with the Jerusalem architect had a follow-up a few months later, when I took a trip to the West Bank city of Hebron with Breaking the Silence. An NGO established in 2004, BTS intended to give on-duty, discharged, and reservist IDF personnel the chance to recount their distressing experiences while serving in the occupied territories. These testimonies are collected to educate the Israeli public about the reality of Palestinian lives under Israeli military control. However, some BTS publications and public appearances outside the country have raised the military and civil authorities' severe condemnations for defaming the Israeli army's reputation by spreading unproven accusations.

Outraged when the ongoing public campaign against the group made a false allegation about a leading figure in the organization, I decided to join a trip to Hebron organized by Breaking the Silence, despite my determination never to travel to that city. The historical site of the Cave of the Patriarchs there has become a focus of continuing daily conflict since a group of about eight hundred Israeli settlers and Yeshiva school students occupied a few compounds close to the sacred monument. However, we traveled instead to an area close to Hebron, South Hebron Mountain, which hosts both old-age Palestinian villages and recently built Jewish communities. I also made an additional trip a few months later to Hebron, described later on.

I spent the bright Friday morning in the company of ten young and middle-aged Israeli citizens and two Breaking the Silence guides. It had taken me fifty years to cross the Green Line border and see the striking views of the West Bank hills, woods, and spread-out villages and towns. We first stopped at Khirbet Susya, a small Palestinian village where people dwell in caves less than a mile from the attractive new buildings on the nearby hill of the Jewish settlement. The settlement was founded in 1983, and its name is taken from the nearby ancient Jewish town of Susya, whose archeological findings date it to the first millennium.

We were depressed and embarrassed as we listened to our Palestinian hosts, and later observed the pitiless measures carried out by Israeli authorities, the army included, to force the Palestinians to evacuate their grazing-season cave-dwelling territory and move to an urban center a few miles away. Only the support of European NGOs has enabled them to stay on, defend their legal rights, build temporary huts to replace caves destroyed by the military, and provide alternative means for water supply (their waterholes were also damaged). We did not visit the nearby Jewish settlement, aware that the company of Breaking the Silence guides would not have endeared us to settlers, the self-styled modern-day pioneers who came to salvage our shared ancestors' land. As we were walking out of the site greeted by our hosts, I overheard an Israeli woman, a participant in the visiting group, calling out toward them: "I am ashamed."

We stopped at a Bedouin village, whose inhabitants had moved to the site after the 1948 war. The nearby Jewish settlers of Carmel, who had crossed the Bedouins' land with electricity cables and water pipelines, did not offer their neighbors the privilege of sharing these improved services. That day of excursion in the "land beyond the mountains" (a title of a film based on the report of novelist and journalist Nir Baram), led me to concur with Karen Wainer, who had taken a similar trip, that no end of the occupation and no solution to its inevitable ruthless regime would soon be forthcoming.

On Saturday, I was still too agitated and edgy to erase the previous day's experience from my thoughts. As before, I took "refuge" by expressing that tense mood in a short article, in which I narrated a few major points related to the trip. I conveyed my admiration for the young Breaking the Silence soldiers, who show no fear in confronting a violent opposition of crude nationalists pretending to protect the Jewish people and their national heritage supported by Minister of Justice Ayelet Shaked, a bold right-winger. However, I admitted that, despite my fifty-year avoidance of crossing the Green Line border, I had joined the wide fellowship of reticent good people who have accommodated the reality of occupation and continued with their daily routine, though they are sometimes offended by the BDS accusations. That short expression of personal frustration was published in *Haaretz* the next Friday under the title "I Also Have Been an Occupation Disclaimer" (24 November 2017). To my surprise, that piece received many responses of both support and opposition, and Breaking the Silence posted it on its Facebook page.

A few months later, I joined another trip to Hebron sponsored by Breaking the Silence. In the company of about thirty mostly young men and women, I visited the city itself for the first time. Approaching the site, we first stopped at Kiryat Arba, an urban Jewish settlement built in the early 1970s adjacent to Hebron that hosts about seven thousand residents. We visited the local park named after Rabbi Meir Kahane, founder of the Jewish Defense League (JDL) in the United States and the ultra-nationalist party Kach ("Thus Only"), which was banned by the Israeli government for its racist agenda. He was assassinated in Manhattan on 5 November 1990. I clearly remember the memorial service held in Brooklyn before his funeral. What an irony, stopping unexpectedly in front of an imposing memorial dedicated to that same person, which took me back to that day in Brooklyn.

I visited Brooklyn, home to various Jewish orthodox communities, with a friend in November 1990, looking for an expert to confirm the authenticity of a Torah scroll donated to the gay synagogue in New York (the site of my research at that time). Unaware of the hectic events taking place on that day, we soon bumped into an enormous crowd of mourners who packed Kahane's synagogue and the streets surrounding the site. On leaving a lunch counter, we noticed a group of men heatedly discussing the story of the day with a reporter who interviewed them about the deceased and his accomplishments. Curious about the commotion, we joined in and listened to the words of praise and sorrow expressed by all commentators. Suddenly, the reporter turned to where I was standing behind the dense circle of men (I probably looked a bit different from the mostly Orthodox crowd) and asked who I was and how I reacted to the tragic event. Surprisingly, my response reached the *New York Times*: a colleague informed me the next day that he discovered my presence in New York on reading about the "interview" the day before (6 November 1990). An article by Ari L. Goldman, titled "Grief and Anger at Kahane's Funeral," included the following paragraph:

> In front of a kosher pizza parlor, however, one visitor from Israel had a different sentiment. "I don't think Kahane had something good to bring to the world," said Moshe Shokeid, an anthropologist from Tel Aviv who is spending a sabbatical in the United States. "Kahane planted hatred in Israel. I will shed no tears."

Twenty-seven years later, as I visited a public playground erected by Israeli authorities, named after a Jew who preached hatred and violence against the Palestinians, and situated close to the center of present-day binational conflict, I beheld the first of many disturbing views and experiences of the day trip. Moreover, at the center of Kahane's Park, we came across the revered gravesite of Dr. Baruch Goldstein, American-Israeli physician, resident of Kiryat Arba, religious extremist, and member of the far-right Kahane's Kach movement. Goldstein perpetrated the 1994 Cave of the Patriarchs massacre, in which he killed 29 Palestinian worshipers and wounded another 125. He was beaten to death by survivors of the massacre. Thus, at the very beginning of our journey to Hebron, a site sacred to Jews and Muslims as children of Abraham, we were already confronted by the legacy of two personalities venerated by the self-appointed custodians of Jewish historical rights in the Land of Israel and Hebron in particular. However, the two are intensely reviled by most others who want a peaceful solution to end the regime of occupation.

From this spot, our Breaking the Silence guides led us to the center of Hebron. At last I saw the façade of the impressive monument hosting the Cave of the Patriarchs, a space now serving both as a mosque and a synagogue to local and visiting Jews and Muslims. The site located at Shuhada Street, the main business avenue of Hebron, seemed to be missing the regular city-center business venues, traffic congestion, and human bustling. All shops along the street were shut, permanently locked up under military order. The only cars moving around were those driven by groups of tourists and a few Jewish settlers. Armed soldiers stationed at a nearby police checkpoint controlled the road, apparently abandoned by the town's Muslim population of two hundred thousand residents. It reminded me of Giorgio De Chirico's disquieting surrealistic paintings of empty city squares.

We walked along the street, renamed The Valley of Hebron Road, viewing the few compounds for Jewish settlers. Hosting about eight hundred residents, the sites had been built in the time since Dr. Goldstein's massacre on locations evacuated by Jews after the Arabs' riots and massacre of 1929. Sixty-seven Hebron Jews were brutally murdered in 1929 and the four-hundred-year-old community of about eight hundred residents was evacuated. No doubt, the 1929 massacre of Jews in Hebron remained a dramatic example of the developing conflict between Jews and Palestinians that reached its violent climax in the 1948 war after the failed UN plan to partition Palestine. However, the return of Jews to Hebron since the 1967 war offers another symbolic demonstration, not to mention actual proof, of the tragic reality separating Israelis and Palestinians, led by extremists on both sides who reject any sign of human clemency and political compromise.

After a delay of about an hour, the army personnel allowed us to climb up the hill overlooking Hebron and visit the settlers' site of Tel Rumeida. As it turned out, the Jewish residents who discovered the identity of the Breaking the Silence visitors refused to let us get close to their compound of newly built modern apartment buildings. As we waited for the army's permission to let us go through, a few settlers approached us and tried to incite a noisy debate and a public clash. However, we evaded that provocation as we had evaded the hateful screams of a few local women who aimed epithets toward the visitors looking around the site. We were aggravated by the scene of the Palestinian dwellings overlooking the Jewish apartment complex, whose balconies and windows were barricaded with iron bars to protect against the settlers' aggressive strikes.

At the end of the day we returned to Tel Aviv, depressed by the scene of a few hundred messianic settlers obstructing the normal life of thousands of Palestinian residents and paralyzing the urban center of a major city—as well as avenging the sad end of Hebron's Jewish community. On my return home, I wrote a short "ethnographic" summary of that "fieldwork" experience, recommending decent citizens to take the trip to Hebron. The letter to *Haaretz* (26 February 2018) was published under the title "The Victory of Baruch Goldstein" after the perpetrator of the 1994 massacre at the Cave of the Patriarchs. It was the aftermath of his action and the legacy of his "sacrifice" for the sake of redeeming Jewish Hebron that facilitated the reclamation of a few old Jewish sites, recruiting the most extremist Israeli nationalists to settle at the heart of Hebron regardless of the security risks involved. However, failing to react forcefully to Goldstein's crime and his followers' aggressive settlement strategy, the Israeli government instead instigated security measures, including the closure of the Shuhada Street that paralyzed Hebron's city center.

The extremely aggravating reality taking place about an hour's drive from Tel Aviv had been previously far removed from the daily life experiences of and information available to most of the travelers who had joined the trip guided by Breaking the Silence members. BTS's methods of participation differ from those of most other protest groups, whose activities include demonstrations in public city squares, signing lists of supporters, and promoting meetings and lectures. The BTS trips enabled the participants to get close to the scene of conflict and see for themselves the terms of the continuing occupation so close to home.

A moving response to my trip report came in a letter from retired General Shlomo Gazit, who inaugurated the military-political-economic administration of the territories occupied in 1967 and later headed the IDF intelligence body (introduced in chapter 2). Since retirement, he had openly expressed political positions considered today as "leftist." He authored books and other publications about his thoughts and experiences concerning past and present Israeli security and future options. In his response, he indicated that PM Rabin's hesitation to react strongly to Goldstein's massacre was a grave mistake, setting the stage for the Palestinians' mortal acts of revenge that influenced the demise of the Oslo Accords. I discovered that Gazit had initiated a one-man protest "e-mail movement," forwarding a weekly newsletter to a wide network of friends and acquaintances to inform them of his observations and analysis about current Israeli government policies related to the continuing conflict. He seems deeply worried about the consequences of the continuing belligerent situation. In a personal communication (March 2018), he added, "I will continue writing these memos as long as my body allows it [at ninety-two years old]. These will become my defense account when asked in Heavens 'what have I done to save my country?'"

In conclusion, most politically leftist voluntary protest groups have disappeared or lost much of their impact, including the leading Peace Now movement. Over and above the various Israeli NGOs mentioned above and other groups offering support and protection to the Palestinians, Breaking the Silence currently presents the most visibly potent protest organization in the Israeli public arena. But compared with the history and position of political opposition in earlier days, it enjoys a far less supportive public response.

Unexpectedly, it took me a few more months and a visit to a Columbia University neighborhood bookstore to find the most painful recent record of the violent encounters between Jewish settlers and Palestinian villagers in the hills of South Hebron, the scene reported in this chapter. *Freedom and Despair: Notes from the South Hebron Hills* (2018) is an account by David Shulman, a distinguished Hebrew University scholar of Eastern languages and religions and a founding member of Ta'ayush, a grassroots volunteer organization established in 2000 as an Arab-Jewish partnership to counter the nationalist reactions aroused by the Al-Aqsa Intifada. Its mission advocates for justice and peace through daily nonviolent actions of solidarity in order to confront the Israeli occupation of Palestinian territories. Its members restrict their activities to interfering with incidents triggered by West Bank settlers of infringement on Palestinian subsistence farmers and shepherds' rights of land ownership, limitation on the free movement of their cattle, or victimization of Palestinians through physical attacks instigated by sheer nationalistic malice.

Shulman reports on his occasional visits to the West Bank in the company of Ta'ayush members trying to assist Palestinian victims of vicious attacks enacted by Jewish settlers in the presence of—or collaboration with—Israeli police and soldiers. His detailed record reads like a horror story. His book is an ardent indictment against the Israeli regime of occupation, a testimony of personal shame and agony narrated by an Israeli academic who cannot feel free until his Palestinian acquaintances feel equally free on the Hebron hills. The circle of Ta'ayush involves a few more respected Hebrew University academics, but its wider membership represents a variety of dedicated men and women. My two "educational" trips to Hebron and its surrounding hills offered me a superficial glimpse into the grim reality the Ta'ayush comrades have often actively experienced in conflict situations, involving aggressive disputes, legal claims, as well as their occasional arrests for "disturbing the peace."

In short, Combatants for Peace, Breaking the Silence, and Ta'ayush, represent a wider network of present-day voluntary associations recruiting Israeli citizens dedicated to supporting Palestinians' human rights under the Israeli regime of occupation. However, different from the first intifada era, these deeply committed groups have not formed a forceful unified front of a mass movement advocating for the end of occupation, able to impact public opinion and leave their mark on the national political arena.

I will continue by exploring some critical interpretations of the persistent political impasse and its consequences suggested by leading Israeli intellectuals, among them university colleagues and other influential commentators.

Note

1. Pitsou Kedem is a famous Israeli architect known for his attractive private homes.

16

Israeli and Other Critics' Commentary on the Continuing Occupation

It is not surprising that the mood among veteran AD KAN members seemed mostly somber. They were withdrawing to the personal-family domain, engaged in professional postretirement projects, or volunteering in support of Palestinian humanitarian issues, leaving the stage for a younger generation to take care of the changing national scene. I will conclude their discourse on past and present realities linked to a wider perspective of commentators constructing the present dominant features of Israeli society.

The continuing conflict in the small contested enclave of the "Holy Land" on the shores of the Mediterranean has been a subject of innumerable reports and interpretations by insiders and outsiders. For some time it has been considered one of the most threatening locations, a scene of insoluble conflict affecting world affairs both close and remote. However, the Iraq War, the rise and fall of the Arab Spring, and the devastating situations that developed in the region later (the ongoing warfare and humanitarian disaster in Syria in particular), unrelated to the Israel-Palestine conflict, seem to have reduced its attraction in world media and on the academic stage. In any case, the conflict has incessantly produced multiple types of voices within Israeli society, though those critical of the continuing occupation have been most eloquent. These include leading journalists and public intellectuals who author daily newspaper commentaries, celebrated novelists (e.g., Amos Oz, David Grossman, and A. B. Yehoshua) who have published an impressive list of books, and professionals representing various disciplines. However, it seems an impossible mission to report on that enormous corpus of writings that have attempted to comprehend the intractable conflict, often expressing similar interpretations and conclusions. I have chosen to represent a short list of reviewers with whom I share some personal history or professional kinship.

I begin with a recent record from a few prominent Israeli scholars, among them a political scientist, a psychologist, and two sociologists who tried to reveal the socio-psycho-historical dynamics sustaining the occupation regime since 1967. Not surprising, they all represent leftist perspectives. It seemed needless to me to display a "just" presentation of both sides of the debate. I left the texts of right-wing reporters and ideologues to the discourse with their leftist interlocutors.

Rubber Bullets (1997) by Yaron Ezrahi (d. 2019), a respected Hebrew University political scientist and activist, is the earliest commentary in the following list. His testimony carries the salient personal exposure of his own history and that of his family, unlike most other critics introduced in our records. The narrative starts with the moment that instigated his impulse to explore divisive present-day Israeli national politics: a "revelation" in January 1988, a few weeks after the start of the first intifada, shared with the author's colleagues and his AD KAN associates. As he professes, Israel is a place where the mood and spirit of ordinary lives are affected by politics, where biography can reflect a moment in history. The text integrates the aftermath of PM Rabin's killing and the following political paralysis.

Ezrahi's multifaceted narrative indicates a few major themes, analyzing the impact of Jewish history over the development of the character and status of the Israeli individual versus the ethos of the community and public life; the transformation of a persecuted minority into a powerful force and its application in present-day reality; the right-wingers' enchantment with the sensation of national liberation and wish to use the gained power to extend the Zionist mission over the occupied territories; and, in contrast, the individualistic-liberal-democratic camp's citizens' desire to restrict its relevance to narrower boundaries. Ezrahi eloquently summarizes these contradictory positions in the following statement:

> Modern Israel has been beset by a bitter struggle between those who believe that earth belongs to the living and those who believe that the living belongs to the earth—that it is their duty to make sacrifices to ensure that the land under Israeli control will remain the land of the Jewish people. (p. 71)

Rubber Bullets takes its name from the technical solution the Israeli army invented during the first intifada to stop the demonstrators without killing and seriously wounding them. However, he suggests, these "gentle" bullets represent Israel's intention to reframe the conflict, to see it not as a war of survival but as a struggle between a civilian population and an occupying force. The rubber bullets symbolize the inherent tensions between nationalism and democracy, between the ethos of a national home for the Jewish people and the universal values of freedom and equality—the founding blocks of Zionism. The election of Netanyahu as prime minister in 1996 (following the killing of PM Rabin) indicated the persistence of considerable support for religious-nationalist visions of unachieved chapters of a Jewish epic. Not surprising, on both the Israeli and Arab sides, moral and religious absolutists are inclined to demonize each other and justify extreme forms of violence, reinforcing each other's epic vision.

Ezrahi's evocative closing scene portrays his climb up to the Mount of Olives in East Jerusalem to visit the grave of his great-grandfather, who died in 1929. He ruminates: "How far can the commitment to the value and freedom of the individual coexist with the commitment to Judaism, Jewish communitarianism, Jewish religious practices, Jewish culture, and the memory of our fathers?" (p. 294).

Leon Sheleff's *The Thin Green Line* (2005), published posthumously, recounts the vision and life commitment of a close colleague of mine at the department of sociology and partner to the founding of AD KAN, who passed away suddenly in 2003 after delivering a paper at the Van Leer Institute in Jerusalem. The "Green Line" embodies Israel's internationally recognized pre-1967 borders with its Arab neighbors. The post-1967 Jewish settlements in the occupied territories are deemed "beyond the Green Line." That extension of settlements broke the Israeli geographical bodyline into a sort of a fluid jellyfish-shaped frame. For many young Israelis, the Green Line map is no longer a potent picture of their homeland. Sheleff alluded to that pre-1967 map as a symbolic peaceful return to a national body contained within legitimate stable boundaries.

At this junction, it seems compelling to narrate my unexpected meeting with the Green Line and its mundane ramifications in the real sense of the term. Sometime during the first intifada, I was cited by the police for a speed violation (115 kilometers per hour, above the 100-kilometer max) on my way to Jerusalem and was ordered to appear before a traffic court there. Naturally, I was nervous at having to show up for the first time as a defendant in a court of law.

Fending for myself with no convincing excuse to the alleged misdemeanor, and before I made my "presentation," the judge exclaimed, "*Shetach efker!*" (no-man's land) and dismissed my case. It took me a while to comprehend that I had been caught speeding on a piece of road (recently constructed close to the site of Latrun monastery) going through an area considered "no man's land" on both sides of the Green Line that separated Israel and Jordan until 1967. Therefore, that zone was not under Israeli (or Jordanian) jurisdiction. I was at first dismayed by the judge's incomprehensible exclamation that let me off with no penalty—but then, deeply amused, I cried out, "Am I free until the arrival of the Messiah?" I must have benefitted from the efforts of another offender's lawyer who discovered that loophole of legal reality. However, the judge pretended not to hear my humorous remark at that scene of incredible absurdity. Although a surrealistic end of the story played out on the road to Jerusalem, it was nevertheless a symbolic reminder of a geopolitical border almost forgotten in daily Israeli life. An AD KAN friend, puzzled to discover that the Green Line had a life of its own, informed me that a local newspaper reported on my exceptional experience.

Sheleff, born and raised in apartheid South Africa and combining a career in law and sociology, could not reconcile with the reality of a Jewish-Israeli regime subjugating another people and controlling their land. Although not religious in a conventional orthodox manner of belief and practice, he felt committed to Jewish history, culture, and morality, and he regularly attended a liberal synagogue. His professional expertise had served his volunteering activities, such as defending victims of human rights injustices in court and representing Gadi Algazi, later professor of history at TAU, whose suit was among the first publicly announced cases of Israeli conscientious objectors.

The subtitle of his book offers a testimony to the man's character and his program for future evolution: *From Intractable Problems to Feasible Solutions in the Israeli-Palestinian Conflict*. The first paragraph informs us of his mood at the time of writing:

> It was a period of despair, particularly among those of Left-wing persuasion in the peace camp, at the breakdown of the Oslo peace process and the dissipation of the sanguine hopes for an end to the century-long dispute with the Palestinians. (p. 9)

However, examining the causes of failure on both sides, he keeps an optimistic view, claiming that there are amicable and easily applicable methods for resolving the presumably intractable problems "through a proper re-definition of the issues." The following chapters deal with the major issues, such as "Figment of the Imagination," in which he discusses a solution for the undivided Jerusalem. He envisions it becoming the capital of two independent states, resembling other cities of international standing and fulfilling a unique role of global institutions—capital cities that are "artificially created." He moves on to suggest a solution to the future accommodation and peaceful interaction between the two states: establishing a confederation. The two populations today are inextricably intertwined: Jewish settlers in the West Bank, Palestinians working in Israel, and the Arab minority citizens in Israel who have close ties with their brethren in the occupied areas. A confederation is therefore an ideal solution.

However, these imaginative solutions cannot be implemented before the Israeli officialdom is prepared to refer to the State of Israel and the State of Palestine in equal terms, showing sensitivity to the Palestinians' plight and legitimate aspirations. Sheleff found support for his visionary picture of a binational accommodation in the failed story of the Oslo Accords, whose promoters, he mentioned, are named in some right-wing quarters "the Oslo traitors." In contradiction, he argued, it was the first intifada that raised public awareness and gave birth to the protest movements that led to the Oslo peace treaty. The treaty failed because of mistakes committed by both sides. However, the time is ripe for a new experiment following the pains of the second intifada. Sheleff, an ardent optimist, undoubtedly believed strongly that it was not a delusional program: "I am writing this in the midst of a climate of general frustration and despondency, aware of the total disparity between the vicious reality of today and fervent hopes of previous years, between the present poisonous atmosphere on both sides, and the yet persistent, lingering belief in the need for and possibility of reconciliation" (p. 170).

Fifteen years have passed since he left that dreamlike document in view of our grave reality. However, Sheleff was not a fanatic or a delusional character. It is enough to mention the lesson from South Africa, his birthplace. Who would have predicted that in 1994 the white minority regime would peacefully give up its coercive domain over the black majority, permit free elections for all, and establish the government of national unity? Equally, who would have predicted the 1998 Good Friday Agreement in Northern Ireland?

TAU psychologist Daniel Bar-Tal's *Living with the Conflict* (2007) concentrates on the psychological dimension that dominates most intractable, apparently insoluble conflicts. The background of that complex syndrome includes collective memories, the ethos of the conflict, and a collective emotional orientation (p. 30). Societies in conflict nourish contradictory historical collective memories and a self-invented communal past. On the Israeli side, the final collapse of the Oslo Accords with the start of the far more violent second intifada (suicide bombers, etc.) in 2000 revived the old historical mentality of a society under siege, the Jewish tragic experience implanted in the epitaph "the world against us." The long history of anti-Semitism and the more recent Holocaust trauma made the Jewish-Israelis suspicious and distrustful of other world societies' intentions. More specifically, the conflict is being perceived by the Israeli public as a battle of the survivors against the inheritors of the Nazi tormentors rather than as a clash between two national collectives fighting for their existence.

Bar-Tal calls on Victor Turner's (1969) interpretation of the function of rituals and ceremonies in society as reminders of their members' collective memories that recruit them to act against their common enemies. Thus, he scans the Israeli panorama of symbolic dedications and annual commemorations of the birth of a nation, the Holocaust, the Israeli wars, and the fallen soldiers. Some educational methods that might impose the collective memory of victimhood include high school students' regular trips to concentration camps in Poland. Equally effective are the TV news reports that vividly demonstrate terror casualties and add a dramatically tragic impression to the atmosphere of tension and fear.

The incessant engagement with collective memory creates shared orientations of fear and hope regardless of political leanings. Despite the sociopolitical polarization of Israeli society between left and right, "security" (*bitachon*) remains a major symbol in the Israeli ethos—easily employed to recruit public support and deep commitment during any national threat. It is no surprise that the second intifada in 2000 had detrimental consequences for both sides. The Israeli peace camp lost about half of its hold compared with its support during the 1990s, and the 2006 Second Lebanon War caused further damage to its sway in Israeli society. Therefore, Bar-Tal concludes that the shift from an intractable conflict to a peace process demands a change in the psychosocial foundations of the engaged societies. It requires a change of the hegemonic psycho repertoire of collective memories of animosities, violence, fear, and hatred. Otherwise, the conflict may survive for generations, exemplified by the Irish case.

Bar-Tal's exposition of the roots of the existential experience of fear are reminiscent of Juliana Ochs's ethnography *Security and Suspicion* (2011) presented earlier, which was conducted during the second intifada. Ochs, the alien anthropologist, had offered direct observations to the "native" psychologist's exploration of the history and symptoms of national fears.

A Half Century of Occupation (2017) by Gershon Shafir, a sociologist and former student and colleague at TAU who left for the United States years ago, raised my interest. I was curious how my ex-compatriot would evoke from afar his perspective on his previous homeland. I was drawn to the subtitle's claim of the *World's Most Intractable Conflict*, especially considering other no-less-insoluble conflicts such as the unsettled India-Pakistan Kashmir conflict, the Kurds in Turkey, Tibet and China, etc. However, Shafir, who started his thesis recording the historical saga of the establishment of the State of Israel, the periodical wars, the reality of occupation, the intifadas and their aftermath, concentrates on the following dilemma: "Why does Israel hold the contemporary world record of belligerent occupation for more than a half century?" (p. 84).

Though he does not reveal any new major insight to respond to his query, he has developed his argument by focusing on the Jewish settlement enterprise in the West Bank. No doubt, that project has been the subject of critical attacks by leftist protagonists for a long time. It was a recurrent subject in AD KAN's events, posters, and oral slogans, such as "One- Two- Three: Demolish Kiryat Arba" (the Jewish settlement close to Hebron's Cave of the Patriarchs). However, Shafir defines the new settlement drive in the biblical occupied territories, led by the Gush Emunim movement, as "a revolution within a revolution": the Zionist strategy of colonization revived but radicalized the ethos of the Zionist pioneering mission exemplified by the mostly secular agrarian settlements of the pre-1967 era (the Kibbutz and Moshav cooperative farming villages). They established instead semi-urban communities reinterpreted through a religious lens. Moreover, the new movement advocates pushing new settlements into the locations of ancient Jewish towns and villages that today host a dense Palestinian population to undermine the possibility of a two-state partition. Thus, he interprets the continuing occupation as representation of Israel's wish to continue the history of colonization, of nation-building, as substitute to secular Zionism.

Shafir relates the drastic weakening of the peace movement that lost its influence in the 1990s as consequence of the violent suicide bombings inside Israeli borders as well as the loss of hope of a peaceful accord under the growing power of the neo-Zionist settlers' political constituency. The old peace movement has been replaced by numerous small NGOs representing specific human rights issues. The leftists, concentrated mostly in the "state of Tel Aviv," no longer view themselves as capable of reversing through electoral means the historical trend that promotes ongoing colonization (pp. 196–97). In a more general viewpoint about the mainstream's accommodation with the unending occupation, he introduces the emotional mechanism of denial applied in similar situations: "The practice of denialism frequently displaces guilt from the perpetrators of wrongdoing onto the victims" (p. 13). A similar interpretation was suggested earlier by Ariella Azoulay and Adi Ophir, representatives of philosophy and cultural studies, in their vast Hebrew canvas portraying the history and ramifications of the Israeli occupation system (*This Regime Which Is Not One*, 2008). Their work highlights the cognitive "blindness" caused by the continuing baffling public perception of the occupation as a "temporary" phenomenon (p. 13).

I move now to represent a different type of commentator expressing viewpoints outside the context of a strictly professional perspective. Nir Baram, a young author, the son of a leading figure in the Labor Party governments, wrote a most evocative semi-ethnographic chronicle recounting his journey among communities of Jewish settlers and indigenous Palestinian villages in the West Bank. The title, *In a Land beyond the Mountains*, which I mentioned when describing the trip to South Hebron Mountain, reflects on his intuition and conviction that contested land and its belligerent peoples represent a reality far remote from most Israelis' lives. They read and speak about the occupation, the settlements, and some unpleasant conflicts that happen there occasionally, but they have no idea how that area looks and how people of both nationalities actually live there. For the majority of Israelis, that territory embodies a foreign land they prefer to avoid in daily life. We are reminded of David Shulman's (2008) passionately expressed indictment against the occupation and its removal from most Israelis' daily consciousness. Shulman made it a personal duty to travel regularly with his Ta'ayush comrades to protect Palestinians confronted by aggressive Jewish settlers in the Hebron hills.

In retrospect, Baram embraced the role that mainstream Israeli anthropologists have given up for ethical-political reasons. He met with West Bank residents, Jews and Palestinians who were pleased to express their feelings, experiences, and hopes about the political future of their communal existence in a shared contested land. As for the Jewish settlers, they stood firmly by the vision of their project regardless of the wishes of their Palestinian neighbors, despite severe condemnation by their leftist compatriots and threatening criticism from outside of Israel.

The Palestinians, however, remained adamant about their hopes for the Israelis' retreat from the West Bank and the establishment of an independent Palestinian state with its capital in Jerusalem. Moreover, they expressed their expectation for the implementation of Palestinian refugees' "right of return" to the villages and towns they evacuated as they fled Israeli forces during the 1948 war. They believed the Oslo agreements had been a deceit strategy that allowed the Israelis' continuing control of "Area C" (part of the West Bank), intended for a later redeployment. Area C is not included under the immediate jurisdiction of the Palestinian Authority, therefore enabling the expansion of Jewish settlements in the West Bank.

Israeli settlers mostly rejected the idea of establishing a Palestinian state that would maintain the West Bank Israeli outposts or a unified state for both nations. They were willing to accommodate the continuing presence of Palestinians in the West Bank, who they believed were entitled to honorable and safe life—but under the authority of Jewish dominance. On the whole, they viewed the long-assumed plan of two independent states as a lost option. They considered the Israeli residents of Tel Aviv (implying leftist Israelis) as lacking a true Zionist spirit, remote from Jewish cultural-religious traditions. They looked nostalgically to the days of 1967, when, under the miracle of victory and return to the biblical sites, a national euphoria engulfed and unified all sectors of Israeli society.

In the end, Baram concluded his journey in deep distress. Both sides have demonstrated reluctance to accommodate each other on any terms. The Palestinians' claims go back to the pre-1948 situation, while the settlers employ the status quo (which he calls "the phantom time") to expand their presence in old and new sites, thus averting the possibility of a two-state solution. Therefore, the model of separation between Israelis and Palestinians seems to have collapsed geographically, demographically, and politically. Baram expressed his deeply rooted hopes for a change of moral values in Israeli society that would emphasize equality between Jews and non-Jews, end the occupation, and institute a mode of appeasement despite the vanished models for coexistence entrenched in our political map. As I finished reading his text, I wrote a note: "A document of despair." The book also became the source for a documentary film under the same title, *The Land beyond the Mountains*.

About a year later, Amos Oz (d. 2019), probably the leading Israeli author of our generation, published *Dear Zealots: Three Pleas* (2017).

The small book includes a list of missives directed to the right-wingers, secular and religious fanatics who sanctify the Land of Israel, the West Bank settlers, and their supporters. Oz expressed his disappointment, fear, and revulsion at the transformation that Israeli society has experienced in recent years. He painted an imaginary surrealistic ladder of its present-day social construction: Rabbis in black coats at the top, followed by West Bank settlers, traditional religious observers, simple-minded Israeli citizens comprising the audience sought after by the religious redemption missioners, and, at the lowest rank, "the enemies of Israel": leftists—the seekers of peace, human rights defenders, the sarcastically named "beneficent souls" (*yefey hanefesh*).

Oz described the two dangerous options implied by both the extreme right and the extreme left advocators. The extreme leftists who envision a binational state are pathetic dreamers. How can one expect a couple sharing a happy bed after one hundred years of spilling blood and tears? But without a two-state solution, the continuing growth of the Palestinian population will inevitably raise a dictatorship of fanatics, fearful of the loss of a Jewish majority, who will govern the Palestinians and the Jews in the opposition camp with "an iron fist." However, a dictatorship where the minority suppresses the majority will not survive for long, as such a framework has never existed elsewhere in the modern era. Oz's prescription had no guarantee for a bright future if Israel gave up the occupied territories following a peace treaty, but the alternative seemed much worse. He ended his "prophetic" pleas expressing his fear and shame over the fanaticism and violence that seem to have taken on a growing presence in Israeli public life. No doubt, another document of despair.

The same year, 2017, Micah Goodman, an Israeli scholar of Jewish history and philosophy, published *Catch 67*, raising a hectic debate among the leftist Israeli political spectrum. Goodman tried to present "an objective" observation of the inclusive position—fears, ideologies and hopes—of all parties to the conflict: the Israeli rightists, their leftist compatriots, and the Palestinians. His basic conception considered the political views of individuals who opposed or supported retreating from the occupied territories, and how these views represented a deeper layer of their personalities. Thus, these views constitute a key element of their identity as Jews and Israelis. The Israelis' fears are nourished by the historical records of persecutions and disbelief in the assurances of peace contracts under the safeguards and promises of foreign powers. However, the leftists who represent a liberal universalistic orientation are not convinced that withdrawal guarantees peace, but they have no doubt that the continuing occupation is a recipe for a catastrophic eventuality. The rightists, by contrast, do not necessarily believe in messianic redemption, but are convinced that retreat from the occupied territories is an equally certain road to a catastrophic national tragedy, mostly on the grounds of security and topography. Departing from the West Bank peak zones overlooking Israel's lower sea-level terrain would be a logistical/security nightmare. But Israelis on both sides feel they are not to blame for the Palestinians' repeated mistakes: rejecting the United Nations' internationally confirmed plan of partition and initiating and losing two wars and more land. Moreover, they presume the Palestinians have declined the conceding terms of withdrawal from the occupied territories that PMs Barak and Olmert proposed to Chairman Arafat in 2000 and to his successor Abu Mazen in 2008.

At the same time, Israelis of all convictions do not comprehend the extent to which their denial of the Palestinians' claims for the "right of return" is a demand for the Palestinians to change their sense of identity. That misconception adds to the right-wingers' growing religious constituency and its messianic trends, who repudiate the leftists' suggestion to withdraw from cherished biblical sites in the West Bank.

For the Palestinians, however, the key experiential element that effected their existential sense of presence in the world is a notion of humiliation. That humiliation is nourished not only by the debacles of the 1948 and 1967 wars but also by the degradation of Islam by Western cultures represented by Israeli colonialism. The Israelis' fears that generate the various means of daily protection from Palestinian attacks (checkpoints, interrogations, curfews, and other invasive measures enforced in the occupied territories) intensify the Palestinians' sense of humiliation. They are equally trapped in a painful "catch": in order to make peace they have to betray their brethren—the refugees' "right of return"—as well as give up control of their religious center in Jerusalem. Thus, the idea of a Palestinian state alongside Israel implies a transformation of their national-religious identity.

Consequently, both Israelis and Palestinians consider themselves victims of historical and present-day circumstances. That conviction leaves little space for mutual understanding and empathy. In sum, Goodman's perspective offers no escape from the historical, demographic, geographical, religious, security, or emotional predicament of Catch [19]67. That tragic confrontation leaves Israelis and Palestinians alike with no path to a peaceful coexistence for the foreseeable future.

Goodman's book gained wide coverage in Israeli media. However, former PM Barak attacked his pessimistic assertion, accusing him of adopting the right-wing ideological conception of the conflict situation. He denied Goodman's tendency to display a model of equality between the fears of rightists and leftists. The leftists, however, are far more convinced about the safe terms of security arrangements supported by international recognition of the two-state solution. A former PM, minister of defense, and army chief, Ehud Barak claimed that Goodman's position actually buttressed a delay of crucial decision-making, enabling the further expansion of West Bank settlements, forgoing any plan of withdrawal, and consequently prioritizing the "integrity of the Land of Israel" (*shlemut ha'aretz*) over the "integrity of the nation" (*shlemut ha'am*), torn between left and right.

Barak's assessment of the leftists' accommodating position was supported by Shlomo Ben-Ami, distinguished TAU professor of history who served as foreign minister and was part of Barak's delegation at the 2000 Camp David summit with PLO chairman Arafat and President Clinton. However, Ben-Ami, according to his records, blamed the Palestinians, who rejected the peace plan that offered them an Israeli retreat from all territories close to the 1967 border, including the Arab neighborhoods in East Jerusalem, and extended their hegemony over the Temple Mount. Barak and Ben-Ami have thus demonstrated the leftists' conviction about sharing lives with the Palestinians, ready to take risks for the sake of peace. No doubt, we observe a conflict of ideology and reality—dual convictions about land-security-political conditions—that continually widens the chasm, tearing apart major Israeli social-political constituencies.

In conclusion, Israeli scholars, literary figures, and other engaged commentators, speaking in various styles and with diverse reasonings, leave few optimistic assessments and prescriptions for a peaceful solution acceptable by both sides to the enduring binational conflict. Thus, one wonders, does the Israeli-Palestinian case embody an "iconic" example of an intractable conflict as suggested by Shafir (2017)? And last, does that picture of interminable deadlock offer an answer to the riddle of our story—the absence of protest in academia since the failure of the Oslo promise? Before we conclude that apparently naïve query, we will turn to a review of some of the main blocks of Israeli society from the anthropologist's point of view.

17

Israeli Society Revisited

An Anthropological Perspective

Israeli anthropologists have typically refrained from exploring generally "the structure of Israeli society"—its social components and cultural features, the dynamics and changes of economic, ethnic, demographic, ideological, and political realities. They often investigate a specific major issue (e.g., Weingrod's focus on Israeli ethnicity, 1985; Handelman's exploration of Israeli nationalism, 2004; Bilu's inquiry of cultural traditions in Israel's urban periphery, 2010) or produce edited volumes on various social components (e.g., Marx 1980; Herzog et al. 2010; Markowitz et al. 2015). However, the mission of revealing a compact theoretical portrayal of Israeli society has been a major project for leading Israeli sociologists. I assume it is beyond the reader's patience at this stage to absorb the immense production of these works. I will mention only S. N. Eisenstadt, the Jerusalem progenitor of Israeli sociology, his students D. Horowitz and M. Lissak, and last, B. Kimmerling, representative of the "third generation" from the Jerusalem school. Those cited above and many others have all inquired into the history of the Zionist project in Palestine and the transformations it went through before and after the 1967 war. Each emphasized the enormous impact of that war, the formative moment of modern Israeli history. It is enough to view the titles of their publications to comprehend the complexity and the mood of their assessment: Eisenstadt's *The Transformation of Israeli Society* (1985); Horowitz and Lissak's *Trouble in Utopia* (1989); Kimmerling's *The Invention and Decline of Israeliness* (2001).

A major theme that connects most of the sociological discourses about the continuing transformations of Israeli society relates to the decline of Israeli hegemonic secular metaculture and its political bearers. These discourses continually evoke the fall of the founding regime in view of facts, myths and stereotypes, nostalgia, or deep resentment. The era of creation recalls the founding generations of the state, mostly Ashkenazi Zionists induced by socialist ideas of the day, whom later generations have blamed for most national ills and social grudges, and the emergence of an altered social-political order, a sociological saga most cogently rendered by Kimmerling (2001).

No doubt, my experiences and conclusions, as well as those of AD KAN participants, must have involved insights revealed by the researchers mentioned above as well as in the writings of others in earlier chapters. However, the following chronicle of my engagement with a few chosen fields of ethnographic research before and after 1967 (summarily introduced in chapter 1), as well as my reports in public forums, demonstrates the anthropologist's observations in vivo, representing some of the dynamics to which the composite sociological discourses and other portrayals of Israeli society have alluded.

As reported earlier, my engagement with Israeli social realities started long before my introduction to anthropology, in the field of the post-1948 immigration of Diaspora Jews to the newly established Israeli state. That preoccupation came to its completion with the ethnographies introducing Moroccan Jews who settled in rural communities (e.g., *The Dual Heritage* 1971/1985, *The Predicament of Homecoming,* with S. Deshen, 1974). In retrospect, though the strategy of absorbing the mostly Middle Eastern–Mizrahim newcomers in the geographical periphery of the state was apparently successful at the start, it yielded immense adverse social consequences later. As it turned out, the idea of settling the various immigrant groups in the territories gained in 1948 did not result in the ideological vision of the "melting pot" (*kur ha'hituch*). These rather segregated communities, remote from the central urban, industrial, administrative, and cultural settings, turned into the social-economic-geographical "periphery" of Israeli society. That failure harmfully impacted younger generations, who blamed the veteran Israeli elite and their political organs (often perceived as the Ashkenazim-led Labor Party, Mapai) for discriminating against and depriving their parents' generation of their equal share and rights in the Promised Land.

That developing notion of deprivation expanded into a wider field of ethnic, communal, and personal humiliation, which led to accusations of demeaning attitudes of the Ashkenazim toward the Mizrahim's (Orientals') cultural roots, traditions, and manners. That new ethnic designation assigned to all those who came from different non-European countries replaced the traditional "Sephardim" identification related to the descendants of Jews who were expelled from Spain in 1492. The protest agenda against the veteran regime was often promoted by younger intellectuals, among them successful academics, who also blamed leading Israeli scholars for their biased perception of the contributions of "Arab Jews" to Jewish culture along past and present history (e.g., Shenhav 2006). No doubt, the developing anti-establishment atmosphere had its consequences in the wider political arena with the growing attraction of Mizrahim voters to the right-wing Likud Party in particular. Comprehending the developing grassroots mood, the Likud Party opened its ranks early on to young, energetic leaders from among the Mizrahim constituencies.

Moreover, a new party called Shas, which catered to a large Orthodox Mizrahim audience, was soon founded, headed by charismatic leaders, Rabbi Ovadia in particular (e.g., Leon 2016). Actually, the emergence of Shas had been encouraged by the Ashkenazi Orthodox religious leadership and congregations who looked down on the Mizrahim's apparently less rigorous requisites of Torah learning and their more lenient upkeep of Jewish ritual tenets. Studying Moroccan Jews during the 1960s/1970s, I was impressed by their more moderate religious approach compared with the strict scrupulous comportment of Ashkenazi Orthodox Jews. They were far more tolerant in daily life of their coreligionists' devout conduct, which made me feel comfortable in their company, even when attending synagogue services.

I cannot forget a particular bar mitzvah party when the local Moroccan rabbi congratulated the community for having me among them, emphasizing that "good manners [*derech eretz*] preceded the Torah by twenty-six generations," a traditional homily intended to acknowledge one's warm acceptance in the community (although I am not a scrupulous religious practitioner). Naturally, I was careful to respect religious comportment in the public domain by wearing a skullcap, observing the Sabbath rules, etc. I doubt one could conduct fieldwork at that time in an Ashkenazi Orthodox community tolerated by "good manners" only. I described that aspect of Moroccan Jewish culture in my ethnographic reports as "Religion of Tradition."

That more relaxed normative conduct, I explained, was related to the life of Jews in Muslim lands. In particular, Jews closely integrated into the economic and daily life of their host societies, including their religious leaders, who were often equally engaged in economic activities. Jews were not separated socially, economically, and culturally in Muslim countries as they were in European Christian societies. At that time, I assumed the Mizrahim's model of more lenient religiosity might change the landscape of religious life in Israel. However, the Ashkenazim's dominant position in Israeli society, including the Orthodox sector's prestigious Yeshiva schools and their control of government's organs, the administration, and generous funds for religious services, left the Mizrahim's religious leaders and traditions in a disadvantaged position. They gradually adopted the Ashkenazim's norms of religious conduct, their system of orthodox education, their style of personal conduct, and their appearance. Although the Shas Party exclusively represents a Mizrahim constituency, it nevertheless has emulated the culture and organizational strategies of an ultra-Orthodox Ashkenazi party.

No doubt, my early assumption about the potential impact of Middle Eastern Jewish cultural traditions on the social-religious texture of Israeli society proved mostly mistaken. Moreover, as already indicated, religious parties of all shades and ethnic backgrounds have been inclined to adopt right-wing ideologies and join rightist government coalitions. Furthermore, despite some early assumptions that Mizrahim Jews might serve as a cultural-political bridge with the Arab world, current observations reveal that they are inclined to develop anti-Arab sentiments. I remember the Moroccan immigrants in the village I studied who often reminisced about their life among the Muslims, claiming that they could safely conduct their economic, religious, and communal life. In contrast, the rising nationalistic trend among a substantial sector of the Mizrahim constituency has further contributed to the weakening of the more liberal Israeli electorate of the "center" and "leftist" parties.

My next project during the early 1970s, completed in collaboration with Shlomo Deshen, a close friend and Manchester/TAU alumnus (*Distant Relations*, 1982), offered a discerning view of the Arab minority—Christians and Muslims—who remained in Israel after the 1948 war compared with the Jewish newcomers from Arab countries (the Mizrahim)—the "second Israel." The study of Arab residents in Jaffa (a former major city in Palestine, now joined to Tel Aviv) displayed the modes of their existential adjustment to the new civil-economic-political-cultural environment under the regime of a Jewish majority, and residing adjacent to Jewish neighbors.

I reported at that time on the pending decline of the "Arab lists"— political factions based on family or personal ties and affiliated with major Jewish parties, mostly on the leftist spectrum. Instead, a growing majority among the Israeli Arab electorate supported the advancement of separate Arab independent parties, Hadash in particular (Shokeid and Deshen 1982: 121–38). In recent years, however, all Arab parties have merged into one (the Joint List) to ensure that they do not fail the minimum votes required per Knesset delegate.

These developments have excluded the Israeli-Arab electorate from consequential participation in the arena of political life. Independent, exclusively Arab parties cannot join Israeli coalition governments headed by left or right Jewish parties. No PM candidate can risk inviting to his/her coalition alliance any independent Arab party associates who might express Palestinian nationalistic claims or feel alienated from issues pertaining to the Jewish majority. That potential partnership would delegitimize any of that government's decisions related to national Jewish interests, especially withdrawal from Palestinian territories. As such, although they have equal citizenship rights and represent about 20 percent of the Israeli electorate in the Knesset, they have mostly played a symbolic demonstrative role in the blueprint of Israeli democratic construction. Thus, while the Mizrahim's electorate became oriented toward the right-wing parties, the Arab electorate was excluded from active participation in the political arena. That reality also weakened the center-left parties' prospects for a potential power hold that would influence national priorities, investments, and long-term planning, particularly in regards to the Arab-Israeli conflict.

My last research of a major issue in Israeli life prior to the eruption of the first intifada took me to New York, where I observed the stigmatized *Yordim* ("those who go down"), mostly Israeli-born citizens who left the country and took permanent residence in the United States. Leaders and public opinion viewed that phenomenon with much concern, considering it a threat to the security of a nation surrounded by hostile countries and a contradiction to the ethos of the Zionist project. The title of the ethnography *Children of Circumstances* (1988) represented the observations, revealing the triggers of the Israelis' migration, which were mostly the consequences of impromptu, unforeseen circumstances, such as leaving for professional studies, travel, visiting relatives, marrying American spouses, representing Israeli agencies overseas, etc.

However, those unplanned temporary migrations soon turned into permanent residences abroad. In any case, no one among my close informants during the early 1980s claimed that he or she had left Israel for political reasons. They typically explained, "We were stuck" (*nitkanu*), and they often expressed regret for their unpremeditated departure. Moreover, many among them conveyed right-wing attitudes, a manifestation of their continuing national loyalties (contrary to my own political sentiments).

Here again, the reality of the 1980s changed dramatically, as emigration from Israel in recent years has taken on a different mode of intention as well as public perception. The stigma associated with *Yordim* (the slur itself has actually vanished) and the justifications for leaving Israel have mostly disappeared from private and public discourse. No doubt, that profound change presents a mix of an innate social-ideological-national transformation, as well as an economic one, as the growing forces of globalization move talents and other human resources among the central hubs of modern technology and business. I remind the reader: *Children of Circumstances* appeared during the opening year of the first intifada, a moment communally and personally remote from present-day Israeli-Palestinian realities.

Thus, my research on Israeli life from the late 1960s to the mid-1980s focused on ethnographic fields that seemed to reflect on issues related to vital elements of social cohesion in a newly constructed society. But, most important, the deep changes that affected these field-sites during the last decades exemplify the immense transformation Israeli society has gone through within a relatively short historical time. No doubt, however, the intifada and its disappointing aftermath must have influenced my change of field-site, outside the Israeli national arena. But regardless of that detour, I was called upon to expose a wider picture of major trends in Israeli society. Preparing for these presentations revealed the complexity of the Israeli social texture and the continuing changes of its social construction.

In 2002 I delivered the Franz Boas lecture (mentioned earlier in a different context in chapter 13) at the Berlin Institute of Ethnology, where I was expected to present some key issues in contemporary Israeli society. I decided to compose a virtual picture of the multifaceted Israeli social structure, a socio-photo as if taken from a plane circling over the country. Titled "The Five Banks Tapestry of Israeli Society" (2003a), it presented a jigsaw-puzzle model of five "banks," an image originating in the post-1967 Israeli geopolitical terminology application to the West Bank (a land its devotees call by the biblical names Judea and Samaria). It considered the ardent constituency of the post-1967 West Bank Jewish settlements as representing a major slice—ideological/political, social, and economic—of the construction of present-day Israeli society, comparable with four other slices: (1) the Coastal Bank, a mostly metropolitan and better-off area, politically divided between left- and right-wing supporters (though probably more leftists), more secular and liberal, and containing a majority of Ashkenazim as well as the middle and upper-middle classes of the Mizrahim; (2) the Peripheral Bank, composed of the relatively disadvantaged members of the population, mostly Mizrahim, many of whom reside in the more remote locations of Israel's geography—"the periphery"; (3) the Ultra-Orthodox Bank, whose mostly Ashkenazim members have shown a remarkable demographic growth, concentrated in some crowded neighborhoods of Jerusalem, the city of Bnei Brak, and other locations in the country; (4) the growing Israeli Arab Bank (Muslims, Christians, Bedouins, and Druze), a constituency concentrated in a few geographical enclaves in the Center, Galilee, and Negev regions. These imaginary banks are undoubtedly not "pure" in their social composition.

The analysis at that time raised the question: how do these five socio-economic-political-cultural banks, locked in continuing competition, conflict, and fierce cultural antipathies, manage to act together to present a functioning unified society without displaying fatal antagonisms that threaten its binding national framework? For this present discourse, I reiterate the first rationale suggested at that Berlin presentation, related to Gluckman's work in tribal Africa (e.g., 1962), whose insights made important contributions to conflict theory. Despite the deep divisions, gaps, and conflicts that separate the Israeli banks, they (mostly the Jewish constituencies) are woven together by visible and invisible threads in a system of continuing or ad hoc relationships and mutual interests (Gluckman defined as "cross-cutting ties") that link up individuals and group members of belligerent parties (African lineages or tribes in Gluckman's observations). Israeli Arabs too, in spite of their grievances and resentments, do not aspire at this time to break away and join a Palestinian state separate from Israel.

This five-banks description and interpretation seemed at the time a reflexive exposition, an exploratory report about some major social-political realities in Israeli society. However, twelve years later (2014), during a term-long stay at the Vienna IFK (cultural studies institute), I was again scheduled to present an overview of present-day Israeli society. As before, Israeli society had gone through myriad transformations, often within a short period. Well known were a few easily depicted historical moments that caused dramatic changes in Israeli social and political life, such as the 1967 and 1973 wars. But other recurrent developments of momentous consequence had intermittently taken place, albeit ones less discernible by public perception and international scrutiny as major turns in Israel's societal structure and its cultural-political-economic consequences. Israel was still in a process of nation-building, particularly considering the new societal components disembarking on its shores.

Addressing the social map of 2002 again in 2014, I added to the five-banks design the ongoing emergence of a few more constituencies (2015c): the arrival of (1) a wave of Jewish immigrants from Ethiopia since the 1980s; (2) a larger wave of immigrants from the former Soviet Union since the 1990s; and (3) a new labor force of hundreds of thousands from Eastern Europe, East Asia, and Africa to replace Palestinians no longer able to work in Israel (in industry, construction, agriculture, services, etc.) following the outbreak of the first intifada in 1987. Although the majority of foreign workers were allowed to stay in the country for a limited period (four years on average, except those who cared for the elderly and disabled, mostly Filipina women who could stay on with their wards), many stayed on illegally and often established family households. In addition, there was an influx of (4) undocumented migrant workers and asylum seekers from Africa who entered Israel on foot via the Sinai Peninsula since the late 2000s. These last waves of newcomers concentrated in central cities and towns, often changing the urban landscape, developing low-class and ethnically segregated neighborhoods. For example, the Tel Aviv Central Bus Station area has become a hub of foreign labor and refugee concentration. Also, run-down neighborhoods hosting the recent wave of Jewish immigrants from Ethiopia have developed in other urban locations.

The reconstructed, simplistic design of this socio-spatial-ethnocultural-political tapestry represents a far less homogeneous and integrated Israeli nation than outside observers often assume. Moreover, that morphological perspective does not reflect on the changes that surfaced within the respective bank "slices." The picture of Israeli society suggested above, resembling a Picasso profile in cubist style, was also alluded to, from a sociological perspective, by Kimmerling (2001: 237), who identified seven cultures challenging one another for control of the basic rules of the national game: access to and criteria for the distribution of public resources, as well as the identity repertoire of the polity.

Thus, for example, the growing messianic convictions among the "religious nationalists" (*datiim leumiim*), members of the Jewish Home Party (Ha'Bayit Ha'yehudi), replaced the accommodating modern-Orthodox political movement—the MAFDAL Party. The new party leadership has changed its ideological orientation, enthusiastically endorsing the expansion of settlements in the West Bank.

The growing settlers' constituency counts among its members nearly 400,000 residents in 125 locations, compared with 50,000 during the 1980s (*Haaretz*, 9 June 2017: 22, Central Bureau of Statistics database). For many years, until the right-wing Likud took over, the former MAFDAL Party was a loyal partner to leftist coalition governments (led by the Labor Party).

No less significant has been the increasing demographic, social, and cultural division due to the fast growth of the ultra-Orthodox (*Haredim*) constituency. Hardly visible in the public arena, concentrated in a few exclusive neighborhoods, and removed from political engagement during the first decades of statehood, its members conduct a "state" of their own. They have never been enthusiastic about the Zionist state founded by secular Jews removed from the "world of the Torah," not guided by divine rules and messianic beliefs. Although they depend on the government's services and financial support, they have continually avoided compulsory military service—the quintessential symbol of national allegiance and social unity. However, they have gradually gained considerable political influence, joining coalition governments mostly interested in supporting its growing population and independent system of Yeshiva schools. As already indicated in earlier discussions, although they are not involved in the current secular or religious nationalist agenda, they are nevertheless comfortable with right-wing politics and its yearning for the biblical Land of Israel.

The arrival of nearly a million of Jewish immigrants from the former Soviet Union actually occurred after the first intifada. That immense wave of migrants, viewed as "high-quality" newcomers, was warmly welcomed; they were considered well educated and capable of integrating relatively smoothly in various sectors of a modern technological society (compared with, for example, Ethiopian Jews, a wave of whom had also recently arrived). However, this new large group of citizens soon revealed a strong right-wing orientation (probably as a reaction to their position as an ethnic minority in Soviet society). That political stance found its impact in the founding of Yisrael Beiteinu (Israel Our Home), a right-wing secular party catering mostly to the Russian constituency.

The emergence of two strong right-wing parties, one religious (Ha'Bayit Ha'yehudi) and one secular (Yisrael Beiteinu), dramatically influenced the Israeli political arena. They became natural partners to right-wing coalitions headed by the larger Likud Party, an alignment unobtainable for a left-wing coalition. Moreover, as I have already indicated, the few ultra-Orthodox parties, although not committed to the vision of securing land in the West Bank (unauthorized by divine intervention), have accommodated a right-wing coalition government. That is also the case with the Shas (Mizrahim) religious party.

The abovementioned enclaves of Ethiopian Jews, foreign labor, and refugees added to the human diversity and social complexity of Israeli society, raising serious issues of socioeconomic integration and controversial policy rulings, in particular, the growing population of asylum seekers (forty thousand) from Eritrea and Sudan who arrived via the Sinai Desert during the 2000s. Concentrating mostly in downtown Tel Aviv, they have become a source of bitter complaints by local residents and have led to polarizing public debate and government administrative actions intended to limit their presence in the country (Shokeid 2015c). However, the presence of newcomers probably had only a secondary influence on major trends in the national political arena compared with the other social dynamics taking place during that period.

Twenty-five years since the end of the first intifada and the ensuing Oslo Accords, we confront a society that has gone through immense territorial, demographic, social, ideological and political change. These shifts have all impacted the somewhat precarious divide of the equal-sized left and right in national politics. In particular, the Labor Party lost its leading position in national politics during the first stages of statehood. In contrast, the Likud Party, although led by old-guard Ashkenazi disciples of the charismatic ideologue Ze'ev Jabotinsky's right-wing Zionist minority (versus David Ben-Gurion's Socialist Zionist movement majority), continually gained the popular vote among the less-privileged electorate. The smaller leftist constituencies and affiliated parties have also lost their influential stance: the Kibbutz Movement as a strong national-political force in particular has declined, compared with the dramatic growth of right-wing militant sectors—religious, messianic, and secular—opposing withdrawal from the occupied territories and supporting conservative policies in the legal domains.

Considering our major theme: in the evolving new social-ideological-political national order, the eminent position of leading intellectuals, a mainstay of the veteran Labor leftist regime (respected authors, poets, political thinkers, columnists, etc.), as well as the prominent standing of leading academics, has greatly diminished in the public arenas. A most obvious confirmation of that claim took place at the time I wrote the above "diagnosis." Early in June 2017, it was publicly announced that, at the request of Minister of Education

Naftali Bennett, Asa Kasher, the TAU emeritus professor of philosophy, had authored a code of ethics to guide Israeli academics' demeanor on campus, to be confirmed by the Council of Higher Education (the MALAG). Known as the author of the code of ethics for the Israeli army, Professor Kasher considered himself competent and rightful, taking on the authority of instructing his academic colleagues about their normative conduct: in particular, that they should avoid expressing personal ideological-political views unrelated to the subject of their teaching in front of their students.

No doubt, Minister Bennett, chair of the right-wing religious party Ha'Bayit Ha'yehudi, which represents the constituency of West Bank settlers in particular, considered the academy a hub hosting notorious "leftists" who naturally advocate for their intransigent anti-occupation ideas in front of their vulnerable young students. Moreover, he likely suspected academics of punishing those who believe otherwise and dare express in class their ideological-political opposition.

For the first time in many years, a storm of protest erupted throughout Israeli academia, one strongly conveyed in most daily newspapers, radio and television programs, and various networks of academic associations. Renowned scholars expressed their revulsion in articles, letters, and discussions in various public forums. Most commentators were amazed at this ruthless and clumsy attempt to silence freedom of academic expression. Not a few critics announced that they would intentionally break the rules of the code if confirmed by the MALAG.

Despite my decision to avoid the task and emotional investment of publicly dissenting, I wrote the shortest letter in that literary genre on the first day of the code announcement, which was published in *Haaretz* a few days later on 14 June 2017:

> The recent good news of the code of ethics created in the name of the Education Minister and his philosopher, prove more than anything else the guilt of Israeli academy that continued perform for many years sealed off from the reality of occupation and the regression of basic values of democratic rule. Except for a few individuals (Profs. Daniel Baltman, Daniel Bar-Tal, Oren Iftahel, Mordechai Kremnizer, Zeev Sternhal, and others) who continued to express their protest from the courtyards of campuses where social-political silence dominates the scene suitable to the green loan squares in Denmark and Iceland's campuses. The Minister and his philosopher must have forgotten the Professors' silence in German academic institutions. The code of ethics will tender a Kosher certificate to the already thunderous silence.

Professor Kasher was severally criticized for his pompous comportment, becoming in his old age a philosopher for rent by political operators, acting against the basic values of academic freedom. Surprisingly, Kasher, a respected philosopher on campus, often attended AD KAN activities during the first intifada and was invited to participate in public events in appreciation of his impressive oratory skills expressing leftist moral convictions (also quoted earlier). Was this another example of Gordon's (2018) "how good people become absurd"?

Anyhow, the Kasher code of academic ethics and the following two-week storm of vocal and printed protest revealed the twofold situation that Israeli academics have faced in recent years: the erosion of their position and impact in the public arena as influential guides in social-political issues and their apparently voluntary retreat from societal involvement, an escape into the "pure" academic realm of work and professional engagement. Although MALAG did not approve the Kasher code of ethics, the shadow of that gross attempt to discipline academia remains a potent threat to the future of free expression on Israeli campuses.

From a personal perspective, reflecting on my major ethnographic engagements reported in this chapter, the growing tolerance toward Israeli emigrants—the previously stigmatized *Yordim*—seems to encapsulate the end of an era of deeply entrenched solidarity of "a nation in arms." I repeat a short summary suggesting some of the inner causes that, along with exogenous global trends, have changed the public mood and opened the door for the *Yordim*'s departure from their homeland, free of guilt, to join the waves of our era's world migrations. These causes include the growing division of convictions about options and terms for terminating the conflict with the Palestinians, the question of the fate of the nation as a democratic society under the regime of occupation, and the advent of right-wing Knesset members' contested appeals to change or elaborate on the national constitution, thus weakening the liberal nature of Israeli legal foundations. No surprise, the wave of Israeli emigrants in recent years includes some of the most promising students and scientists who chose to embark on their professional and academic careers elsewhere in the United States and Europe; this is a stark change from past years, when mostly those who could not secure tenure-track positions in Israeli universities looked for opportunities elsewhere. Were I to suggest a title for a new ethnography about the status of the *Yordim* these days, I would adjust 1988's *Children of Circumstances* to *Children of Smart Planning*.

At this junction, reviewing recent stages in the evolution of Israeli society that seem to coincide with my own record of ethnographic experiences, I am reminded of Clifford Geertz's exploration of the history of his work, narrated in *After the Fact* (1995). *After the Fact* reviewed the changes that took place during his life-long career both in the societies he studied and in the discipline of anthropology. The towns he studied in Indonesia and Morocco, but no less the anthropologist himself and the terms of his craft, have changed dramatically.

Incidentally, Geertz's monograph is based on the Jerusalem-Harvard Lectures first delivered in Jerusalem in 1990. I remember attending his lectures and hosting him during a day trip to Tel Aviv. A most evocative moment during that visit occurred while visiting the leading ultra-Orthodox Yeshiva academy at nearby Bnei Brak, a major enclave of religious Jewish residents. No doubt, Geertz was overwhelmed by the sight of the huge study hall packed with one hundred or more young students engaged in Talmud discourse, whom we observed from a small window in an upper-floor corridor. It was a sight imported from a lost world, the turf of classical ethnographers.

Though of Jewish extraction, Geertz did not reveal any sentiment toward Jewish traditional culture or a particular link to a Jewish social milieu (actually, it was a surprise to discover his natal roots). As mentioned in an earlier context, I do not remember the themes of our conversations during that visit. These occurred during the heyday of the first intifada; could one keep silent on that subject? One must assume he was well aware of the ongoing conflict and the protest on campus, approached by AD KAN member Sasha Weitman to help release Gaza lawyer Abu Shaaban. But it did not seem appropriate at this time to engage in hectic Israeli politics with a celebrated guest who maintained a poker face ...

However, we were not surprised or offended ten years later, in 2002, when Geertz abruptly canceled his trip to Israel to receive an honorary doctorate from Tel Aviv University. His cancellation followed an eruption of violence in response to Operation Defensive Shield (29 March–10 May 2002), PM Sharon's invasion of the West Bank intended to halt Palestinian terror attacks during the second intifada, suicide bombers in particular. The massive retaliation against major Palestinian locations prompted an international uproar condemning the harsh treatment of the Palestinians. In a personal e-mail message, Geertz apologized for canceling:

I am still troubled as to whether I have acted appropriately or not. I simply find myself in the end unable to contemplate the image of my accepting an honorary degree in Tel Aviv amidst an invasion. ... It is not the security situation which bothers me, for I am certain that I would be well-protected, it is simply that the prospect of a general war in the Middle East is not something I can contemplate without objection. (8 May 2002)

I responded to his letter: "I am not surprised. I am appalled by 'my' government's wisdom that repeats the Lebanon disaster. Unfortunately, only mice learn from experience."

Why do I recall that apparently unrelated and disturbing story now? The unexpected embarrassing situation facing the most prominent late-twentieth-century anthropologist that connected him with the realities that triggered the writing of this text highlights the complex emotions that engulf Israeli academics connected to international academia. In any case, throughout his communication with the TAU administration, Geertz did not display an aura of higher moral standing, which compares favorably with my experience with Daniel Segal, related earlier, when Segal personally admonished me for participating in "a Zionist degradation and marginalization of Palestinians" and emphasized his Jewish ethical responsibility.

In his professional-biographical text, Geertz did not say much about himself. In documenting the transformations experienced by the societies he studied, he was able to serve his platform by commenting on the essence of the anthropological project:

> Anthropology is in fact rather more something one picks up as one goes along year after year trying to figure out what it is and how to practice it than something one has instilled in one through "a systematic method to obtain obedience" or formalized "train[ing] by instruction and control." ...
>
> Of all the human sciences, anthropology is perhaps the most given to questioning itself as to what it is and coming up with answers that sound more like overall world views or declarations of faith than they do like descriptions of "a branch of knowledge." ... The matter is ad hoc and ex post. You see what you have been doing after you have been doing it. (1995: 97, 98)

Behind that cloud of uncertainty over the essence, theory, and practice of anthropology, and avoiding a commentary on the reality at home typical to earlier generations of anthropologists, Geertz's moving personal testimony expressed how joyful he was over his career as an ethnographer, highlighted by the last sentence: "But it is an excellent way, interesting, useful and amusing, to expend a life" (p. 168).

I envy Geertz, whose work greatly influenced my own professional evolution, who could look back at his life's work with such contentment. As much as I have enjoyed my ethnographic ventures, I could never remain a reserved observer, free of deep personal concerns about the changing sociopolitical circumstances of the people I studied. True, that applies to the studies of Israelis in particular: Moroccan immigrants, Jaffa Arabs, Israeli *Yordim* in the United States, Ethiopian Jews, and downtown Tel Aviv refugees. No doubt, moving away to study among the gay community in New York offered for a while a taste of "classical" anthropologists' "guilt-free" professional enjoyment, going after the "fact," in Geertz's terminology. But, despite my temporary "escapade" abroad, my Israeli identity never allowed me to maintain a moral distance from the broader social-political context of Israeli society.

Epilogue

> *Israel is one place where the mood and the spirit of ordinary lives are affected by politics, where biography has come to be above all a reflection of a moment of history, where people like us wait for the news reports as if they were daily verdicts on our personal lives.*
> —Yaron Ezrahi, *Rubber Bullets: Power and Conscience in Modern Israel*

Although we are both members of a small country and a small academic community, and although we were similarly active during the first intifada and afterward, Hebrew University political scientist Yaron Ezrahi and I rarely met. Israeli universities regularly operate as disconnected islands, and the fifty-minute drive between Jerusalem and Tel Aviv keeps them apart, maintaining a notion that they represent somewhat different moral entities. Not surprising, AD KAN, the trigger of our narrative emerging at TAU, included dedicated participants from the Open University located in a nearby Tel Aviv neighborhood. However, although the record of activities and commentaries related in our text have expressed my intense personal engagement, I have tried to restrain an intimate and emotional display of life history and state of mind, which Ezrahi and Shulman (also at the Hebrew University) more openly revealed. They mostly based their records relating to the intifada on their personal activities, engaged as they were in the struggle against the brutality and injustices of the occupation.

No doubt, a few reputable academics from the Hebrew University have publicly criticized politically and legally problematic developments in the national arena. But since the early days of the first intifada, AD KAN remained the only case where academics on campus recruited an impressive number of senior and junior faculty, as well as many students, founding a viable protest movement against the continuing occupation of Palestinian territories and control of their native residents. However, since the celebrated signing of the ill-fated Oslo Accords, no other acute social or political issue in Israeli life has triggered a similar organized response at TAU or elsewhere in Israeli academia.

Naturally, writing up the story of AD KAN also offered me an opportunity to reveal my frustrations and deep worries in observing the political mood and impending transformation of Israeli society, especially its legal and ethical values. The idea of a return to the first intifada days and their aftermath cannot be separated from one's morning reading of the news or daily radio listening, apparently a compulsive habit, illuminated by the opening excerpt, of "people like us." From a young age, Israeli women and men are trained to regularly attend to the latest reported violent incident involving Palestinians and Jews as well as the international coverage of the ongoing "intractable" conflict. Most Israeli young people (excluding the ultra-Orthodox) spend a few years in the military (IDF), conscripted to the defense of their country. Moreover, that sacrifice takes place under the overwhelming shadow of the Holocaust, a permanent powerful reminder of a long history of national suffering and persecution. That period must leave its mark both ways: among those who develop deep animosities toward the Palestinians they have encountered during conflictual situations, and among those who feel guilty for the harsh or humiliating treatment they have conducted during acts of reprisal or control in Palestinian territories (e.g., the Breaking the Silence organization).

At this late stage of reflection on past and present, exercising again the terms of the "ethnographic present," I recount a recent experience I probably got into as consequence of writing the present chronicle. In October 2018, I joined a weeklong trip to Poland in the company of about fifty Israeli travelers, mostly Jewish Orthodox congregants, intended to explore Jewish history there. It was actually a semi-ethnographic adventure for me, as I was the only visibly secular participant, similar to an anthropologist's position among a neighboring tribe. As it turned out, the journey was exclusively limited to Jewish sites that carried a religious or tragic element in recent Jewish records. For the first time, I came face-to-face with the horrific displays of human savagery as exemplified by the concentration death camps. Exposed to these "archeological" memorials, I also experienced moments of resentment toward my co-travelers, who ended each visit calling for God's mercy, revenge, or forgiveness for their own sins following reciting of the traditional prayer *el maleh Rachamim*, dedicated to the souls of the dead, or evocative chapters from Psalms.

For many years, I avoided visiting these scenes of horror, even when I would stay close to one of these sites. My discomfort in particular stemmed from the tradition of Israeli high school youths taking trips to Nazi death camps in Poland. No doubt, the journey must be an intense educational experience, indoctrinating a powerful nationalistic message of "the world against us Jews" and raising strong antagonistic feelings toward potential enemies who threaten Israeli security (the Palestinians in particular). However, sharing at last that "Israeli experience" in vivo, while in the company of Orthodox Jews, carried a threefold message also relevant to our discourse: (1) comprehending the impact of the Holocaust more than ever before, as told and observed on the national ethos and political arena; (2) grasping the "stubborn Jewish mind"—never giving up believing in the love of Jehovah, his commends and promises, regardless of all atrocities targeting his loyal disciples committed under his gaze; and (3) comprehending the ominous power of ideology—nationalistic, racial, religious, etc.—distorting human minds. That last "revelation" took me back home, reminding me of the terrible price that Israelis pay for their dedication to the mythical vision of "liberating the land promised to the Jewish people" and that Palestinians pay for their own rigid dream of the "right of return—to Jaffa, Haifa, etc."

The trip to Poland also offered a moment of reminiscence about the recent visits to Hebron and its neighboring Jewish settlements, the embodiment of a ruthless agenda in the name of a divine calling. Added to the aggravation of that memory is the subject of our text: why do "we" enlightened Israelis, academics in particular, remain paralyzed to confront a minority of aggressive messianic dreamers who have hijacked our national political and moral compass?

No need to repeat in detail the reasons given for this query, asked by AD KAN veterans and other thoughtful commentators who have relayed the transformation of Israeli society throughout recent decades, in particular the changing circumstances on the ground—the winning march of the settlers' project, the decline of the liberal political constituency, the expansion of the right-wing and Orthodox sectors (also conceived as "the religionization of Israeli society") (Peled and Peled 2019). I am not in a position to comment on the "exceptional" personal characteristics of AD KAN's core members.

A short review of world academia reveals a list of charismatic figures who stood firmly without a supportive team and spoke "truth to power"—for example, the British E. P. Thompson, the American Noam Chomsky and the Israeli Yeshayahu Leibowitz. Even today, respected Israeli academics, including historians, philosophers, law scholars, social scientists, and others, publicly express their critical opinions on issues of politics and morality. But their impact is of limited scale, exposed to a circle of leftist listeners and readers, often vilified by right-wingers.

The Israel Anthropological Association had rarely engaged in political issues during its annual meetings. However, in 2018, a few of its members introduced a resolution opposing the government's decision to incorporate the few Jewish colleges operating in the occupied territories (the West Bank) under MALAG's academic authority. The resolution also proclaimed that the association would not collaborate with those institutions on any professional activity, including conferences, discussion groups, and other events convened on its premises. The resolution was supported by 64 percent of the attending members, and 32 percent opposed it (76 out of the association's 109 members participated in the vote). No doubt, this was a landmark in the history of the organization.

As many may testify, academic units are not necessarily a land of harmony and affection. However, when considering the AD KAN record, I posit that a concerted academic response requires the critical combination of two phenomena: first, it must take place in a college setting involving a group of like-minded, self-assured, cooperating colleagues who experience a notion of *communitas*—a deep sharing of alienation and moral anguish arising from current events observed in the public forum; second, it must occur with the emergence of other publicly exposed manifestations of deep resentment beyond the gates of campus. This was the story at TAU, when a small circle of friends in the social sciences faculty recruited like-minded colleagues in their disciplinarian departments and in other faculties. Carried along in the zeitgeist of the day—an atmosphere of simmering frustration outside academia—they found support, a model to imitate, and allies in other similar protest collaborations evolving in neighboring professional, political, and civil constituencies.

Despite the declining political and human circumstances concluding fifty years of Israeli occupation of Palestinian territories, as well as a right-wing government's threats to Israeli democracy, we are still waiting for the historical moment that might revive the zeitgeist of the first intifada and instigate the formation of another uprising of academics protesting in the public forum. In the meantime, however, one cannot blame them for collaborating with the "enemy." The public image locates them at the left side of the political map, sneeringly nicknamed *smolanim* (leftists) by right-wing propagators implying they are "traitors."

Nonetheless, I cannot close our extensive discourse about the "intractable conflict" and its inactive academics without pointing to the "black hole" in our narrative: the missing partners, the Palestinians. Although I have not reported on them in the last chapters, they are not passive spectators. It was their homemade first intifada that triggered the political earthquake and the protest movements, a process that culminated with the Oslo Accords. One cannot exonerate the Palestinians who are as divided—socially, culturally, politically (Fatah, Hamas, Islamic Jihad, etc.)—as the Israelis are, if not far more, deliberating as they do about the options, targets, and tactics of reaching a solution to save their people from continuing suffering.

I introduced Palestinian professionals and political activists in earlier chapters who took part in AD KAN's activities. However, beyond linking to a few renowned Palestinian figures (in particular Edward Said, Sari Nusseibeh and Salim Tamari), I refrained from a more comprehensive examination of Palestinian intellectuals'/academics' terms of engagement (and disengagement) in the scene under investigation. I did not have the information or the linguistic competence in Arabic to tackle the subject, nor did I intend to take on the mission beyond the borders of Israeli society.

This text has incorporated the words and ideas of a long list of researchers and commentators who reported on the "intractable" Israeli-Palestinian conflict, as well as on the transformation of Israeli society since the first intifada. Some suggested (often in pessimistic terms) that these changes would eventually affect Israeli society. Anthropologists, however, are not expected to predict the future of their studied arenas. But years later, they can sometimes revisit their ethnographic sites and review the changes that have taken place since they departed from the field (see Shokeid 2020). Would I survive waiting for good news from the Holy Land?

I end our ethnographic account and critical discourse returning to Fassin's claim (2018: 8) about the mission of public ethnography: "What is at stake … is the sort of truth that is produced, established, and, in the end, told." I hope that I have validated this objective throughout the chronicle of the circumstances of academics' successes, and more often failures, in trying to mend the world around them.

References

Alimi, Eitan Y. 2007. *Israeli Politics and the First Intifada: Political Opportunities, Framing Processes and Contentious Politics*. London: Routledge.
Arendt, Hannah. 1963. *Eichman in Jerusalem: A Report on the Banality of Evil*. London: Faber and Faber.
Arian, Asher, and Raphael Ventura. 1989. *Public Opinion in Israel and the Intifada: Changes in Security Attitudes 1987–88*. Tel Aviv: Jaffe Center for Strategic Studies, Tel Aviv University.
Arieli, Yehoshua. 1992. *History and Politics*. Tel Aviv: Am Oved. In Hebrew.
———. 2000. "The Intellectuals in Politics." In *Binuy Uma*, edited by Dani Yaacobi, 9–23. Jerusalem: Magnes Press. In Hebrew.
Azoulay, Ariella, and Adi Ophir. 2008. *The Regime Which Is Not One: Occupation and Democracy between the Sea and the River (1967–)*. Tel Aviv: Resling Publishing Ltd. In Hebrew.
Banda, Julien. 1955 [1928]. *The Betrayal of the Intellectuals*. Boston: Beacon Press.
Baram, Nir. 2016. *In a Land beyond the Mountains*. Tel Aviv: Am Oved. In Hebrew.
Bar-Tal, Daniel. 2007. *Living with the Conflict: Socio-Psychological Analysis of the Jewish Society in Israel*. Jerusalem: Carmel. In Hebrew.
Behar, Ruth. 2003. "Ethnography and the Book that Was Lost." *Ethnography* 4(1): 15–39.
Bellamy, Richard. 1997. "The Intellectual as Social Critic: Antonio Gramsci and Michael Walzer." In *Intellectuals in Politics: From the Dreyfus Affair to Salman Rushdie*, edited by Jeremy Jennings and Anthony Kemp-Welch, 25–44, London: Routledge.
Ben-Ari, Eyal. 1989. "Masks and Soldiering: The Israeli Army and the Palestinian Uprising." *Cultural Anthropology* 4(4): 372–89.
Benvenisti, Meron. 1992. *Fatal Embrace*. Jerusalem: Keter Publishers. In Hebrew.
Bilu, Yoram. 2010. *The Saints' Impresarios: Dreamers, Healers, and Holy Men in Israel's Urban Periphery*. Brighton, MA: Academic Studies Press.
Bloch, David. 2007. *Aristotle on Memory and Recollection: Text Translation and Reception in Western Scholasticism*. Leiden: Brill.

Borofsky, Robert. 2019. *An Anthropology of Anthropology: Is It Time to Shift Paradigms?* Honolulu: Hawaii Pacific University, Center for a Public Anthropology.
Brym, Robert, J. 1980. *Intellectuals and Politics*. London: George Allen & Unwin.
Cohen, Stanley. 1988. "Criminology and the Uprising." *Tikkun* 3(5): 60–62, 94–95.
Cohen, Uri. 2006. *The Mountain and the Hill: The Hebrew University before and after National Independence*. Tel Aviv: Am Oved. In Hebrew.
Coser, Lewis A. 1956. *The Functions of Social Conflict*. New York: Free Press.
———. 1965. *Men of Ideas: A Sociologist's View*. New York: Free Press.
Dahrendorf, Ralf. 1969. "The Intellectual and Society: The Social Function of the 'Fool' in the Twentieth Century." In *On Intellectuals: Theoretical Case Studies*, edited by Philip Rieff, 49–52. New York: Doubleday and Comp, Inc.
Deshen, Shlomo, and Moshe Shokeid. 1974. *The Predicament of Homecoming: Cultural and Social Life of North African Immigrants in Israel*. Ithaca, NY: Cornell University Press.
Eisenstadt, Shmuel. N. 1985. *The Transformation of Israeli Society: An Essay in Interpretation*. London: Weidenfeld and Nicolson.
Ellis, Deborah. 2006. *Three Wishes: Palestinian and Israeli Children Speak*. Groundwood Books.
Ezrahi, Yaron. 1997. *Rubber Bullets: Power and Conscience in Modern Israel*. Berkeley: University of California Press.
Fassin, Didier, ed. 2018. *If Truth Be Told: The Politics of Public Ethnography*. Durham, NC: Duke University Press.
Freedman, Robert, ed. 1991. *The Intifada: Its Impact on Israel, the Arab World and the Superpowers*. Miami: Florida International University Press.
Fried, Morton, Marvin Harris, and Robert Murphy, eds. 1968. *War: The Anthropology of Armed Conflict and Aggression*. New York: Natural History Press.
Gal, Reuven, ed. 1990. *The Seventh War: The Effects of the Intifada on the Israeli Society*. Tel Aviv: Hakibbutz Hameuchad. In Hebrew.
Gans, Chaim. 2008. *A Just Zionism: On the Morality of the Jewish State*. Oxford: Oxford University Press.
Gazit, Shlomo. 1999. *Trapped*. Tel Aviv: Zmora- Bitan. In Hebrew.
———. 2016. *At Key Points of Time*. Rishon LeZion: Yediot Ahronot Books. In Hebrew.
Geertz, Clifford. 1995. *After the Fact: Two Countries, Four Decades, One Anthropologist*. Cambridge, MA: Harvard University Press.
Gelber, Yoav. 2018. *The Time of the Palestinians: Israel, Jordan and the Palestinians, 1967–1970*. Hevel Modi'in Industrial Park: Kinneret, Zmora, Dvir-Publishing House Ltd. In Hebrew.

Gingrich, Andre. 2005. "German Anthropology during the Nazi Period: Complex Scenarios of Collaboration, Persecution and Competition." In *One Discipline, Four Ways: British, German, French, and American Anthropology*, edited by Barth Fredrik, Andre Gingrich, Robert Parkin, and Sydel Silverman, 11–136. Chicago: University of Chicago Press.

Gluckman, Max. 1962. *Essays on the Ritual of Social Relations*. Manchester: Manchester University Press.

Gonzalez, Roberto J. 2004. *Anthropologists in the Public Sphere: Speaking Out on War, Peace and American Power*. Austin: University of Texas Press.

Goodman, Micah. 2017. *Catch 67*. Tel Aviv: Kinneret, Zmora-Bitan.

Gordon, Robert. 2018. "How Good People Become Absurd: J. P. van S. Bruwer, the Making of Namibian Grand Apartheid and the Decline of Volkeunde." *Journal of Southern African Studies* 44(1): 1–17.

Gracia, Jorge J. E. 1999. "Philosophy in American Public Life: De Facto and De Jure." *Proceedings and Addresses of the American Philosophical Association* 72 (May 1999): 149–58.

Graeber, David R. 2004. *Fragments of an Anarchist Anthropology*. Chicago: Prickly Paradigm Press.

Gramsci, Antonio. 1971 [1929–35]. *Selection from the Prison Notebooks*. New York: International Publishers.

Grossman, David. 1988. *The Yellow Wind*. Tel Aviv: Siman Kriaha Books. In Hebrew.

Grunberger, Richard. 1971. *A Social History of the Third Reich*. London: Weidenfeld and Nicolson.

Hacham, David. 2016. *Gaza in the Eye of the Storm: The Inside Story of the Intifada*. Moshav Ben-Shemen: Modan Publishing House Ltd. In Hebrew.

Haffner, Sebastian. 1978. *Anmerkungen Zu Hitler*. Munchen: Verlag.

———. 2000. *Geschichte Eines Deutschen*. Munchen: Deutsche Verlag-Anstalt.

Halbwachs, Maurice. 1992. *On Collective Memory*. Chicago: University of Chicago Press.

Handelman, Don. 2004. *Nationalism and the Israeli State: Bureaucratic Logic in Public Events*. Oxford: Berg Publishers.

Hannerz, Ulf. 2010. *Anthropology's World: Life in a Twenty-First-Century Discipline*. London: Pluto Press.

Harkabi, Yeoshafat. 1986. *Fateful Decisions*. Tel Aviv: Am Oved. In Hebrew.

Herzog, Esther, Orit Abuhav, Harvey E. Goldberg, and Emanuel Marx, eds. 2010. *Perspectives on Israeli Anthropology*. Detroit: Wayne State University Press.

Horowitz, Dan, and Moshe Lissak. 1989. *Troubles in Utopia: The Overburdened Polity of Israel*. Albany: State University of New York State.

Jacoby, Russell. 1987. *The Last Intellectuals: American Culture in the Age of Academe*. New York: The Noonday Press.

Jenni, Kathie. 2001. "The Moral Responsibilities of Intellectuals." *Social Theory and Practice*. 27(3): 437–54.
Kaminer, Reuven. 1996. *The Politics of Protest: The Israeli Peace Movement and the Palestinian Intifada*. Brighton: Sussex Academic Press.
Kanafani, Ghassan. 2000 [1969]. *Palestine's Children: Returning to Haifa and Other Stories*. Washington, DC: Three Continents Press.
Kaufman, Arnold S. 1968. *The Radical Liberal: The New Politics; Theory and Practice*. New York: Simon and Schuster.
Kimmerling, Baruch. 2001. *The Invention of Israeliness: State, Society, and the Military*. Berkeley: University of California Press.
King, Mary Elizabeth. 2007. *A Quiet Intifada: The First Palestinian Intifada and Nonviolent Resistance*. New York: Nation Books.
Klemperer, Victor. 1998. *I Will Bear Witness: A Diary of the Nazi Years 1933–1941*. New York: Modern Library.
Leon, Nissim. 2016. *Mizrachi Ultra-Orthodoxy and Nationalism in Israel*. Jerusalem: Van Leer Institute and Ha-Kibutz Ha-Meuchad. In Hebrew.
Lesser, Alexander, ed. 1981. "Franz Boas and the Modernization of Anthropology." In *Totems and Teachers: Perspectives on the History of Anthropology*. New York: Columbia University Press.
Lewis, Oscar. 1967. *La Vida*. London: Martin Sacker & Warburg
Lilla, Mark. [2016] 2001. *The Reckless Mind: Intellectuals in Politics*. New York: New York Review of Books.
Lockman, Zachary, and Joel Beinin, eds. 1989. *Intifada: The Palestinian Uprising against Israeli Occupation*. London: I. B. Tauris Publishers.
Lustick, Ian. 1993. *Unsettled States, Disputed Lands: Britain and Ireland, France and Algeria, Israel and the West Bank–Gaza*. Ithaca, NY: Cornell University Press.
Mannheim, Karl. 1968 [1952]. *Essays on the Sociology of Knowledge*. London: Routledge & Kegan Paul.
Markowitz, Fran, Sharot Stefan, and Moshe Shokeid, eds. 2015. *Towards an Anthropology of Nation Building and Unbuilding in Israel*. Lincoln: University of Nebraska Press.
Marx, Emanuel, ed. 1980. *A Composite Portrait of Israel*. London: Academic Press.
Mendels, Doron, ed. 2007. *On Memory: An Interdisciplinary Approach*. Oxford: Peter Lang.
Merton, Robert K. 1957. *Social Theory and Social Structure*. Glencoe, IL: Free Press.
Michael, Sami. 2005. *Pigeons at Trafalgar Square*. Tel Aviv: Am Oved. In Hebrew.
Mishal, Shaul, with Reuben Aharoni. 1989. *Speaking Stones: The Words behind the Palestinian Intifada*. Tel Aviv: Hakibutz Hameuhad. In Hebrew.
Myerhoff, Barbara. 1978. *Number Our Days*. New York: Simon and Schuster.

Nassar, Jamal R., and Roger Heacock, eds., 1990. *Intifada: Palestinians at Crossroads.* New York: Praeger.
Nisbet, Robert A. 1997. *The Degradation of the Academic Dogma.* New Brunswick, NJ: Transaction Publications.
Ochs, Juliana. 2011. *Security and Suspicion: An Ethnography of Everyday Life in Israel.* Philadelphia: University of Pennsylvania Press.
Okely, Judith, and Helen Callaway, eds. 1992. *Anthropology and Autobiography.* ASA Monographs 29. London: Routledge.
Oz, Amos. 2017. *Dear Zealots: Three Pleas.* Moshav Ben Shemen: Keter Books. In Hebrew.
Palmer, Bryan D. 1994. *E. P. Thompson: Objections and Oppositions.* London: Verso.
Palmer, David Scott. 1994. *Shining Path of Peru.* New York: St. Martin Press.
Parsons, Talcott. 1951. *The Social System.* London: Routledge.
Peled, Yoav, and Horit Peled. 2019. *The Religionization of Israeli Society.* London: Routledge.
Perry, Donna J. 2011. *The Israeli-Palestinian Peace Movement: Combatants for Peace.* Palgrave.
Price, David H. 2004. *Threatening Anthropology: McCarthyism and the FBI's Surveillance of Activist Anthropologists.* Durham, NC: Duke University Press.
Pogrund, Benjamin. 2014. *Drawing Fire: Investigating the Accusations of Apartheid in Israel.* London: Rowman & Littlefield.
Rabinow, Paul. 1977. *Reflections on Fieldwork in Morocco.* Berkeley: University of California Press.
Reed-Danahay, Deborah E. ed., 1997. *Auto/Ethnography: Rewriting the Self and the Social.* Oxford: Berg.
Riding, Alan. 2011. *And the Show Went On.* New York: Vintage Books.
Rieff, Philip, ed. 1969. *On Intellectuals: Theoretical Studies Case Studies.* New York: Doubleday & Comp, Inc.
Ringer, Fritz K. 1969. *The Decline of the German Mandarins: The German Academic Community, 1890-1933.* Cambridge, MA: Harvard University Press.
Rosaldo, Renato. 1980. *Illongot Headhunting 1883–1974: A Study in Society and History.* Stanford, CA: Stanford University Press.
Said, Edward W. 1978. *Orientalism.* Pantheon Books.
———. 1980. *The Question of Palestine.* London: Routledge and Kegan Paul.
———. 1996. *Representations of the Intellectual: The 1993 Reith Lectures.* New York: Vintage Books.
Sanders, Mark. 2002. *Complicities: The Intellectual and Apartheid.* Durham, NC: Duke University Press.
Sanjek, Roger. 2013. *Ethnography in Today's World: Color Full before Color Blind.* Philadelphia: University of Pennsylvania Press.
Sasson-Levy, Orna, and Tamar Rapoport. 2002. "Body, Ideology and Gender in Social Movements." *Megamot* 41(4): 489–513. In Hebrew.

Schalk, David L. 1979. *The Spectrum of Political Engagement*. Princeton, NJ: Princeton University Press.

———. 1991. *War and the Ivory Tower: Algeria and Vietnam*. Oxford: Oxford University Press.

———. 1997. "Are Intellectuals a Dying Species? War and the Ivory Tower in the Postmodern Age." In *Intellectuals in Politics: From the Dreyfus Affair to Salman Rushdie*, edited by J. Jennings and A. Kemp-Walch, 271–85. London: Routledge.

Scheper-Hughes, Nancy. 2000. "Ire in Ireland." *Ethnography* 1(1): 117–40.

Schiff, Ze'ev and Ehud Ya'ari. 1990. *Intifada: The Palestinian Uprising—Israel's Third Front*. New York: Simon and Shuster.

Scott, Alan. 1997. "Between Autonomy and Responsibility: Max Weber on Scholars, Academics and Intellectuals." In *Intellectuals in Politics: From the Dreyfus Affair to Salman Rushdie*, edited by J. Jennings and A. Kemp-Walch, 45–64. London: Routledge.

Shafir, Gershon. 2017. *A Half Century of Occupation: Israel, Palestine, and the World's Most Intractable Conflict*. Oakland: University of California Press.

Shapira, Anita. 1997. "The Labor Movement and the Hebrew University." In *The History of the Hebrew University: Origins and Beginnings*, edited by S. Katz and M. Heyd, 677–89. Jerusalem: Magness Press.

Sheleff, Leon. 2005. *The Thin Green Line: From Intractable Problems to Feasible Solutions in the Israeli-Palestinian Conflict*. Bloomington, IN: Xlibris Coproduction.

Shenhav, Yehuda. 2006. *The Arab Jews: A Postcolonial Reading of Nationalism, Religion, and Ethnicity*. Stanford, CA: Stanford University Press.

Shils, Edward. 1969. "The Intellectual and the Powers: Some Perspectives for Comparative Analysis." In *On Intellectuals: Theoretical Studies Case Studies*, edited by Philip Rieff, 25–48. New York: Doubleday & Comp. Inc.

Shokeid, Moshe (Minkovitz). 1963. "The Social Structure." In *Ghazvin Area Development Project Reconnaissance Report*. Vol. 2: F3–20. Tel Aviv: TAHAL (Water Planning) Ltd., Iran Branch.

———. 1971. "Fieldwork as Predicament Rather than Spectacle." *European Journal of Sociology* 11: 111–22.

———. 1984. "Cultural Ethnicity in Israel: The Case of Middle Eastern Jews Religiosity." *Association for Jewish Studies Review* 9(2): 247–71.

———. 1985 [1971]. *The Dual Heritage: Immigrants from the Atlas Mountains in an Israeli Village*. Manchester: Manchester University Press. Augmented edition: New Brunswick: Transaction Books.

———. 1988. *Children of Circumstances: Israeli Emigrants in New York*. Ithaca, NY: Cornell University Press.

———. 1988/89. "The Manchester School in Africa and Israel Revisited: Reflections on the Sources and Methods of an Anthropological Discourse." *Israel Social Science Research* 6(1): 9–23.

———. 1992a. "Commitment and Contextual Study in Anthropology." *Cultural Anthropology* 7(4): 464–77.

———. 1992b. "Exceptional Experiences in Everyday Life." *Cultural Anthropology* 7(2): 232–43.

———. 2001. "For the Sin We Did Not Commit in the Research of Oriental Jewry." *Israel Studies* 6(1): 15–33.

———. 2002. *An Israeli Voyage: Tel-Aviv, New York and Between*. Tel Aviv: Yedioth Books. In Hebrew.

———. 2003a. "The Five Banks Tapestry of Israeli Society." *Zeitschrift fur Ethnologie* 128: 233–48.

———. 2003b [1995]. *A Gay Synagogue in New York*. New York: Columbia University Press. Augmented edition, 2003: Philadelphia, PA: University of Pennsylvania Press.

———. 2004. "Max Gluckman and the Making of Israeli Anthropology." *Ethnos* 69(3): 363–86.

———. 2007a. "Anthropological Texts: Mirrored Memories of Researchers and Subjects." In *On Memory: An Interdisciplinary Approach*, edited by Mendels Doron, 275–98. Oxford: Peter Lang.

———. 2007b. "When the Curtain Falls on a Fieldwork Project." *Ethnos* 72(2): 219–38.

———. 2009. "What Is There to a Name? The Ethnographer and His Moroccan Subjects in Shokeida." In M. Shokeid, *Three Jewish Journeys through an Anthropologist's Lens*, 341–51. Brighton, MA: Academic Studies Press.

———. 2015a. *Gay Voluntary Associations in New York: Public Sharing and Private Lives*. Philadelphia, PA: University of Pennsylvania Press.

———. 2015b. "From Engaged Mediator to Freelance Consultant: Israeli Social Scientists in the Service of Immigrant Absorption." In *Towards an Anthropology of Nation Building and Unbuilding in Israel*, edited by F. Markowitz, S. Sharot, and M. Shokeid, 91–106. Lincoln: Nebraska University Press.

———. 2015c. "Newcomers at the Israeli National Table: Transforming Urban Landscapes and the Texture of Citizenship." *City & Society* 27(2): 208–30.

———. 2020. "The Lifespan of Ethnographic Reports." *Anthropology and Humanism*.

Shokeid, Moshe, and Shlomo Deshen. 1982. *Distant Relations: Ethnicity and Politics among Arabs and North African Jews*. New York: Praeger and Bergin.

Shulman, David. 2018. *Freedom and Despair: Notes from the South Hebron Hills*. Chicago: University of Chicago Press.

Smith, Gavin. 1999. *Confronting the Present: Toward a Politically Engaged Anthropology*. New York: Berg.

Steinberg, Matti. 2008. *Facing Their Fate: Palestinian National Consciousness 1967–2007*. Tel Aviv: Yediot Ahronot. In Hebrew.

Strong, Simon. 1993. *Shining Path: A Case Study in Ideological Terrorism*. London: Research Institute for the Study of Conflict.

Swedenburg, Ted. 1989. "Occupational Hazards: Palestine Ethnography." *Cultural Anthropology* 4: 265–72.

———. 1992. "Occupational Hazards: Reply to Moshe Shokeid." *Cultural Anthropology* 7: 478–95.

Thompson, Edward P., ed. 1970. *Warwick University Ltd: Industry, Management and the Universities*. Harmondsworth: Penguin Books Ltd.

Turnbull, Colin. 1972. *The Mountain People*. New York: Simon and Schuster.

Turner, Victor W. 1969. *The Ritual Process: Structure and Anti-Structure*. Ithaca, NY: Cornell University Press.

Turner, Victor W., and E. M. Bruner, eds. 1986. *The Anthropology of Experience*. Urbana: University of Illinois Press.

Van Teeffelen, Toine. 1978. "The Manchester School in Africa and Israel: A Critique." *Dialectical Anthropology* 3: 67–83.

Vine, David. 2011. "Public Anthropology in Its Second Decade: Robert Borofsky's Center for a Public Anthropology." *American Anthropologist* 113: 336–39.

Vogelgesang, Sandy. 1974. *The Long Dark Night of the Soul: The American Intellectual Left and the Vietnam War*. New York: Harper and Row.

Walzer, Michael. 1977. *Just and Unjust Wars: A Moral Argument with Historical Illustrations*. New York: Basic Books.

Weingrod, Alex, ed. 1985. *Studies in Israeli Ethnicity: After the Ingathering*. New York: Gordon and Breach.

Weinreich, Max. 1946. *Hitler's Professors: The Part of Scholarship in Germany's Crimes against the Jewish People*. New York: Yiddish Scientific Institute-YIVO.

Weiss, Erica. 2014. *Conscientious Objectors in Israel: Citizenship, Sacrifice, Trials of Fealty*. Philadelphia: University of Pennsylvania Press.

Zweig, Stefan. 1964 [1943]. *The World of Yesterday*. Lincoln: University of Nebraska Press.

Index

AAA. *See* American Anthropological Association
academic encounters, 120
academics, 1, 52, 185
   American, 38–39
   French, 44–45
   German-Austrian, 41–42, 43
   Israeli, 36–37, 53, 54, 110, 176–77, 180
   Peruvian, 45–46
   South African, 47–48
AD KAN (protest organization), 1, 14, 15, 25, 53, 93, 101–102, 106
   advertisements, in *Haaretz*, 82
   box of records, 64–65
   buttons, 74–75, 78
   conferences, 59, 60, 61–62, 71–72, 91, 99–101, 104
   demonstrations, 72, 73, 98, 99, 104
   flyers, 70–71, 78, 108
   inauguration of, 63, 88
   media coverage, 79, 80–81, 82, 84, 88
   membership, 68, 69, 77, 126–27
   opposition of, 76–77
   Peace Now meeting with, 101
AD KAN participants (mentioned in the text)
   Arbel, Benjamin, 129
   Berman, Ruth, 100, 130–31
   Biletzki, Anat, 68, 128
   Ehrlich, Avishai, 74, 136–37
   Ezra, Ovadia, 131
   Friedman, Ariella, 60, 65, 77, 89, 128, 141
   Gershoni, Israel, 79, 87–88, 134–36
   Gilat, David, 132–133
   Jacobson, Dan, 139–140
   Maor, Uri, 60, 68, 99, 130
   Neuman, Joseph, 68
   Sand, Shlomo, 138–39
   Shapiro, Jonathan, 60, 87–88
   Sheleff, Leon, 58, 59, 64, 109, 157–59
   Shohamy, Ilana, 137–38
   Slonim, Ora, 89
   Smorodinski, Meir, 80, 87
   Volkov, Shula, 79
   Weitman, Sasha, 69–70, 133–34
   Yechiali, Uri, 131–32
Al-Aqsa Intifada, 31, 112, 134, 153
Alimi, Eitan, 30, 31
American Anthropological Association (AAA), 39–40, 41, 123
anthropologists, ix–x, 2–3, 14
   American, 39–41
   German-Austrian, 42–43
   Israeli, 167
   South African, 47
anthropology, 8, 9
   British, 11
   ethnographic present, xi, 67
   public anthropology, xi, 186
   reflexivity in anthropology, 3, 12, 111, 121

apartheid, 47–48, 49–50, 51, 92
Arab code of honor, 13, 117
Arabs, Israeli, 13, 26, 50, 61, 120, 143, 170–71, 173
Arafat, Yasser, 29, 98, 117
Arendt, Hannah ("*the banality of evil*"), 91–92, 97
Arian, Asher and Raphael Ventura, 26
Arieli, Yehoshua, 36–37
articles, 60, 61, 89, 90, 96
   in *Haaretz*, 110, 124–25, 149
   in *New York Times*, 150
Ashkenazim, 50, 94, 136, 145, 169, 170
Azaria, Elor, 92n1

Banda, Julien, 33
Barak, Ehud, 166
Baram, Nir, 162, 163
Bar-Tal, Daniel, 159–60
Bar-Yosef, Yariv, 89
BDS. *See* Boycott, Divestment, Sanctions
Behar, Ruth, 4
Beinin, Joel, 19
Bellamy, Richard, 34
Ben-Ami, Shlomo, 166
Ben-Ari, Eyal, 26–27
Ben-Gurion, 54–55
Bennett, Naftali, 176–77
Benvenisti, Meron, 22
Berlin, Germany, 43–44, 112–13
Bezalel School of Architecture, 146–147
Bilu, Yoram, 167
Bloch, David, 5
Boas, Franz, x, 39, 116, 172
Borofsky, Robert, xi
Boycott, Divestment, Sanctions (BDS), 41, 48, 52n1, 110, 120, 122–23
Breaking the Silence (protest organization), 108, 146, 147–48, 149, 151, 154
Brit Shalom (covenant of peace, Hebrew University), 53
Brooklyn, New York, 149–50
Bruner, E. M., 2

Bush, George H. W., Sr., 73, 91
Butler, Judith, 86

Callaway, Helen, xi
Catch 67 (Goodman), 164
Cave of the Patriarchs, 17, 139, 141n3, 148, 150–51, 152. *See also* Hebron, Israel
CFP. *See* Combatants for Peace
Checkpoint Watch, 141n5
Chomsky, Noam, 37, 38, 185
civil disobedience, 21–22, 24, 56, 81
Clinton, Bill, 166
code of honor, 13, 117
Cohen, Stanley, 96–97
collective action, 30–31
collective memory, 3, 159–60
colonization, 161–62
Combatants for Peace (CFP), 142, 143, 154
communitas, 52, 64, 112, 124, 128, 137
concentration camps, 183–84
conflict, x, 21–22, 28, 115–16, 117, 155
   of ideologies, 166
   as intractable, 159–60, 161, 186
   theory, 134, 172
conscientious objectors, 143
cooperative communities, 7–8, 161
Coser, Lewis A., 34
Council of Higher Education (the MALAG), 177, 185
Custodians of the Land of Israel (right-wing protest organization), 76–77

Dahrendorf, Ralf, 35
Dear Zealots (Oz Amos), 163–64
Diamond, Stanley (*Dialectical Anthropology*), 120–121
discriminatory laws, 49
Drawing Fire (Pogrand), 48–49

Eisenstadt, S. N., 167
Ellis, Deborah, 117
ethnographic present, xi, 67, 183
ethnographic research (fieldwork), ix, x, 2, 4, 8–9, 12–14, 114, 168

public ethnography, xi
reflexivity in, xi, 4
ethos, cultural, 117
extremists (right wing), 29, 31, 100, 150, 151, 164
Ezrahi, Yaron (*Rubber Bullets*), 156–57, 182

Fassin, Didier, xi, 186
fieldwork. *See* ethnographic research
five banks of Israeli society, 172–174
foreign workers, 174
Friedman, Thomas, 107–8
Funkenstein, Amos, 79

Gal, Reuven, 26
Gaza, 18–19, 20, 23, 25
Gazit, Shlomo (e-mail movement), 17–18, 152–53
Geertz, Clifford, 69, 70, 179, 180, 181
Gelber, Yoav, 17
Gingrich, Andre, 42–43
Gluckman, Max, ix, x, 48, 173
Goldstein, Baruch, 139, 141n3, 150, 151, 152
Gonzalez, Roberto J., 39
Goodman, Micah, 164, 165–66
Gordon, Robert, 47
Gracia, Jorge J. E., 36
Gramsci, Antonio, 34
Green Line, 17–18, 49, 148, 157–58
Grossman, David, 118–19
Grunberger, Richard, 91
Gulf War, 102
Guzmán, Abimal, 45–46

Haaretz (newspaper), 56, 74, 75, 79, 83, 90
articles in, 110, 124–25, 149
letters to, 81, 85, 105–6, 152, 177
Habibi, Emile, 104–5
Hacham, David, 21, 22–23, 24–25
Haffner, Sebastian, 129
HaKampus Lo Shotek (protest organization), 109
A Half Century of Occupation (Shafir), 161

Halper, Jeffrey, 111
Hamas, 23, 25, 28, 31, 145
Handelman, Don, 167
Hannerz, Ulf, 67
Haredim (ultra-Orthodox), 175, 179
Harkabi, Yeoshafat, 28–29
Hebrew University, 7, 53, 153, 182–83
Hebron, Israel, 107, 108, 147–48, 149, 150–52
Heidegger, Martin, 42
Herzog, Esther, 167
Hoover, J. Edgar, 40
Horowitz, Dan and Moshe Lissak, 167
Husseini, Faisal, 98, 99, 100

identities, 11, 56, 74, 114, 181
ideologies, 12, 51, 166
IDF. *See* Israeli Defense Force
immigrants, 2–3, 8, 87, 175, 176
In a Land beyond the Mountains (Baram), 162
intellectuals, 1, 11, 56–57, 113
responsibility of, 38
social role of, 33–36, 51–52
intifada (uprising), first, 1, 2, 4, 16, 25
aftermath of, 183
Al-Aqsa (Mosque) Intifada, 31, 112, 134
civil and military leaderships, 23–24
reporting on, 18–19, 20–21, 22–23, 26, 30
intractable conflict, 159–60, 161, 186
Israel
founding of, x, 5, 12, 16, 18
Jaffa, 12–13
Jerusalem, 100, 182
Tel Aviv, 1, 7, 11, 64, 95, 11, 182
Israel Anthropological Association, 9, 57, 111, 185
Israeli academics, 36–37, 53, 54, 110, 176–77, 180
Israeli anthropologists, 167
Israeli Arabs (Arab minority), 13, 26, 50, 120, 143, 170–71,173
Israeli (army) Defense Force (IDF), 1, 16, 55, 92n1, 108, 141n1, 146, 157, 177, 183

Israeli emigrants, 14, 87, 171–72, 178
Israeli settlements, 114, 161
Israeli settlers, 163
Israeli society, 5, 12, 167, 181
   ethnic designations of, 169
   five banks of, 172–73, 174
   human diversity, 176
   social-religious life of, 169–70
   transformations of, 144–45, 172, 183, 186
Israeli universities, 53–54, 55, 94

Jacoby, Russell, 38
Jenni, Kathie, 36
Jerusalem (political visions), 100
Johnson, Lyndon B., 38
justice, 115, 116, 117

Kach movement, 99–100, 105
Kahane, Meir, 149, 150
Kaminer, Reuven, 66
Kanafani, Ghassan, 118, 119
Kasher, Asa, 177, 178
Kaufman, Arnold S., 35
Kennedy, John F., 40
kibush naor (enlightened occupation), 17
Kimmerling, Baruch, 167, 168, 174
Klemperer, Victor, ix
Knesset (parliament), 24, 71, 94, 96, 104, 171
kur ha'hituch (melting pot), 168

laws, discriminatory, 49
"learned helplessness," 140
Lebanon War, 57, 119, 134, 141n1, 160
Leibowitz, Yeshayahu, 37, 57, 74, 94, 112, 185
Leon, Nissim, 169
Lesser, Alexander, 39
letters, 9–10, 56, 57, 60, 69–70, 76
   to Friedman, T., 107–8
   to *Haaretz*, 81, 85, 105–6, 152, 177
Lewis, Oscar, 2
Likud party, 29, 107, 169
Lilla, Mark, 52
Lissak, Moshe, 26, 167

Lockman, Zachary and Joel Beinin, 19
Louw, N. P. van Wyk, 47–48
Lustick, Ian, 19–20

MALAG. *See* Council of Higher Education
Manchester University, 115–16
Mannheim, Karl, 52
Markowitz, Fran, 167
Marx, Emanuel, 167
"masking" strategy, 27
massacre, 119, 139, 141n3, 150, 151, 152
mathematicians, 68–69
McCarthy, Joseph, 40
McCarthyism, 38, 40–41
Mead, Margaret, x, 11, 40, 56
melting pot (*kur ha'hituch*), 168
memory, 2, 3, 4–5, 159–60
Meretz Party, 99, 110, 113, 133, 139
Merton, Robert K., 34
Michael, Sami, 118, 119
Milgram, Noah, 94
Milgrom, Yermyau, 90
military service, 12, 27, 55, 131, 143, 175
   exemption from, 83, 146
   refusal of, 57, 110–11
Mishal, Shaul, with Reuben Aharoni, 19
Mizrahim, 50, 94, 136, 143, 169, 170
Musée de l'Homme, 44

Nathan, Abie, 101–2
Nationality Bill, 123–24
Nazi regime, 42–43, 44
Ne'eman, Yuval, 72–73
Netanyahu, Benjamin, 107, 114, 129–30
Netherlands-Israel Development Research Project, 45
newspapers. *See also Haaretz*
   Al Hamishmar, 81
   Coteret Rashit, 80
   Ha'ir, 94, 96
   Résistance, 44, 45
   Yediot, 9, 10

New York Times, 150
no-man's land (*shetach efker*), 158
Noyman, Giora, 80
Nusseibeh, Sari, 75, 102–3

objectors, conscientious, 143
Ochs, Juliana, 144, 160–61
Okely, Judith and Helen Callaway, xi
Open University, 82, 182
Operation Defensive Shield, 179
Orgler, Yair, 76
Oslo Accords, 27, 32, 105, 106
    failure of, 28–31, 64, 107, 159
    Oslo (dramatic play), 32
Oz, Amos, 163–64

Palestine, 7, 17–18, 49–50, 59
Palestine Liberation Organization
    (PLO), 17, 26, 27, 28, 66, 75, 101
Palestinian academic institutions
    (closing of), 15, 87, 93, 94
Palestinians, x, 17, 61–62
Palmer, David Scott, 45
Peace Now (protest organization), 66,
    89, 90, 91, 99, 101
Perry, Donna J., 142, 143
Peru, 45–47. *See also* Shining Path
Peter, Sinai, 57
petitions, 60, 83, 87, 93, 124, 146
Pfeffer, Georg, 43–44
Physicians without Borders, 141n6
PLO. *See* Palestine Liberation
    Organization
Pogrund, Benjamin, 48–51
Poland, 43, 160, 183–84
political parties, 54, 145–46, 174–75
    Likud, 29, 107, 169
    Meretz, 99, 110, 113, 133, 139
    Shas, 169, 170, 176
political realities, 65, 164–65
Pot, Pol, 47
Price, David H., 40–41
protest organizations, 57–58, 63, 67,
    69, 106, 112–13. *See also* AD
    KAN
    absence of, 109, 131, 132–33, 134,
    135–36, 138

Breaking the Silence, 108, 146,
    147–48, 149, 151, 154
Combatants for Peace, 142, 143,
    154
Custodians of the Land of Israel
    (rightist), 76–77
Peace Now, 66, 89, 90, 91, 99
SISO (Save Israel Stop the
    Occupation), 140
Ta'ayush, 153–54
Twenty-First Year, 57–58, 67, 68,
    126, 146
Yesh Gvul, 57, 59, 83
protests, ix, 1, 19, 23–24, 89, 99

Rabin, Yitzhak, 24, 27, 31–32, 63, 107,
    139
Rabinow, Paul, 4
Reed-Danahay, D. E., xi
reflexivity, 140–41, 173
    in anthropology (ethnography), xi,
    3, 4, 12, 111, 121
refusal, of military service, 57,
    110–11
Riding, Alan, 44
Rieff, Philip, 34
"right of return," 163, 165
right-wingers, 72, 104
Rosaldo, Renato, 2
Rosenfeld, Henry, 111
Rubber Bullets (Ezrahi), 156, 157

Sabra generation, 7, 15n1
Said, Edward, 18, 19
Sanders, Mark, 47–48
Sanjek, Roger, xi, 67
Sarid, Yossi, 113
Sartre, Jean Paul, 45
Schalk, D. L., 33, 36, 38–39
Scheper-Hughes, Nancy, xi
Security and Suspicion (Ochs), 144
Segal, Daniel, 119–20
Sendero Luminoso (Shining Path),
    45–46
settlements, Israeli, 114, 161
settlers, Israeli, 163
Shaaban, Abu, 62–63, 69–70, 75, 80

Shafir, Gershon, 161, 166
Shamir, Yitzhak, 73, 86
Sharon, Ariel, 28, 112, 114, 139, 145, 179
Shas Party, 169, 170, 176
Shenhav, Yehuda, 169
Shils, Edward, 35
Shining Path (Sendero Luminoso), 45–46
Shuhada Street (Hebron), 151
Shulman, David, 153, 162
smolanim (leftists), 186
sociology, 7, 8, 22, 111
soft sciences, 68, 79–80
Steinberg, Matti, 29, 30, 135
Strong, Simon, 45
Swedenburg, Ted, 121

Ta'ayush (protest organization), 153–54
Talmon, Jacob, 37
Tamari, Salim, 19–20
Tel Aviv University (TAU), 1, 4, 9
 faculty, 66, 70, 74, 80, 83, 126
 senate, 93–94, 95, 96, 97
territories. *See* West Bank
Thompson, E. P., 35, 185
The Three Wishes (Ellis), 117–18
transcendent pluralism (Perry), 142
Turnbull, Colin, ix
Turner, Victor W., 64, 128, 160
Turner, Victor W. and E. M. Bruner, 2
Twenty-First Year (protest organization), 57–58, 67, 68, 126, 146

two-state solution, 71, 161, 163, 164, 166

ultra-Orthodox (*Haredim*), 175, 179
United Nations (UN), 165
universities, 35, 53–54, 55, 95
UN resolution 242, 71
Uprising. *See* intifada

The Valley of Hebron Road, 15
Van Teeffelen, T., 121
Ventura, Raphael, 26
Vienna, Austria, 43, 95, 173
Vine, David, xi

Wainer, Karen, 146, 147
Walzer, Michael, 117
war, 16–17, 155
 Gulf War, 102
 Lebanon War, 57, 119, 134, 141n1, 160
Weingrod, Alex, 167
Weiss, Erica, 143
West Bank (also territories), 28–29, 115, 163
Wilson, Woodrow, 39

Yediot (newspaper), 9, 10
Yesh Gvul (protest organization), 57, 59, 83
Yordim. *See* Israeli emigrants

Zionism, 18, 86, 137, 143, 157
Zweig, Stefan, 1, 5

www.ingramcontent.com/pod-product-compliance
Lightning Source LLC
Chambersburg PA
CBHW051543020426
42333CB00016B/2073